AGENT TATE

AGENT
TATE

The Wartime
Story of Harry
Williamson

Tommy Jonason & Simon Olsson

AMBERLEY

First published 2011

Translated from Swedish.

Amberley Publishing
The Hill, Stroud,
Gloucestershire, GL5 4EP

www.amberleybooks.com

British Library Cataloguing in Publication Data.
A catalogue record for this book is available from the British Library.

ISBN 978 1 4456 0481 7

Typesetting and Origination by Amberley Publishing
Printed in Great Britain

CONTENTS

Introduction

On 2 May 1945, two days after Hitler ended his life, and five days before his successor, Admiral Dönitz, would accept unconditional surrender, thus ending the war in Europe, a final message from Germany was delivered to an agent in Britain. For the German intelligence service, the agent was known under the code name *Leonhard* or Agent 3725. The message gave encouragement, and thanks for a report on the mining of the inlet to the Kola Peninsula. In addition, the Germans responded to a question about a suitcase with personal papers and valuables the agent had left in Hamburg in 1940.

The man who received the message, and who the Germans thought was a valuable agent, was in fact a British double agent, with the cover name TATE. Born as a Dane with the name Wulf Schmidt, he changed his real name to Harry Williamson during the war, and became a British citizen. He was one of the agents of the British Double-Cross system, which carried out a game with double agents giving misinformation and deception to the Germans. During the Second World War, MI5 managed to achieve a remarkable success. All agents sent by the German Abwehr were caught, and no agent managed to perform espionage or sabotage of any value. The British were not content with imprisoning or executing the agents, instead they used them, if possible, as double agents, with considerable success. The organisation for this was called the Double-Cross system, which was controlled by a committee with members from several authorities, with the Oxford historian J. C.

Masterman as chairman. TATE was the double agent who served the longest, from the moment he landed in September 1940 by parachute in Willingham, to the end of the war in May 1945. Considerably more than 1,000 radio messages, with misleading information or operations with disinformation, were provided via radio transmissions from TATE.

Wulf Dietrich Christian Schmidt was born on 7 December 1911, in Aabenraa, a small town situated on the east coast of the southern part of Jutland, in North Slesvig in Denmark. His father, William Schmidt, was of German descent and a respected lawyer and royal notary in the town. Wulf's Danish mother Helene, born Bruhn, came from a country house with surrounding farmland, and she was Danish in her manners and nature, while his father was more of a Germanic character.

Wulf was of small stature with dark hair, unlike his two sisters and one brother, who were tall and fair-haired. Much to his father's resentment, Wulf remained small in stature. His beloved mother died when he was only eight years old, and he was brought up by his strict father in an almost Prussian manner. The loss of his mother was a severe blow, and Wulf never really got over it. Her ashes remained for many years in an urn on his father's desk, and he never told his children where she was eventually buried.[1] Long after the war had ended in 1945, Wulf came to Denmark to search for her grave, but he never found it.

Wulf had his paradise at his maternal grandparent's large country house at Skovbølgaard in South Jutland. His happy summers at the estate made him often express his wish to work in farming when he grew up. This had drastic consequences when Wulf finished school, and discussed his future prospects with his father. William stated categorically: 'You have always said you want to be a farmer, so therefore you will become a farmer.' His father sent him away as an agricultural student to a farm, which Wulf soon discovered in reality was more like working as a slave. Wulf had soon had enough of life as a starving serf on the farm, and, for once, told his father what he really thought. He was then sent to an equestrian school in Eutin, between Lübeck and Kiel in Germany, where he spent six months learning to ride and drive horse-carriages.[2]

On 31 October 1931, the nearly twenty-year-old Wulf Schmidt was drafted into military service as a recruit at *Gardehusarregimentet* in Copenhagen. The documentation from the army shows that he was 166 cm tall, skinny, dark-haired and had blue eyes.[3] Wulf dreamt of making a career as an officer, like his paternal grandfather, Hans Otto Schmidt, who had been a *Leutnant* in the Hussars, during the German siege of Paris in the war of 1870–71.[4] Now he felt that there was a goal and a career waiting for him in his life, and he enjoyed the comradeship, well away from his father's sarcasm. Riding caused no problems, but he had problems with the rifle and sabre-fencing. Wulf was in fact left-handed, and if this had been discovered by his superiors, he would immediately have had to leave. Wulf, who throughout his life would be stubborn and determined, easily solved this problem by simply training up his right hand. He managed his education and training very well, and was therefore sent to an officer school to become an officer.

Wulf was proud of his career and splendid grades; now he had really achieved something in his life. His father had always expressed his displeasure during Wulf's upbringing but perhaps this would finally impress his father and make him feel proud of Wulf. However, Wulf's hopes were dashed when his father decided that he definitely could not proceed with his career in the Danish army. Wulf's dream of a future remained only a dream. The reason was that his older brother Kai, his father's favourite, had joined the Luftwaffe. It was unthinkable to have sons on either side in case of a war between Denmark and Germany.[5] In February 1933, Wulf Schmidt with a heavy heart resigned from the Danish army, once again deeply disappointed. Having now been forced to leave the Danish army, the distraught Wulf had to seek out new work. His father arranged a place on a course in farming machinery in Zeesen, south-east of Berlin. But after only two days Wulf heard about an opportunity which the father of one of his friends had to offer. A horse dealer was looking for a man who could take some young horses to Argentina.[6] Wulf, who was now accustomed to and fond of horses, gladly undertook the mission, with a promise of work for the Dane who owned a farm in Argentina, the destination of the horses being transported. He probably also felt a desire to get as far away from his father as possible.

Therefore, in June 1933, Wulf Schmidt travelled to Argentina from Anvers in Antwerp. He got work as an inspector and controller on the farm until he became ill in 1936, and in April that year returned to Europe. Wulf now began to study agronomy at the University of Berlin. However, his time at the university would be short. During a visit to his grandmother's farm he received information that a German firm, *Compagnie Afrikanische Frucht* in Hamburg, was searching for personnel for their banana plantations in the Cameroons. One requirement was that he would become a member of the Danish Nazi Party.[7] Wulf agreed to embark on this exciting enterprise and in October 1936 he sailed to Cameroon. This was done against the wishes of his father, who had not even been informed in advance.[8] The company had large banana plantations in the Cameroons, which had been a German colony between 1884 and 1918. Wulf got work as a foreman on a plantation at the foot of the Cameroon Mountain.

In 1938 Wulf returned to Germany because he had been informed that his former employer was offering work in Argentina.[9] Unfortunately, Hitler got in the way of his plans. Most South American countries had introduced visa requirements; Jews emigrated in increasing numbers from Germany, and the borders of the South American countries were closed. It was impossible to get a visa, a big disappointment for Wulf. But he also took part in Nazi activities. In a report written by the *StatsPoliti* (the police) from Aabenraa on 10 November 1938, it was stated that the day before they had, among the participants in a German Nazi march, noticed the Danish citizen Wulf Schmidt.[10]

Unable to get work in Europe, he returned to the banana plantation in Cameroon in January 1939, but when the war broke in September 1939, living there became more difficult. Therefore, he went back to Hamburg, where he arrived on 13 March 1940.[11] When Wulf came to Hamburg, he had an outstanding salary of 800 Reichmarks[12] from his employer. However, when he went to the bank to get his money, he was told that all foreign accounts had been seized by the German government. We can imagine his consternation; Wulf had lost his savings. We know that Wulf had a temper, and he was frustrated, raging, and penniless. Now he owned basically only the clothes he was wearing.[13] In Hamburg, Wulf received orders to go to the local immigration office to register, where he met a Herr Schmidt. He told Wulf that he had a friend, a certain 'Herr Doctor' Scholtz, who would probably be interested in Wulf's experiences in Africa and his journeys; maybe he could even arrange a job for him. A meeting was, therefore, arranged at the Phoenix Hotel,[14] opposite the Central train station in Hamburg.

At the meeting, Dr Scholtz (or *Leutnant* Huckriede) wanted to hear about Wulf's background, but seemed, to Wulf's disappointment, quite uninterested in his travels and experiences in Argentina and Cameroon. Apparently more interesting was what he had observed in various ports. Dr Scholtz finally asked Wulf to write down his story in detail. A few days later, Scholtz said that a company in Copenhagen could employ Wulf, and he was going to be sent to England on the firm's behalf. When he came back he should report everything he saw and heard about the morale of the people, and the food situation. The trip was, however, cancelled, and soon afterwards, on 9 April 1940, Denmark was invaded by the Germans.

After that, he was instructed to travel to Denmark on a mission of espionage. In spite of the occupation, Denmark still had a certain autonomy. Dr Scholtz introduced him to a Dr Werner, probably Dr Karl Praetorius, head of the economic section of the Abwehr in Hamburg and an important person concerned with the handling of agents. The mission consisted of finding out about Danish factories which had changed their production of civilian goods to military armaments, and companies which had commercial contacts with Britain before 9 April. Also, information was needed about the names of Danish ships in British service, and contact was to be made with sailors who worked on these ships to find out what they had seen.[15] Wulf, however, did not succeed in his espionage mission in his home country and it was a total failure.

Dr Scholtz asked if he was willing to undertake a much more important job instead. One way or another they would get Wulf Schmidt into Britain. Wulf hesitated and was doubtful as this reeked of danger, but Scholtz pointed out, as an unspoken threat, that he was now in great financial debt to them. He was told that before the mission he had, among other things, to learn Morse and codes for the encryption of his messages. Wulf was going to learn telegraphy from a certain Petersen together with a Swede named Gösta Caroli, in Hamburg. The two Scandinavians soon became good friends, but Caroli would eventually play an important role in Wulf Schmidt's mission to England.

Gösta Caroli was born in 1902, and had in his youth travelled several times to Canada, where he had worked on a farm that bred silver foxes. He started his own company breeding silver foxes in Sweden, which ended in bankruptcy. After that he lived the life of a vagabond around Europe, making his living from occasional work, and writing travel stories, for Swedish papers. Eventually, he came to Hamburg, where he got work in 1937 on the *Hamburger Tageblatt*, the official newspaper of the Nazis. Soon he got in contact with Abwehr, and carried out two spy missions for them in the Birmingham area in England in 1938 and 1939. He sent his reports by letter but the results were poor. When the war started, they tried to get him into Britain on a ship, SS *Mertainen*, carrying iron ore from Narvik to Britain. The ship was, however, sunk by German bombers outside Trondheim in April 1940, on the voyage from Narvik to England. Caroli was now once again back in Germany where the Abwehr intended to train him as an agent and send him back to Britain, now as a spy with radio equipment.[16]

When the course in Morse telegraphy was finished, Wulf was able to send 100 characters and receive 80 characters per minute (a qualified telegraphist managed at least 130 characters). They also received lessons on radio equipment, and *Hauptmann* Bruhns (his real name was Böckel) gave short courses on military matters, such as the equipment which the British Army and Air Force used, their airports, anti-aircraft artillery, camouflage, map reading, and he was also their teacher in meteorology. He explained that the information from Britain which the Abwehr were most interested in was the location of new airbases, what sort of defences they were equipped with, roads, radio communications, staffing, equipment, data on aircraft types, and number of aircraft. Secondary areas of interest were troop movements, the morale of the British people, the situation concerning food, roadblocks, evacuations, transportation, and factories with production for the armed forces. They would also regularly broadcast weather reports,[17] important information for the Wehrmacht.

Major Nikolaus Ritter was the head of the Luft department in *Abwehrstelle* Hamburg, and was responsible for the agents who were sent to Britain. He had spent many years in the USA before, in 1936, beginning work for the Abwehr, where his career advanced rapidly. Eventually, he only took orders directly from Admiral Canaris. He was in charge of Operation *Lena*, in which Wulf Schmidt and Gösta Caroli took part: the recruitment of agents in Britain before the expected invasion in September 1940. None of Ritter's handful of agents, including one woman, 'the beautiful spy' Vera Eriksen, succeeded; nearly all were caught and some of them executed.[18] Soon Ritter's career declined, especially after his whole network of agents in the USA were revealed and arrested in 1941.

Finally, on 25 August 1940, Wulf Schmidt was informed that they would leave Hamburg the following day, to embark on his espionage mission in England. After he had performed his mission, he had been promised a good job in the colonies after the war, and 7,500 Reichmarks; if he should die, 10,000 Reichmarks would be given to his sister. Wulf Schmidt, who had been given the designation Agent 3725 and the code name *Leonhard*, was ready for his mission.

The Double-Cross system managed to engage around 120 double agents during the war, most of whom had minor roles.[19] But there was a group of agents which was considered to be the great double agents, consisting of names such as GARBO, TRICYCLE, ZIGZAG, and also TATE, or Wulf Schmidt/Harry Williamson. There are recently published books about the first three mentioned agents.[20, 21, 22, 23, 24]

One book has been written about Wulf Schmidt, Harry Williamson, Agent 3725, *Leonhard* (he had many names), by the journalist and researcher Günter Peis: *The Mirror of Deception*, published in 1976.[25]

He is also mentioned in Ladislas Farago's *The Game of the Foxes* from 1971,[26] and in David Kahn's *Hitler's Spies* in 1978,[27] but these books were all written long before MI5's secret files became available to the public in the 1990s. That is why these books are filled with serious errors and are in parts completely unreliable. However, the advantage is that they relied heavily on German sources, which are now hard to find. The well-known writer Nigel West, who met Wulf in person, as did Günter Peis, wrote about him in his books *MI5: British Security Operations, 1909–45* in 1983,[28] and *Seven Spies Who Changed the World* in 1991,[29] and TATE is briefly mentioned in most books about secret intelligence operations in Britain during the war. It was when Nigel West's book was published in 1991, that his relatives for the first time found out the truth about what he really had done during the war, which was shocking news for some of them. His name for the rest of his life, Harry Williamson, which he used during and after the war when he became a British citizen, was revealed in the newspapers first in 1992, shortly before he died.

However, there is no comprehensive book of later date, based on the new information that has become available in recent years, about this interesting and unusual man. We believe that his remarkable life is well worth writing a book about. With the help of files from the National Archives in Kew, NARA in Washington, Danish archives, and new data from several other sources, we have managed to create a more complete picture of him, and write this book.

I

England Next

On 25 August 1940 a unit consisting of Wulf Schmidt, Major Nikolaus Ritter, the radiotelegraphy teacher Petersen, Brandt (a radio operator), and a military driver (Hinsch) started their journey in two cars from Hamburg towards Brussels, where they arrived on 27 August. The enterprise to send Wulf Schmidt as an Abwehr agent to England had started. In Brussels they went to the headquarters of *Eins Luft* (Referat IL) at Rue de la Loi. Now followed several trips by car, from Brussels to Paris (the Abwehr *Eins Luft* headquarters was in Hotel Lutetia), and back to Brussels again. Very odd, but the reason was that they had problems finding anyone in command in both Abwehr offices. At least they had opportunities to make several further tests of the radio equipment. But it must have been interesting for Wulf to see something of these countries on these outings by car, while the tension was probably increasing each day before his uncertain mission. But he was guarded, and Ritter warned Wulf that he was not allowed to talk to anyone on his own initiative.

They wined and dined and later in the evening, in Paris, Ritter introduced Wulf to a woman named Vera, with a Russian-sounding last name that he afterwards did not remember. This was of course Vera Eriksen, who in October would be landed by seaplane in Scotland as an agent in Major Ritter's Operation *Lena*, in which Wulf and Caroli were also involved. Some people still call her the 'Beautiful Spy', so the company must have been pleasant. She was accompanied by some *Oberleutnant*, possibly with the name Sturrege. The three had dinner together at the restaurant 'Ardennaise'. The night was spent in the Metropole Hotel.

They decided to go back to Brussels again, the reason being that the Luftwaffe pilot, who would fly Wulf to England, could not come to Paris. On 30 August, they went back to Brussels and the *Eins Luft* headquarters. In the afternoon, *Oberleutnant* Karl Gartenfeld, the pilot they were waiting for, arrived for his special mission to deliver agents with his *Staffel Gartenfeld*. He had flown from Rennes in France, and with him he also brought Gösta Caroli. It was decided that he would fly to England a few days after Wulf.

The security around the operation was supposed to be tight. The Abwehr was concerned about possible Allied agents in Belgium who could ruin the whole mission. Therefore, they were staying in different places. The responsible Abwehr chief, Major Ritter, his assistant *Leutnant* Georg Sessler, and his chauffeur Karl Schnurre were living in Hotel Metropole in Brussels, while the crew of the aircraft stayed at different hotels in Amsterdam, all wearing civilian clothes. The two main figures of the operation, Wulf Schmidt and Gösta Caroli, lodged at a boarding house close to the old north railway station in Brussels. Ritter, who trusted the two agents, allowed them to stay there without guards, which would prove to be a mistake. Caroli got involved with a servant girl, and told her about their mission. But the problem was solved by a severe threat against the girl and her father, in case they dared to tell anyone.

Gartenfeld had a long discussion with the unit regarding the location where Wulf, or Agent 3725, would be dropped. From the beginning it was planned that the drop would be performed the same evening, on 30 August, but there was no flight that night as the weather was too bad. Major Nikolaus Ritter continued to Antwerp, and Wulf never met him again. The next morning Gartenfeld handed some money to Wulf and Gösta Caroli, but he did not have much. Wulf, therefore, went to

Eins Luft, where he managed to persuade a civilian, Dr Kirchof, to call Bruhns in Hamburg. Bruhns ordered that 200 Marks should be given to Wulf, of which Caroli would have half, and Wulf changed some of their Reichmarks into the local currency. The bad weather continued for several days. Meanwhile, Wulf received instructions about parachute jumping and also met several other people during the days of waiting. A *Kapitän-Leutnant* Tornow arrived. He would now take care of Wulf and Caroli. He introduced Wulf to a Major Wenzlau at *Eins Luft* and also a Major Thoran, who had arrived from Berlin. Wulf got the impression that both Wenzlau and Thoran were affiliated to the General Command in Berlin. The Abwehr obviously had high hopes of what their agents would accomplish.

On 5 September, it was decided that Gösta Caroli should depart first instead of Wulf, despite the fact that the plan from the beginning had been that Wulf would go first. Caroli would actually fly the same night, and he was not going to use the heavier ZBV transmitter with its own parachute. He would jump with his radio equipment (a transceiver) strapped to his body. Caroli also received his other equipment, including a gun. Wulf was present at the airport when Caroli's flight departed on its journey to England.[1] At least they had spent almost a week together in Brussels.

A few days after Gösta Caroli had left, Wulf met two other agents, Fritz and Johannes. Wulf managed to make Fritz's radio equipment work, which had been unreliable. He discovered that new models of radio equipment existed, which Caroli had been equipped with. This would make it possible to avoid the heavier extra ZBV transmitter, which needed its own parachute. He would thus be able to jump from a higher altitude, and thus the weather was not so important anymore. Through *Oberleutnant* Weber, who was the head of the radio department, Wulf managed to get the newer and more compact equipment, which they tested with good results. In the coming days Wulf was fitted with the rest of his equipment, and had time to socialise with the others in the organisation.[2]

On 12 September it was once again decided that Wulf would set off on his flight, but it was cancelled because of bad weather. When he was at the airport, he noticed a collection of equipment which he heard belonged to Kurt Goose (or Hans Reysen), whom he had met during his training in Hamburg. He would later be called GANDER by the British as a double agent. Gartenfeld's unit had now received additional aircraft for the transportation of their agents. From *Kapitän-Leutnant* Tornow he received a fake British identification card in which Wulf wrote the name Williamson. He also received a ration book where he wrote the same name.

The identity card and ration book, with which all agents were equipped, were generally forged by the Abwehr in a clumsy way, and were easy to spot. Firstly, the first and last names were often in the wrong order, and everything but the signature was written in the same handwriting. Usually the authorities only wrote the registration number and the name on the card, the rest being filled in by the card owner. Several different handwriting styles should therefore be seen on the card. The address was written in the continental way with the name of the city before the street address and the date should not be before 20 May 1940 (new cards were probably introduced then). Foreigners needed information from their Aliens Registration Certificate written at the bottom of the left page of the ID card, which often was missing, and the card should have been folded by hand, not machine-folded as the German cards were.[3] Numbers were sometimes written in a continental way, the number '7', for example, is written in different ways in Britain and the rest of Europe, and also the style of written letters vary. The registration numbers and the addresses on the cards often revealed directly that they were fakes because the double agent SNOW had provided them for the Abwehr and he in turn had informed MI5, who could easily check the numbers and addresses from their lists.

Through a telegram, Wulf received information that, in an emergency, he could turn to a pianist in a dance band, Bernie Kiener (actually a double agent code named RAINBOW in British service). He was given his address (169 Lordship Road, London N16), but he was asked to be careful as there was a possibility that Kiener was under surveillance. The password would be 'How is Mr O'Brien?' and the answer was 'Mr

O'Brien is still in Guy's Hospital'. (A few weeks after he arrived, he received a request from the Germans asking if he had met Bernie Kiener, which he had not). He was also given the address of a Daisy Lopez, Santo Amara d'Oeiras, Av. Carlos Silva 33, Lisbon, where he could send a postcard with a secret message written with invisible ink, in case his radio equipment failed. In that way the Germans would understand why his radio transmissions had ceased, but he was certainly not allowed to contact her for any other reason. In case he was unlucky and was arrested, he had been instructed to invent a good cover story which would clear him until the invading German troops arrived, which they promised would be soon. If his life was at stake, he was, however, allowed to reveal the true story.[4]

His mission was to be performed in the area restricted by London–Bedford–Cambridge–Chelmsford (he had one map with him which only covered parts of the area): to examine obstacles to landings of aircraft in the fields, the location and calibres of anti-aircraft batteries, the location of new airfields and their fuel supplies, and to check how many aircraft were refuelled there to give an idea of the fuel capacity, the morale of the civilian population, and ongoing evacuations. Of course any other military information was of value. The reports should be encoded with a special cipher disk, and the transmissions should take place between the hours of midnight and 2.00 a.m., but did not have to occur every night. A first communication was expected within eight to ten days. The radio operator Brandt, who would receive his messages in Morse, recognised his style of transmitting. Wulf, however, stated in the hearing later that, because he was instructed to send only 30 to 40 characters per minute even though he was able to manage 90 to 100, it would probably be difficult to recognise his 'fist'.[5]

The transmitter and receiver were not very large, and were wrapped in air bags and strapped to his body with the batteries strapped to his legs.[6] The equipment also included a shovel to bury the parachute, a pistol with six shots and eight Pervitin (amphetamine) pills to stay alert.[7] He also brought with him £132 (4 £5, 62 £1, and 100 10s notes, and also 8s 5½d in coins) and $250 (including two $50 notes). The pound notes were actually those that Wulf originally brought with him from the Cameroons. He had been given permission by Dr Scholtz to change them for approximately 2,600 German Reichmarks, a beneficial exchange rate of around 20 Reichmarks to £1 which would later surprise the British.[8] (In the plans for the German invasion it was decided that the exchange rate for £1 should be set as 9½ Reichmarks after the defeat of Britain. In all conquered countries on the European continent, the exchange rate was always very favourable for the Reichmark.) Now, the same pound notes came in handy to use again. The dollar notes he had received because the Germans were short of English currency. Moreover, he had his genuine Danish passport with his own name, but they had removed a page that showed that he had travelled through Germany in 1938, and the amount of money he had been paid out from German banks (this was always noted in the passport), and the fake British identification card and ration book with the name Williamson.[9] He chose the name Harry Williamson because that was the only English name he could think of – a District Commissioner in the Cameroons, whom he had met.[10] This name he would later use during his life in England after the war. On his identification card with the name Williamson was a London address. MI5 knew it was false, as it was one of those SNOW had delivered to the Abwehr.[11]

Wulf also had a personal agreement with Gösta Caroli, unknown to the Germans, to meet him at the Black Boy Inn[12] in Nottingham. They would meet sometime between midday and 6.00 p.m. on the 10th, 20th or 30th, and they would continue each month until they met. The Germans were sure that the invasion would soon be successfully performed, and that Wulf could then feel safe. To begin with, however, he would follow the civilian population fleeing from the invading forces and continue with his reports to the Germans.

His personal valuables and other possessions were now deposited in a suitcase at the Phoenix Hotel. Wulf later stated, during interrogation by the British, that he was not particularly pro-German. Because of his travels abroad, he felt almost like a man without a homeland. But it had seemed impossible to get a job, and the Germans made an attractive promise of employment in the colonies after the war. There was, however, no signed contract and Wulf had not sworn any oath to Germany.[13]

The departure had now been postponed several times, but on 19 September 1940 at 10.00 p.m. the aircraft at last took off from Brussels. After the war Wulf still remembered the names of the crew: the pilots *Leutnant* Wolfgang Nabel and *Hauptmann* Karl Gartenfeld, *Feldwebel* Wagner was the radio operator, *Feldwebel* Suessman the observer and *Unteroffizier* Achtelik assisted with the parachute jump.[14] In contradiction it is stated in a file from the National Archives[15] that it was a small aircraft with only one pilot. Wulf was naturally getting more nervous for the flight, the parachute jump, and an unknown fate in England, but was perhaps relieved by some optimism concerning his mission; after all, his good friend Gösta Caroli had been working for some weeks as an agent in the country.

After about a 1½-hour flight they were over Cambridgeshire and Agent 3725, Wulf Schmidt, made his first ever (and only) parachute jump. He estimated that he jumped from about 3,500 metres during his interrogation by the British later. He landed undetected east of the village of Willingham, ten miles north of Cambridge, close to an air defence command post, about 100 yards from a searchlight. He was very surprised that he was not discovered, as there were personnel at the searchlight. The presence of an anti-aircraft defence was due to the fact that RAF Oakington was located nearby.[16] Because of the wind and his heavy load, the landing was hard; the wind got hold of him for the last seventy feet, and he drifted away out of control. He got stuck in a phone line on his way down and he dragged it down with him. The landing was rough, and he injured his hand and sprained his right ankle. Wulf had no training in parachuting and one important part of such training is the landing procedure to avoid injuries. In addition, he had broken his wrist watch on a strut when he jumped from the aircraft. He had to cut himself loose from the telephone line. The landing was in a field beside a small road called Priest Lane,[17] which led to Willingham, about two miles away. About five minutes after he landed he heard sirens from Willingham, which warned of an air attack.

The next morning, he hid his equipment in several places in the fields. The parachute was hidden in a haystack while his parachute harness, overall and flying helmet were covered up in a ditch. He found a large hedge with an opening, and hid the radio equipment under branches of the hedge, and covered it with some long grass. Additional equipment ended up in another haystack as the ground was too hard for digging with his shovel.

After this he went to the village of Willingham to buy a new watch, and some aspirin for the pain in his foot.[18] He bought a new Ingersoll watch in a barber's shop and aspirin in a chemist on Church Street, and *The Times* at the newsagent of Mrs Fields, then he used the village water pump to wash his swollen ankle. Next he had breakfast in a small café.[19] His English, which he had learned in Cameroon, was good but with a distinct foreign accent. Since he, a stranger, had appeared in a rural area, washed his feet with the village pump and spoke English with a foreign accent, he immediately aroused suspicion. When he was on his way back to his hidden equipment in the fields near Half Moon Bridge, around 10 a.m., one of the villagers became suspicious and asked to see his identification card. A soldier in the Home Guard, Tom Cousins, took care of Wulf and brought him to the headquarters of the Home Guard at the Three Tuns pub. There he was interrogated by Lieutenant Colonel Langton of the 1st Cambridgeshire Battalion of the Home Guard. With suspicions clearly aroused, they phoned the County Police in Cambridgeshire, and at lunchtime Wulf was transferred to the police station in Cambridge for further questioning. The Chief Constable personally called Captain Dixon, who was the Regional Security Liaison Officer (RLSO) of MI5. It was decided that Wulf would spend the night in the cell, but the next morning, 21 September 1940, he would be transferred to Camp 020 in Latchmere House in West London.

The whole time, MI5 and the police had known that an agent would soon arrive by parachute. Gösta Caroli had revealed this during interrogation at Camp 020, shortly after his arrest on 6 September. So the police and MI5 were on the alert to catch the next arriving Abwehr agent, No. 3725 with cover name *Leonhard*, the Dane Wulf Schmidt. They even knew his name.

During the war all captured suspects in the UK were interrogated at Camp 020, with detention of varying duration. After having been engaged in this activity in scattered and substandard premises (for example in Wormwood Scrubs prison), it was realised that MI5 needed premises in a safe place in a more remote and protected location, sheltered from public scrutiny, where suspected enemy agents could be isolated and subjected to interrogation in an orderly manner. They found a suitable place, the Victorian estate Latchmere House at Ham Common in the suburbs of Richmond in West London. The buildings were surrounded by a large area belonging to the estate, at the end of a small road lined by a screen of trees.

The property and surrounding land had already been purchased by the War Office during the First World War, and was then used as a hospital and the rehabilitation home for 'shell-shocked' officers. Latchmere had an annex with thirty rooms, well suited for detaining prisoners. An additional wing was built in 1941, a two-storey building with ninety-two cells, which were equipped with interception microphones, often placed in the ceiling.[20] The value of these was, however, quite limited, because most prisoners were aware of the risk of bugging, and the task was demanding with a staff who needed education and brains to know what was important. In the main building there were three floors with the offices for interrogation situated on the first floor. There was a tall wooden fence around the entire perimeter so Latchmere was hidden from prying eyes, and the entire inner area was surrounded by double barbed-wire barriers. There was only one entrance/exit, manned by military police. Special passports were required for admission, and all visits were recorded.

Eventually, the staff consisted of some twenty-five people who managed the interrogations, around a hundred soldiers with four or five officers who took care of the security watch, and there were about fifty female office workers.[21] The new area was also called 'Ham'. This institution opened on 10 July 1940, and on 27 July the first twenty-seven inmates arrived, consisting mainly of British fascists, often members of the British Union of Fascists. In December 1941 it was given the name Camp 020 by the military authorities. The name came about because of the existence of a similar institution, Camp 001, a hospital wing at Dartmoor Prison.

The officer who became the head of Camp 020 at the inauguration was a remarkable and bombastic man, with a colourful way of writing, who later became a legend. He was Lieutenant Colonel Robin Stephens, born in Alexandria of British parents in 1900. He received his education in a French school in Egypt and he finished in Dulwich College, after the family had moved to England in 1912. When he was eighteen years of age, he entered the Royal Academy in Woolwich and later the Quetta Cadet College in India, and then joined the Indian army, where he participated in five military campaigns on the north-west frontier. He returned to Britain in 1933, and in September 1939, as a captain, he was contacted by the Security Service. Robin Stephens was a very colourful person and a lot of Camp 020's history is linked to his personality. He mastered several languages, Urdu, Arabic, Somali, Amharic, French, German, and Italian, and was very widely travelled.

His personality corresponded to what one would expect of a commander at a secret facility for the interrogation of suspected spies, with a sinister reputation as a temperamental, authoritarian person. A typical comment was that he was 'disliked by most of the people he came into contact with, because of his almost Nazi behaviour and vile temper'.[22] He was always perfectly dressed in a Ghurka Rifles uniform, and physically he resembled a stereotypical Gestapo officer from the film world. He wore a monocle, earning him the nickname 'Tin-eye',[23] which, however, no one dared to use in his presence. Employees have said that he had a short fuse when it came to those he suspected of working for the enemy. His menacing manner and behaviour was, however, mainly window dressing. His female staff liked him for his politeness and humour. He was also a generous host and arranged parties for the staff, with good food and plenty of good wines and other beverages.[24] His disgust of the enemy was evident with an almost morbid feeling of hatred, a feeling he tried to convey to his staff, and which he considered to be necessary for all interrogators.

Because of all the secrecy concerning Camp 020 and its terrible commander, a vicious rumour existed after the war about secret executions and even faked executions to crack the agents.[25] Stephens may be deemed to have been a xenophobe, and often used derogatory descriptions of inmates from other countries, such as: 'Italy is a country populated by small-sized posturing inhabitants', 'weeping and romantic fat Belgians', 'of all the obstinate, immoral and immutable Spaniards, he was undoubtedly the most pigheaded'.[26] He was a product of the time, and he enjoyed making sweeping and disparaging comments to impress and entertain others. Although Stephens was considered by many as an unpleasant oddity, it was well known, not least by himself, that he was a master in his work to establish the suspect's guilt, break his resistance, scare him, to then gain his trust, and if considered appropriate, the MI5 officer Tommy Argyll, or TAR Robertson from the Seaforth Highlanders, would take care of the agent for training as a double agent. He was the head of section B1(a), which handled captured agents, and was going to be a very important person in working with Wulf Schmidt, and one of the most important members of the Double-Cross organisation.

On the subject of interrogators, Stephens stated that there were two types: 'the breaker', who managed to break the prisoner, and 'the investigator', who could obtain and report relevant data. 'A breaker is born and not made', that is, has an innate talent that only some possess. Robin Stephens wrote down his experiences during the war in a book entitled *A Digest of Ham*. It begins with a history section on the activities of Ham[27] (Camp 020), then an interesting section of twenty-five pages on how to interrogate spies, followed by a longer section of 'Case Histories', which deals with 200 separate suspected agent cases where 350 individuals are mentioned. His language is very colourful, vivid, and very entertaining. This subsequently was published in a book from the National Archives in 2000 entitled *Camp 020, MI5 and the*

Nazi Spies, with a foreword by Oliver Hoare, an expert on intelligence work. Stephens had a blunt exterior but with a psychological insight that made him a master of the interrogation of suspected agents. Stephens himself said: 'The story of Ham is stranger than fiction, indeed, as a work of fiction it would violate the probabilities.'[28]

During the interrogations, the goal was to clarify whether the detainees were guilty, to get as much vital information about enemy intentions as possible, and to recruit inmates as double agents in the Double-Cross system. The development of interrogation methodology at Latchmere relied a lot on 'trial and error', and accumulated experience; there were no pre-written manuals on the subject. Newly caught agents had to undress and undergo physical searches. Possible tags sewn into clothing were checked. The teeth were examined to identify any toxic materials, or capsules for secret invisible writing; chemicals for invisible writing could also be impregnated in clothing or in the seams. The agents got special prison clothes: flannel trousers, a coat, and a six-inches-wide diamond-shaped white piece of cloth, which was sewn on, easily visible on their clothing. As a next step, data such as name, date and place of birth, nationality, address, weight, and height were taken. Photos were taken, both in civilian clothes and in prison uniform. The photo with civilian clothes could then be used for further research without revealing that the agent was sitting in Camp 020.

A medical examination was conducted by Dr Harold Dearden, who was a psychiatrist and well-known expert in criminology.[29] At the hearings, he was often dressed in rather shabby civilian clothes, with cigarette ash here and there, and with uncombed white hair. Wulf Schmidt became fascinated by this odd, elderly man, who was reading a trade magazine. He had looked up at Schmidt briefly, but continued later to read during the hearing.[30] He often had disagreements with Stephens. Later, Stephens said: 'Strange people psychiatrists, even in war.'

It was important that the hearings began as soon as possible and the initial hearing was crucial to break the prisoner, and to get what they wanted. The prisoner came into a room, where a panel of officers was sitting with their backs against the window, often with Stephens as chairman. It was almost exclusively the chairman who conducted the inquest. Each prisoner's possessions and relevant documents were placed on the table. A secretary wrote down the hearing in shorthand. The suspect had to stand up during the entire hearing. Questions and statements were fired at a rapid pace, often without even waiting for the response, and the prisoner was allowed to speak only when he was asked. It has been stated that Wulf Schmidt had to stand naked in front of the panel, in spite of the presence of a female secretary.[31] A clear distance should to be kept from the prisoner, no familiar tone. According to Stephens:

> The penalty for espionage is death. If the spy tells the truth he may live. There is no guarantee; it is a hope, not more. The quicker the spy realises that fundamental position the better. Psychology and discipline should produce the results. Arrest must be efficient. The less said the better. The quicker the handcuffs are slipped on the more pronounced is the effect of stark reality. The quicker ill fitting and shabby prison garb takes the place of sartorial elegance the more profound and depressing is the effect. No chivalry. No gossip. No cigarettes ... Figuratively, a spy in war should be at the point of a bayonet.[32]

The atmosphere was reminiscent of a trial. The accused was informed that, based on his response, it would be determined whether he should be executed or not. Any assistance from civilian authorities was not to be expected, and a trial would never be necessary.[33] Sometimes they would show material from already executed spies. Once the questioning began, it was 'Truth in the shortest possible time' which was the aim.[34]

Surprisingly, in view of Stephen's blunt personality, there was a clear rule that physical violence was never to be used in any circumstances. This was because, 'not only does it produce answers to please, but it lowers the standard of the information'. Moreover, such Gestapo methods reduced opportunities for recruitment to the Double-Cross organisation. On the other hand, refined psychological intimidation was used in a variety of forms.

At one point, however, violence was used, and it was actually Wulf Schmidt who became the victim of this. An officer from MI19 (the department in charge of the interrogation of prisoners of war), Lieutenant Colonel Alexander Scotland, assaulted him to get more information, but without success. Scotland was removed from participation in further interrogations at Camp 020.[35] Usually threats of execution because of espionage were used.

Sixteen agents were hanged in Wandsworth or Pentonville prisons and one was shot in the Tower. Stephens regretted that so few cases went to trial and prosecution. The threat of execution was backed up by a desire to give the impression that MI5 was omnipotent, and already knew everything. Thus, it was equally good for the prisoner to admit and tell everything, because most was already known.

Useful information came from ISOS (Intelligence Service Oliver Strachey, after the responsible section head), the signals intelligence at Bletchley Park, which more and more successfully managed to read Enigma-ciphered radio-based traffic. From December 1941 they were able to read all Abwehr radio communications for the rest of the war.[36] If the interrogation team failed to break down the agent quickly during the first interview, sophisticated methods were used such as using 'stool pigeons', who were detained together with the prisoner, but actually worked for the interrogation team. Also 'sympathy men' were used, who with friendly behaviour towards the prisoner tried to win his confidence. There was also a legend about two penalty-cells, number 13 and 14, called 'condemned cells', which was an additional psychological weapon. The message 'You will now be taken to Cell Fourteen' by the interrogators, made the prisoner fear that now the worst was coming, and often many began to cooperate. Stephens was usually able to close a less successful interrogation by using implied threats:

You will now be taken to Cell Fourteen. In time of peace it was a padded cell, so protected that raving maniacs could not bash out their brains against the wall. Some recovered. Some committed suicide. Some died from natural causes. The mortuary is conveniently opposite. Cell Fourteen ... perhaps it is remote, and cold and a little dark. That is all. But the sinister reputation persists ... Results are interesting. Some spies have told the truth and been transferred. Some have committed suicide. Some have passed out for the last time to their judicial hanging – their rich desert. I shall not see you again. I do not know how long you will be there. Petitions will be ignored. Only if you decide to tell the truth will you be allowed to write. But just remember this, that we are winning the war in spite of you – one man only – in captivity. Maybe you are holding back information which is already in our possession. Maybe you are more of a fool than a hero. For the rest, you will be interested perhaps in the movements of the sentry who will cover you every quarter of the hour. Perhaps he comes to check. Perhaps he comes with food. Perhaps he comes – to take you away – for the last time.[37]

The security personnel took part in the mental breakdown of the agents too. The prisoner was put in a solitary cell. The guards wore tennis shoes so they would not be heard in the corridors, and had strict instructions to avoid talking to the prisoner or to answer questions. They appeared blunt and could come up with statements like: 'The guy in your neighbour cell has recently been shot, I should think it's your turn next.'[38] When Wulf Schmidt was picked up for his first radio transmission, the guard, who thought he was being taken to a prison to be shot, asked if he could have Wulf's watch now, because he would not need it anymore.[39]

The use of drugs and alcohol often had the opposite effect; the prisoner became more resistant, relaxed and less tense. The classic technique of 'good cop, bad cop' was used, particularly if the inmate was considered more susceptible to a gentleman's approach. The first interview was with a terse threat of a death sentence as described above, and the prisoner was sent away without the opportunity of defending himself. Later, a more sympathetic officer arrived in the cell, and tried to smooth over the harsh statements of the first hearing if the prisoner was willing to cooperate. After the agent had admitted his espionage mission it often seemed as if a burden had eased, and many were willing to cooperate fully. Several agreed to switch to an active role in the Allied service, or as 'stool pigeons' or 'sympathy men' in the camp.

For prisoners who were detained for a long time the daily routine was like ordinary prison life. Much was boring, but there was access to gardening, a library, rooms for recreation, physical training, and association with other prisoners. Connection with other prisoners could have positive effects. With a source with the 'correct' attitude, an effect could perhaps be achieved on hard-core *Dritten Reich* fanatics. One example is the Belgian Huysmans, who came to the camp in 1943. He was never asked to work for MI5, but did it unintentionally. He told his story to newly arrived prisoners, how MI5 knew everything and silence was meaningless. After his confession he had received positive help and his wife had been smuggled to England so the Germans could not catch her. His advice was that everybody really should follow his example. As a person he was intelligent, well educated, knew several languages and had a very convincing manner.

Visits and writing letters were, however, not allowed; if anything leaked about this institution, the whole system with double agents risked being destroyed. Some were allowed to cook their own food. The rations were similar to what the British Army received, but with more bread and less meat, which however could be complemented with fresh vegetables from the kitchen garden of the prison. In wartime Britain the slogan 'digging for victory' was well known, and it was very appropriate to have Abwehr agents doing this work. Camp 020 was not a Prison of War, and it could not be found in the lists of such camps, which the Red Cross had. It was, therefore, not essential to apply the Geneva Convention to these interned spies; this was a civilian camp under the rules of Home Office. This meant that isolation in a solitary cell was allowed for up to twenty-eight days. You may think this was a juridical detail, but this was still a society built on human rights, a description that could hardly be applied to Hitler's Reich.

Camp 020 was the target for two attacks by bombers, the first one causing severe damage. On 30 November 1940 an air-mine landed on the roof and exploded, which caused severe damage, but only one person was killed, a German prisoner named Bruhn. The secret bugging equipment was destroyed, as was the officers' mess, offices and lodgings;

the telephones, water and electricity were also put out of action. For a while therefore, all interrogations were held in the mortuary. The necessity of a reserve camp in some other place was realised, as was the need for the storage of spent agents. One important part of the agreement with those who took on the work as double agents was that they would avoid execution. Therefore, a new institution was built, Camp 020R in Huntercombe, outside Oxford.

INTERROGATION

On the night of 6 September Gösta Caroli landed at a farm just outside the village of Denton in Northamptonshire. His landing was traumatic as, just like Wulf Schmidt, he had not had any parachute training. He was knocked unconscious, possibly by his radio in the suitcase hanging strapped to his body. The next day he was discovered lying down resting on his parachute in a ditch. He was brought to Camp 020 where he soon confessed everything. After only a few days, on 9 September, he agreed to start working as a double agent, and he was given the cover name SUMMER. During the questioning he soon revealed that another two agents were on their way: his friend Wulf Schmidt and Hans Reysen (or Kurt Goose). This confession was made unwillingly and Caroli was full of remorse, but the interrogators were very skilful. The thing that finally persuaded Caroli to reveal everything about them was a promise that the life of Wulf Schmidt would be spared. What would happen to Gösta himself was of less importance to him. Stephens later wrote:

> For the first and last time in the history of Camp 020 a promise was made to a prisoner; SUMMER was assured that the life of his friend would be spared. It was a momentous decision, and it was to prove felicitous, for upon that promise devolved many of the most spectacular wartime successes of the British counter-espionage service.[40]

So when the interrogation of the arrested Wulf Schmidt started, they had a real ace in their hands, as they already knew quite a lot about him due to Gösta Caroli. This was of course a hopeless situation for Wulf, but in the beginning nothing was revealed to him about their knowledge. As Gösta Caroli's information was so important, the questioning of him about the arrival of Wulf Schmidt can be found in Appendix I.

In an autobiographical letter to his cousin Gisella Alloni in 1989, Wulf described how he

> ended up in a comfortable environment but was not allowed to sit down, nor did he get water or was allowed to go to the bathroom. It was no need to use violence against me, I had already lost the battle. But I never accepted being called a traitor, I was Danish, not German.[41]

This may seem inhumane today, but we must remember that Britain was facing a threat that would mean being totally enslaved by a regime of gangsters worse than the Chicago variety. So the methods used to discover important information about the enemy can be understood and justified. But torturing prisoners half to death was not on the agenda, unlike with the Gestapo. At one interrogation, Wulf was apparently forced to stand naked in spite of the presence of a female secretary. Whether this is fiction or not, we do not know. There is so much uncertainty in our story of Wulf Schmidt that cannot be verified from original sources, the files from Camp 020 and MI5, from his own few documented words, or from the early books by Ladislas Farago 1971,[42] David Kahn 1978,[43] and Günther Peis in 1976,[44] which were almost entirely built on German, often distorted, sources. Unfortunately, many errors in these books still persist in the literature on this subject.

The first interview with Wulf was by military staff because of the impending invasion and Wulf Schmidt managed to keep his cover story intact. During the lunch break, Lieutenant Colonel Alexander Scotland, later head of the notorious London Cage where prisoners were treated almost as if they were in a concentration camp, entered Wulf's cell and started to use physical force. This was discovered and stopped by one of the ordinary interrogation staff of Camp 020. Stephens then decided that only staff employed at Camp 020 would attend the interrogation. But in spite of this, the next day Scotland arrived again with a syringe containing a 'truth serum', but Stephens stopped this bizarre attempt.[45]

In the transcripts it is obvious that Wulf was hardly very fluent in English. First he demanded to see the Danish consul, which was ignored. He further insisted that on 7 July he had travelled by fishing boat from Esbjerg, and arrived north of West Hartlepool on the night of 10/11 July. They did not dare go into the port itself, but rowed him ashore north of Hartlepool. The boat was a sixty-foot brown barge with No. E 134 or 136, and a fisherman was captain. It had brown sails, but mostly used the diesel engine. There were eight in the crew, and they had stopped to fish at times. It had been quite windy, a south-westerly wind. He had paid 500 Danish kroner for the trip, and said that he was a journalist (if they were boarded by the Royal Navy, he would argue that he was going to write a story about fishing), but the reason why he fled to England was that he was forced to escape after he got into a fight with a German soldier in Aabenraa. This happened because the soldier bragged that Denmark was now theirs. He had arrived from the Cameroons in March 1940, and gave a detailed account of his trip back home by boat, and his journey through Germany on his way to Aabenraa. A contributing factor to the exodus from Denmark was that he had worked for the British in the Government Central Bureau in the Cameroons, and received payment from them, not a positive fact when dealing with Germans. Throughout the questioning, the chairman Stephens argued that he was a liar, and that he had in fact been in Germany and was trained as an agent, including radio telegraphy:

> Don't tell me this cock and bull story. Now look here my man, I know more about you than you think. You are in a very dangerous position. You are going to be shot as a spy if you don't start telling the truth.[46]

Wulf wore a coat made in Paris, which aroused suspicion, but Wulf had bought it in Copenhagen. The knife he possessed looked suspiciously similar to the knife used by Nazi stormtroops. The ration book Wulf possessed was discussed. He insisted that he had bought it from a man in a café, and also the identification card. This was an absurd impossibility, according to the questioner, as it was absolutely impossible to obtain these documents from a complete stranger in a café. Furthermore, there was another name, Harry Williamson, on these documents compared with the name in his Danish passport. Wulf said that the name was already there on the identity card and ration book when he bought them and he had only added the address. This was written in an odd way too, not with the number before the street, which was the British way of writing an address. He had paid £10 for the documents and visited the café three or four times. They asked why he did not take the opportunity to arrange lodgings with the same man, instead of sleeping outdoors, but Wulf considered that to be insecure.

The pound notes he had bought from a Dane, who had sold fish in England, and obtaining dollars was no problem in Denmark. The question about what he had been doing during the time after his arrival in July was raised. It was very suspicious that he had not immediately made contact with the police to reveal that he was a refugee, but Wulf said that he thought the Danish consul was in London, and had intended to go there. He also had considered joining the British Army. Initially he had wandered around for some weeks, living on buns and chocolate, and subsequently reached the middle of England. He had avoided towns, afraid to risk being caught by the police, but finally he reached Birmingham. Questions were raised about how he knew it was Birmingham; he had read it in a paper he bought, and talked to people. There he spent three weeks, and had mostly slept in gardens. Then he decided to walk towards Cambridge on his way to London. He never arrived in Cambridge, but reached Willingham (which he continuously called Billingham) after nine days. On his way there he had fallen into a ditch and hurt his hand and strained his ankle.

He was asked why his clothes did not look more worn and dirty, if he had been wearing the same clothes during his long wandering. And how could his trousers remain so well pressed? He had slept outdoors for a couple of nights in Willingham before he was arrested as he did not dare to use hotels. It was pointed out that there were doubts about his story, about what he had really done. His story now covered forty-seven days and they should have been somewhere around 27 August; there was a big gap in the chronology to 20 September. During the interrogation he was now and then interrupted by insinuations that he was lying, and that his real identity was that of a German spy:

> You have not said a single word of truth. If you don't wish to speak the truth, we have methods to make you speak the truth, which will be very unpleasant for you. Do you understand that? Alright. You must make up your mind very quickly what you are going to do, because what will happen to you will be something you never forget.

And where did he cut his hair; the length of his hair was definitely not what would be expected after two and a half months. Wulf insisted that his hair grew slowly. He had shaved using razorblades he had brought with him. And where did he wash his clothes? Wulf said that he brought several shirts, socks and underwear, which he threw away when they were dirty. Stephens, who was in charge of most of the questioning, now started to ask him about his relatives. Wulf told about a sister, and Stephens asked if he wanted them to tell her after he had been shot. Wulf answered 'yes' to this question. His military service was discussed; it was considered strange that he knew about Morse telegraphy if he had been in the cavalry. Further, Stephens, in a sarcastic remark, said that he was not surprised that the Germans conquered Denmark in one day, with people like Wulf in the cavalry. During the interrogation Stephens now and then lost his temper:

> You know the whole story is a stack of lies. We know that. It has been proved. It is very badly told and does not fit in with anything. It is just a question of whether you intend to help yourself or not. We know a good deal about you, you see. Everything is consistent with your having fallen from a parachute a couple of days ago. Your clothes, in the first place, are clean. Your hair has recently been cut. You probably hurt your hand and foot when you landed. Your health is good, which means you have not been living on buns and chocolate for two months.[47]

34

Now the interrogators started to read out for Wulf from the transcripts made during the questioning of Gösta Caroli, where he described Wulf Schmidt and his expected arrival. The transcript had been re-written in such a way that it would appear that Caroli was a traitor. Wulf Schmidt now realised that the game was lost. His reaction was dramatic and came quickly. Completely losing his previously well-kept control, he cursed 'that swine Caroli', and exclaimed that he would now tell everything.[48]

2

Recruited Double Agent

It was not only Gösta Caroli's treason during the questioning of him that made Wulf Schmidt turn around completely and join the British Service. In the German newspapers and radio there was constant news of Britain being a dying country, even if Wulf was somewhat sceptical of this propaganda. But Germany, ruled by a clique of psychopathic gangsters and evil institutions, like Hitler, the Nazis, Gestapo, Abwehr, SS, grotesque racial theories, and an obedient tool in the Wehrmacht, now seemed invincible. Poland, Norway, Denmark, Holland, Belgium, tiny Luxembourg, and France were quickly defeated. Among the German people, the coming invasion of still undefeated Britain was a common topic of discussion, and they were convinced that it would come soon. The propaganda informed the German people that large parts of British cities lay in ruins.[1] Of Buckingham Palace and the Parliament there were only ashes left, people starved and their morale was broken. Perhaps even the Nazis believed in their own words. Capitulation would inevitably come in the reasonably near future, and one of Wulf's missions was to report on the miserable state of the country.[2] The other potential agents had received similar information during their training. Wulf felt as if he had to believe in this, to be able to continue with his task. He hoped and assumed that the invasion would go as planned, and that the Germans would appear before his money was exhausted.[3] He had been told that the invasion might come within fourteen days, so Wulf was advised to have the wine chilled ready for the victory celebration as soon as he arrived in England.

During the journey from Cambridge to Camp 020, the driver of the van made a proper tour of London. Wulf was shocked. The streets swarmed with people, cars, buses, news vendors, and shops were open as usual, with fairly full shop windows. No one seemed to be suffering distress in the least. People stood and looked up into the sky where the last critical phase of the Battle of Britain was going on. He also saw that Buckingham Palace was still standing in its full glory. Not one bomb crater did he see during the trip.

He realised that everything he had heard was untrue. He started to question whether he should actually put his life at stake for such obvious lies.[4] So even before the interrogation started at Camp 020, Wulf had begun to have serious doubts. Even the possibility of a rapid and successful German invasion seemed remote. When later, after only one day of intensive interrogation, he gave up, it was pointed out to Wulf that Caroli's testimony had actually been of only minor importance. The main thing was that the Germans, with their poor preparation and outright lies, had sent him into an unsafe and lost battle, which now he also realised himself.[5]

During the questioning, Wulf now showed a cooperative attitude which was a complete change from his stubborn manner during the initial questioning. He soon revealed everything, especially about his time in Germany and Denmark after he returned from the Cameroons, with a detailed account of the training and preparations for his departure to England. The British carefully went through all involved German personnel, with names provided as accurately as Wulf could remember. He had to describe what they looked like, and many times the interrogation team could work out who was really hiding behind an alias. This gave the British additional important information, which helped to identify Abwehr activities. Much time was also spent on going through the cipher system and the operation of the radio transmissions. The atmosphere was now completely different. Wulf had been surprised because instead of torture or rigorous, harsh questioning including psychological intimidation the tone was now much more pleasant. Unlike British agents of the SOE and other organisations, the Abwehr agents had no training in how to cope with this more subtle style of interrogation.

Dr Harold Dearden, a leading psychiatrist, was a principal interrogator at Camp 020, and was soon able to form a view of Wulf's psyche. The young Dane seemed most of all to need people he could rely on. He had been insecure ever since his youth, and on the run from his very dominant father, who treated him as a Prussian general would have done. The ashes of his mother were kept in an urn on his desk, and later his father refused to say where she was buried. This makes one wonder about the mental health of this man. Respect for authority was deeply rooted in Wulf, which was noticeable during interrogations. Dr Dearden realised that Wulf needed someone to forge links with, and get support from. In addition, Dearden was certain that Wulf Schmidt was actually homosexual. Showing kindness and friendship were important elements in persuading Wulf to come over to the British side. Dr Dearden, who often had the role as 'sympathy man', actually sat down and drank whisky with him.[6] Wulf would, after the war, insist that they tried to get him drunk, something which contradicts the policy at Camp 020 of not using alcohol or drugs, as it often created the opposite effect by boosting the confidence of the prisoner.

Within a week, Wulf found someone to confide in, who could provide support, and whom he could trust: one of the members of the interrogation team, Major (later Colonel) TAR Robertson,[7] one of the most important men in MI5 during the war. Later, the radio operator Russell Lee would become an important friend and supporter of Wulf in his difficult and nerve-wracking work. 'Tin-eye' Stephens also had a final interview with Wulf, where he pointed out that he actually respected Wulf as he had shown 'guts', was brave during the interrogations, and had said that he did not mind exposing himself to danger. Also, when he finally decided to tell everything he had stuck to the truth. Stephens was even generous enough to say that they were probably rather alike, with a taste for travel and living in other countries. But, he warned him, Wulf had still come as a spy, and if he attempted any bluffing or deception the consequences would be merciless.

The Scot, TAR Robertson, was head of the B1(a) department of MI5. Section B was responsible for counter-espionage, and the subdivision 'a' stood for German espionage. He was born in Sumatra in 1909, his father being a Scottish banker, and after school he went to Sandhurst military academy, and ended up in the Scottish Seaforth Highlanders. As a twenty-year-old officer, he lived a luxurious life filled with parties, fast cars and beautiful women, but his father did not approve of this extravagant lifestyle. Officers at that time served only a few hours in the morning, after that he could amuse himself by drinking pink gin, playing golf or taking rides in his MG Midget car. His father got tired of paying the bills, and TAR was slipping into a boring job in the City of London. But MI5 and his friend Guy Liddell, who was head of section B, persuaded him instead to start work with the security services. At that time, personal contacts were essential to be recruited to MI5. The chain-smoking party-man was always elegantly dressed in suits from Saville Row, and later when he worked for MI5 sometimes dressed in tartan trousers, to the secretaries' delight, who adored him for his 'good looks' and friendly manner. According to his secretary Peggy Harmer (one of the last survivors from the MI5 staff of that time) he was 'universally adored by his staff, very good-looking, and terrifically well-organised, but in a relaxed way. He was delightful'.[8] He would become a prominent and highly valuable employee in MI5. During their operations, he came in contact with most new agents, and had an important role in initially determining their fate, and later he gave instructions to and directed the work of the agents. With the ability to listen and to assess people and complex situations, he was extremely valuable for the successful efforts of the British secret service with disinformation, use of double agents, and obtaining important secret intelligence. He later became the head of the radio communications centre (GCHQ) in Cheltenham, and then a farmer, before he died in 1994.[9] According to his obituary in *The Times*, TAR

Robertson in handling agents exploited 'unusual power of persuasion' and had a 'deceptively sympathetic nature'.[10]

Guy Liddell, head of MI5 section B, suggested that perhaps they could use Wulf as a double agent.[11] There were three criteria that should be fulfilled before MI5 could consider someone as a potential recruited double agent, besides, of course, being able to trust the person. The arrest of the person should have occurred quickly after arrival, the agent should not have had time to communicate with the Germans, and the arrest should have taken place without public knowledge. Wulf Schmidt fitted these requirements and was rapidly recruited as a double agent.

At a meeting concerning Wulf's suitability as a double agent, Dr Dearden presented his psychological profile of him, and added that Wulf at the present time felt some anger towards the interrogation team, as they had shaken his pride a little, but that he had a fine sense of humour. TAR Robertson responded:

> You're absolutely right! I have always wondered whom he reminds me of, but when you mention the humour, I know who it is, it's Harry Tate, the comedian and music hall entertainer.[12, 13]

Moreover, there was a good cricket player, a bowler with the same name, someone pointed out. Thus, Wulf Schmidt, with his German code name *Leonhard*, now also had a cover name as a British double agent, and from now on we call him TATE in the text. The phrase Harry Tate has even more meanings in the English language; the Cockney 'rhyming slang' used it instead of 'worried', and in the merchant fleet it was used as a designation for the chief officer, second in rank after the captain. During World War I there was an aircraft known as 'Harry Tate', a two-seater reconnaissance aircraft, RE8, which with 'rhyming slang' became 'Harry Tate', an unfortunate machine with a nasty tendency to spin.[14] 'Harry Tate's Navy' was the nickname of the patrols using small boats to find mines, often fishermen and other civilians, who did not care about the strict rules of the Royal Navy.[15]

The next step now would be to locate his hidden equipment in Willingham. Early one Sunday morning, at 5.50 a.m. on 22 September, a group of five people (surprisingly Dr Dearden had joined then), including TATE, set off by car to Willingham, about ten miles north of Cambridge. In wartime England the trip from Richmond took two hours. The torn-down telephone lines after TATE's violent landing were noted, and a search for his radio equipment was made of the hiding places revealed by TATE: haystacks, ditch and hedge. The radio was found without difficulty; it consisted of transmitter, receiver and batteries in one red and two small black leather bags. They found his parachute with harness, flying suit and helmet, the cipher disk with instructions, a map, some chocolate, two rolls of bandages, a box of pills (containing the amphetamine Pervitin) and a leather package with two more pills (probably cyanide). It is likely that he was equipped with this effective means of committing suicide. Already, at 10.40 a.m., they were back in Latchmere House, and the prisoner was placed in his cell again.[16]

They discussed how the enciphering of his reports should be performed. He had a circular disc of cardboard with a smaller rotating disc attached. Around the two discs were the alphabet and numbers. TATE would set 'L' (as in *Leonhard*) on the internal disk towards the current date on the external disk. Then he used a simple substitution cipher, in which letters from the inner ring, which were in random and not alphabetical order, were exchanged for the letter that was opposite on the larger disc. For the call sign he would use the three letters corresponding to those that stood opposite the first, third and fifth letter from the 'L', on the inner ring. The Germans would then use the letters which stood against the second, fourth and sixth letters as their call sign, and this would therefore be TATE's call sign the next day, when he put his 'L' against the next day's date (see Appendix II).

Later, he received radio messages ordering him to change his 'L' to other letters. Transmissions should be carried out with the message divided into groups of five letters. Numbers were indicated by an 'X' before and after. The usual abbreviations from the international Q code could be used, for example, to communicate about the quality and audibility of the radio signal. TATE had a small card with the most common abbreviations (with the plaintext in Spanish!). All agents had a similar set for enciphering, but the order of the letters in the inner ring varied for each agent, and another character was set to the current date, in Gösta Caroli's case the letter 'G'. Later the Abwehr would send instructions for increasingly complex ciphers to their agents, including TATE. The transmission, in TATE's case, should take place between the hours of midnight and 2.00 a.m., but not necessarily every night. The antenna had to be placed facing the east-west direction (a compass was included in his equipment), prompting the radio technicians to assume that the signals were directed towards Cherbourg (Caroli had instruction to set it up in a north-south direction). TATE had no idea where the receiving station was, but he thought possibly it was in Paris. They put pressure on TATE to tell if there was any second system of cipher, but this was not the case. He had been instructed to send with a speed of 30 to 40 characters per minute, although he was capable of handling 100 characters per minute. The radio operator Brandt recognised his Morse 'fist', but it was doubtful if that was the case with such a low transmission rate. If Brandt sat as a receiver, he would communicate this by calling himself '*Hr. Bra*'.[17]

Surprisingly, any security system for the radio transmissions was never mentioned. The Germans could not be certain that it really was *Leonhard*/Wulf Schmidt, who was sitting with the Morse key, and he should have had a system to inform the Germans if he had been caught. This was extremely important for all British agents who worked during the war. A simple way to ensure that the genuine agent really was sending the messages, was to have an agreement that, for example, letters should be incorrect at certain intervals, or that a certain word should always be included in the transmissions. The recipients could also include questions that needed a particular answer. Often several methods were used together; an arrested agent might be forced to reveal his security checks, and could start with disclosing the first one. If this little detail was missing in the messages, it implied that the agent was communicating under enemy control, or that someone else was doing the transmission. The latter could be controlled by having recordings of the agent's 'fist'. This is very characteristic and easy for someone with a trained ear to recognise, as easy as identifying the handwriting. This may seem remarkable as Morse only consists of 'dots' and 'dashes', but there are individual ways of how certain letters were signalled, or the duration of the 'dashes', or the interval between the 'dots' and 'dashes' for certain letters, or between the letters, which made it possible to recognise the operator. Furthermore, the procedures before and after sending the message were also signs for recognition. This could, however, be imitated by a skilled radio operator, who in this way could even make the presence of the agent unnecessary. Another method of verifying that the agent was free, was to have regular confirmations sent by letters to a prearranged address. Or, the receiving unit could take bearings, and find out if the radio signals really were coming from the area where the agent was supposed to be located.

After taking care of the radio equipment, it was necessary for the technicians to check the circuits and to regulate the operation of the radio. The radio operator responsible was Ronnie Reed, who was born in 1916, and worked as a radio engineer for the BBC. In 1940 he was asked to perform a mission for MI5; he was going to help Gösta Caroli/SUMMER with his first transmission. After that, Reed began his work for MI5, and took part in the supervision of several agents. An odd distinction was when his photo was used on the identity card of the dead man in Operation MINCEMEAT – the body planted in the Mediterranean with false documents. It was considered that Reed 'could have been the twin brother of the corpse'.[18] Reed retired in 1976, and died in 1995.

The battery-powered receiver had the name E.S/o and could receive transmissions with frequencies between 4,140 and 8,810 kHz; the Germans were broadcasting on a frequency of 6,200 kHz. It worked well during the testing. The S88/5 transmitter had an output of three watts and was equipped with two crystals with frequencies of 4,603 and 6,195 kHz. The three-watt transmitter lacked power and all agents with similar transmitters had problems with the range. (When the double agent GARBO transmitted his vital message after D-Day, that the invasion in Normandy was a deception, and that the 'real' invasion would come in Pas de Calais, a 600-watt American transmitter was used, to be sure of a successful transmission.) The length of the antenna was recommended to be 9½–13 metres. They had to change one valve, which had been damaged during the parachute landing.

The test transmission was now performed, with TATE present as an eager enthusiast, to control the range by determining on which radio stations in Britain the signals could be heard. First it was tested in the city of Cambridge on 28 September, with poor results; no one heard anything. Probably the buildings in the city caused poor reception. It was, therefore, decided to make a test transmission out in the countryside, and the next day they tried a place about fifteen miles outside Cambridge – again without success. TATE had to spend the night in a cell at the police station in Cambridge; no hotel room for him at this stage in his career as a double agent. Therefore, they returned to Camp 020 and then transmitted during the nights of 2 and 3 October from TATE's room (which apparently was on a higher level, on the second floor) with an improved antenna. The reason why it was better to send during the night is that the radiowaves bounce off higher layers in the ionosphere which then improves the signal. The results were better now, but with varying degrees of success. The signal could be received in St Erth in Cornwall, Gilnahirk in Northern Ireland and in Thurso in the far north of Scotland (distance about 550 miles). The conclusion was that the antenna that came with the equipment was totally inadequate. With a larger antenna placed higher up, the results were significantly better.[19]

On the nights of 17 and 18 October they again tried to make contact with the Germans, and TATE was supposed to send his first message. The transmissions were made from Scottswood in Barnet, six miles east of Watford. He used his call sign several times (JLN on 17 October), and international codes such as QSA (which is my signal strength?), PSE (please), KKK (make contact). He sent his message several times over the two nights, but never made any contact with the German radio station.

44

TATE's message was that he had landed in the vicinity of Willingham, and injured his hand and ankle. He wondered why he had not had any contact with the Germans. His cover was that he claimed to be British but had grown up in Denmark, and now he asked for instructions to start his work. He had written to Daisy Lopez in Lisbon because of lack of radio contact with the Germans. He wondered if he could send at 8.00 p.m., instead of at night, and he announced that the roads and fields were full of obstacles against the expected invasion, south of Cambridge and, according to rumours, down as far as London. They left Barnet without the slightest contact with the Germans, and were certainly disappointed and discouraged. But, after three days, he finally received a reply to his message. Now he had made contact with his masters, and the game could begin!

There had been a lot of discussion among the people in MI5 about his contact with Daisy Lopez. TAR Robertson, a wise man, was afraid that the Germans would suspect that something was wrong, and ignore TATE and instead rely on other spies. On the other hand, it was a way of showing that he felt confident in the German organisation. Apparently he sent a message to Daisy Lopez in Lisbon, in invisible ink on a postcard, about the difficulty of achieving contact with Germany.[20]

Now, TATE began to carry out his radio transmissions from the second floor of Latchmere House and Camp 020. However, they were rather worried that the Germans would be able to get the bearings of his location, so he soon moved to a riding school nearby. But TATE needed a more comfortable environment for his future radio traffic. He was moved to a house in Radlett, about three miles north-east of Watford, where he lived under round-the-clock surveillance by guards. The Germans were told that he had now moved to a safe place, as a lodger in a house in Barnet about fifteen miles east of Watford, and would have time to engage in the missions they gave him. He enjoyed a certain freedom in Radlett and tours and parties were organised for him at regular intervals. However, he did not like this house and the constant monitoring was frustrating, so his controllers kept looking for another house in the same area that would be more suitable. He was paid £1 per week, which was invested in National Savings Certificates, which he would receive after the war, if he remained in British service and willingly worked for them.[21] In comparison, the minimum wage for a farm worker, working fifty hours a week, was around £3 a week at this time. He was also later taken on a short holiday to the Lake District.

In January 1941 Gösta Caroli, SUMMER, made an unsuccessful escape attempt, but TATE claimed that he had not been involved in the planning. However, he had apparently known about it before, but refrained from reporting it to his superior. They had probably spent Christmas together in Hinxton, where Gösta Caroli sat in one of MI5's safe houses and carried out his radio activities, so he may have revealed his plans to his friend Wulf.[22] We imagine that Caroli's 'treason' was now forgiven by Wulf, who had found his place as a double agent for MI5. It now felt more and more as if Wulf had adapted to his new life as a British double agent, but it was not taken for granted that this new-found loyalty to his new home country would be likely to survive any major shocks. His quiet life went on as usual, interspersed with radio contact with the Germans.

An evaluation of TATE as a radio operator, probably made by Russell Lee, is documented in a report. His skill was clearly recognised: TATE sent 'very good Morse, clean stuff and quite solid'. Moreover, he seemed to practise in his leisure time, and seemed to be increasingly involved in and excited by his work, and he managed to increase his transmission speed. But one wonders if he could demonstrate his skills for his masters in Hamburg, who sat and listened; earlier, he had been given directives to send at a slow speed of 30–40 characters per minute. TATE was so talented that he could even express dissatisfaction with his Morse key, which gives a clear impression of his acquired professional pride. We know that Wulf Schmidt displayed a certain temperament in his communications, and also as a man; he made it clear to the radio experts that he would certainly buy his own new Morse key, if he saw any in the shops. But MI5 was well-stocked with telegraphy equipment and TATE could borrow a larger key, so that he would not get cramp so easily when sending. But when he became more and more skilled he wanted to use his old key again. He preferred to rest his arm across the table when he sent, and if he was nervous or disturbed it had a definite effect on the quality of his signalling. Later, he found a better posture, sitting on a high chair with the key on the edge of the table.

He used the so-called 'Ham Chat', i.e., international abbreviations, such as 'PES' (Please), 'C' (please send), ERE NIL instead of the QRU ('Have you anything for me? I have nothing for you'). He used the international 'Q code' with clear text in Spanish. He ended every broadcast with 'Cheerios'. Gösta Caroli, SUMMER, was equally familiar with this. Unlike Caroli/SUMMER, who always sent his call sign for four minutes before the message was sent, TATE was more impatient and managed to send call signs for only one to three minutes, which underlines the impression you get of Wulf Schmidt's impatience. And it was a sign of a good radio operator, claimed the writer of the report, that TATE could read the signal from the receiver stations in spite of all the interference, which SUMMER did not master. His knowledge of electrical theory was worse.

If there were problems with the equipment, according to his instructions, he would write to Daisy Lopez in Lisbon, but the batteries he had to try to obtain himself. Simple solution Wulf thought, I will buy four 3-volt motorcycle batteries and link them in series, and the problem is solved. But motorcycle batteries in the UK, as in Germany, were of 6 volts, and with the 18 volts he thus would have burnt out his valves, and made the equipment inoperable (but on the other hand, one would expect that he could check the voltage of the batteries).

It had been a good idea to separate the receiver and transmitter for Wulf's parachute jump; Caroli was hit on the head by his suitcase with 9 kg of radio equipment when he landed, which knocked him unconscious. This injury was to affect him for the rest of his life. Apparently the box containing his receiver looked very strange, with an odd shape and covered with some sort of red leather material. No one could walk down the road with this box without attracting attention. But the intention was to hide it after landing, and he protected it with his ground sheet.

The frequency of the signal from Hamburg of 6,200 kHz was very close to regular radio broadcasts in England, which increased the risk of interference problems. On the other hand, it could be advantageous from a German perspective, reducing the risk of detection of the transmission. The British concluded that the German radio security service was worse than the British, because nobody detected TATE's signal although it was sent several nights in a row with varying call codes. The signal could be heard very well by British radio stations far away from the location of the sender. TATE was particularly concerned about the fact that the original antenna was not good enough – it was feared that this would be a blow to his cooperation – but at last he understood, after all the tests, that perhaps he needed a new, more effective, antenna.[23] This revealed a new dimension of Wulf's personality: he was stubborn and obviously sensitive to criticism, even if it was German equipment that was considered inadequate.

THE DOUBLE-CROSS SYSTEM

MI5 was successful when it came to capturing the German agents, who now arrived in a steady stream, and they realised the value of recruiting those who were suitable as double agents. But there were others who did not approve of this. There was a higher authority for security operations, the Security Executive, with Lord Swinton as chairman. He decided that it was not appropriate to negotiate with the captured spies with promises to spare their lives. Even Churchill held the opinion that more agents should end up in court and be executed. Lord Swinton was disliked by MI5 and regarded as incompetent, especially by the head of counter-espionage in Division B, Guy Liddell.

MI5 did not care very much about Lord Swinton's directive, but instead saw the great advantages of double agents. And security work was a challenging and patient long-term project that demanded accuracy and could not be hurried, which Lord Swinton did not understand.[24] More and more double agents recruited to the organisation, however, meant ever more complex operations. First, they had to have control over everything for every agent; there must be absolutely no mistakes in terms of how their imaginary lives and activities developed. There must be no inconsistencies in the double agents' communications with the Abwehr. One double agent exposed by the Germans would pose great risk for the entire Double-Cross operation. There was a need for an all-embracing body, which controlled and directed the activities, and had a comprehensive overview of the various double agents' fictitious businesses, with a coherent structure of information flow without contradictions.[25]

In addition, there was also the delicate question of what information they could allow the agents to disclose to the Germans. Guy Liddell, with the help of TAR Robertson and another MI5 man, Dick White, who was Robertson's immediate supervisor, were behind these ideas and the organisation thus formed. (Dick White later in his career became head of both MI5 and MI6.) This organisation, which would become very successful, was called XX (or 'twenty') Committee and later the Double-Cross system.

The historian John Cecil Masterman, born in 1891, was appointed as chairman. He was a teacher of modern history at Oxford, a brilliant cricketer and tennis player, but an amateur in the intelligence context. When the First World War broke out, he was a student at the University of Freiburg, which led to internment in Ruhleben throughout the war, with the advantage that he learned German. Masterman was not an obvious chairman. He was a gloomy bachelor, with little sense of humour, and was not naturally decisive, but he worked well in a committee as a monitor and coordinator of the delicate question of what should be disclosed to the Germans.[26] The Secretary was the former lawyer J. H. Marriot and in the directorate was also TAR Robertson, who eventually became a lieutenant colonel.

To run the work, a multi-disciplinary team with representatives from organisations such as MI6, War Office, Air Ministry Intelligence, Naval Intelligence Department, GHQ of Home and Home Defence Forces Executives was required. Soon representatives of the London Controlling Station (LCS, the organisation that managed the investigations of refugees in the United Kingdom), the Chief Combined Operations, and even later SHAEF (Supreme Headquarters Allied Expeditionary Force), the global body for the Allied military cooperation, were included.[27] The first meeting was held on 2 January 1941, and thereafter every week at MI5's headquarters at 58 St James Street in Mayfair. A popular feature was the tea and buns served at the meetings. A total of 226 meetings were held before the war ended. The committee managed to almost always reach a decision through consensus. The members were of course very rarely in direct contact with the individual double agent, and often had no hint of their actual identity. During the war about 120 double agents were handled, with varying degrees of activity, most with only a minor role. At most, there were some fifty agents active at the same time. The objectives of the activity were:

1. To control the German intelligence system in the UK. If they managed to establish a fictitious agent business which satisfied the Germans, they did not run the risk of additional, unknown, agents entering the country.

2. To capture quickly new agents when they arrived in the country. This was originally the main target, but the addition of new agents decreased with time, as the Germans were satisfied with their 'reliable' fictitious network of spies.

3. Learning about the personalities and methods of the German secret service.

4. To gather information about the German's code and cipher operations. By the controlled agent activities much very useful information was obtained, which facilitated the work of GC & CS (Government Code and Cipher School) in Bletchley Park, to read the German Enigma-coded radio traffic. If they managed to make the Germans believe that their ciphers and codes were secure, it prevented the introduction of new varieties, which could only be decrypted with great effort.

5. To obtain evidence of enemy intentions and plans through the analysis of the questions asked by the Germans of their agents.

6. To deceive the enemy with disinformation.

7. To facilitate censorship and surveillance.

8. To prevent sabotage by maintaining control of saboteurs, their

methods, and equipment. The German's ineffectiveness in this area surprised everyone. They achieved in practice no sabotage of value.[28]

Over time, the work became increasingly complex. It was a delicate matter to consider what information they would convey to the Germans, and in the beginning there were problems in convincing the defence authorities of the necessity of providing information to the Germans. The question was always what one would gain relative to what was lost, in giving the enemy information. Most of the communication with the Germans was managed by radio traffic, letters with invisible writing, or photomicrographs, as well as personal meetings with the Abwehr in neutral countries. The most important double agents came to be GARBO (Juan Pujol) TRICYCLE (Dusko Popov) and TATE. Other agents with utterly imaginative names were GW (Gwilym Williams), ZIG-ZAG (Eddie Chapman), the Norwegians MUTT (John Moe) and JEFF (Tor Glad), CELERY (Walter Dicketts), BISCUIT (Sam McCarthy), SNOW (Arthur Owens), DRAGONFLY (Mr George), THE SNARK (Mihailovic), RAINBOW (Bernie Kiener), SWEET WILLIAM (William Jackson) and BALLOON (Dickie Metcalf), and others. Gösta Caroli (SUMMER) managed to end his career before the organisation started, but they gained very useful experience for the future work from his behaviour. During the war, the British security services controlled virtually the entire German agency network. There were only a few that are considered to have managed to stay free, but without any influential role.[29] Some key principles guided the business:

1. Double agents were recruited from agents who the Germans sent themselves. It became clear that it was almost impossible to 'create' agents and persuade the Germans to recruit them. But there were some benefits with that as, instead of accepting prime candidates for espionage, the Germans often contented themselves with second class agents. The Germans seemed to have a naive faith in the ability of their agents. In the Abwehr it was important to recruit your own agents to improve your career prospects; almost anyone who wanted to could start an agent and control him. Prestige and career were based on their agent's success, and they therefore wanted to believe the reports which their own agents sent.

2. All double agents should as closely as possible really live the life they pretended to have. It was really important to travel or visit places where factories and air bases were located, which they were going to report on. This gave more credibility in reporting, and details were vital if a physical meeting took place with the Abwehr in a neutral country. The fabricated identity of a sub-agent was 'hung up' on an individual the agent had actually met, in order to provide credible descriptions.

3. No traffic was allowed to be transmitted without written consent from competent controllers.

4. A case officer would always be linked to the agent, who would monitor him daily and know all the details of his case. This was something which was realised after the case of Gösta Caroli. If the agent received requests, it was necessary to keep track of previously reported activities, which the case officer could help to remember. A case officer also lived an intimate life with the agent, to sense the nervous strain an agent was exposed to, and be on hand in case of emergency.

5. A thorough psychological analysis and evaluation of the agent was important, and in this the case officer was also important. A new double agent could, after a few months, feel remorse and turn again and risk revealing everything. A high degree of cooperation would be sought. The agent himself could then begin to get actively interested in 'his' traffic, and make useful suggestions for improvement and even criticism.

6. The business must get started quickly in order to inspire confidence with the Germans. But it was important that a thorough, systematic and detailed analysis of the agent's upbringing and history, background, qualifications and contacts with the Germans were made first. Any warning sign that the agent had been equipped with to use in his radio transmissions to inform the Germans that he was revealed, had to be rapidly established. And they had to find out if the Germans, during the agent's training in Morse, had become familiar with, or recorded his style ('fist').

7. Agents were often not revealed by a sudden stroke of genius or hidden clues, but by the time-consuming studies of the details of the materials previously filed. Only through good documentation of what had been

dealt with, keeping records of journeys, meetings and conversations – in an easily searchable archive – could contradictions be avoided. Often there was a large amount of material. For GARBO there were, for example, fifty volumes, and for SNOW more than thirty-five thick volumes, with documented traffic and activities.

8. In any espionage activities, it is extremely important to keep the agent ignorant and independent of other agents. The risk of leaks and revelations of agent networks were thereby minimised.

9. A designated financial arrangement, which could be generous, was important. Often, the agent received a bonus in the form of a percentage of the money received from the Germans for his work.

10. The question of what risks the agent was exposed to was an important issue. What was the limit for how much disinformation and false material could be sent, before they risked revealing an agent, with subsequent threats against both the agent himself, or his family, and the whole Double-Cross operation? In the beginning, there was concern about undetected agents in the country, which could give the Germans information which would expose a double agent.

11. If the availability of double agents increased, quality should take precedence over quantity. The most important agents were usually men with a low position in society, with ordinary jobs. They could submit small pieces of a puzzle, which gave indirect information about the larger context. Gossip and indiscretion from senior personnel in the Foreign Office or the Ministries was not always equally convincing.

12. For the genuine agents it was often best to stick close to the true facts – for disinformation, it was better to use fictional data from imaginary sub-agents.[30]

The disinformation which was delivered, was carefully and thoroughly designed, often a mixture of truth and false information. The answers to the Germans' requests to their agents could mislead the Germans about actual British plans, and about the strength of the British defence forces. But facts that the Germans could check were only slightly distorted. The disinformation had to be credible, without sensations to begin with, and mixed with true facts in order to gradually build up German confidence in their agent, and then, when it was essential, provide vital disinformation to the Germans, which could be swallowed without difficulty.

They did not always allow the agents to report 'facts' straight, but let the Germans themselves, from several sources with small pieces of the puzzle, draw the conclusions that the British aimed for. If they wanted to give disinformation that destroyers were being equipped with new torpedo tubes, they could allow an agent 'A' to report that he had heard two drunken sailors in a pub at the harbour discuss how much leave they were likely to get. At least one week, it was believed, 'to change the torpedo tubes is no simple story'. And agent 'B' reported that he had seen, from the train, the destroyers in dry docks, while agent 'C' forwarded the information he got on the bus, where he overheard two factory workers complain that they would miss overtime now, while production was converted to the manufacture of torpedo tubes.

With similar small pieces of disinformation they managed to deceive the Germans into thinking that the range of the British radar was a lot shorter than it really was. This, among other things, was important in ensuring the sinking of the cruiser *Scharnhorst* in December 1943.[31] True data could be safe it they 'came too late'. For example, agents were allowed to inform that so-and-so many ships had departed for Malta, when it was already too late for the Germans to intervene. Everything was created with the aim of building up an agent's credibility. An essential tool the XX Committee had access to was ULTRA, the Enigma decryption of coded German radio traffic, which gave an opportunity to be well informed about the impact of their double agents' work. It could also provide information that was safe, for example, to let an agent give reports about where the main Navy units were, when it was known through ULTRA that no submarines were nearby.

In 1941 a German invasion was still a real threat. There was, therefore, a plan to cover what they should then do with their Double-Cross agents, in case of an invasion. This enterprise was called 'Mr Mill's circus', and the plan's official name was Operation HEGIRA (after Muhammad's flight from Mecca in 622). The agents were going to be transported to hotels in remote locations in Wales. This concerned several important agents in addition to our protagonist TATE, such as MUTT, DRAGONFLY, GELATINE, STORK, GW and SNOW. The local MI5 officer responsible was Captain Finney, later replaced by Captain Kimpton, and their office was in Colwyn Bay in Wales. This was deadly serious as at worst the agents were going to be liquidated. TAR Robertson, head of the division B1(a) in MI5 responsible for the double agents, said: 'If there is danger of any of the more dangerous cases falling into enemy hands they will be forcibly liquidated.' Another officer, C. B. Mills (hence the name Mill's Circus), wrote that if German paratroopers landed near a camp with Double-Cross agents, they would be liquidated. From 1942 the invasion threat was considered non-existent, and in 1943 the plan was scrapped.[32]

The greatest achievement performed by the Double-Cross was the disinformation for the benefit of OVERLORD, the landing in Normandy in 1944 (see chapter 9 '1944 & 1945'), which has been frequently described. However, there are critics who claim that the importance of the double agents was overestimated, the Germans knew very well about this double-crossing, and that they did not mind if their agents worked for the British. In this way they obtained information from the Secret Service. The importance of the disinformation concerning the landings in Normandy from the Double-Cross system was exaggerated, and the Germans knew where it was going to happen. By leaks from the French parts of SOE the Germans knew that twenty-six French Resistance groups had orders to perform sabotage to enhance the invasion while there were no such orders for the Dutch or Belgian Resistance organisations, which there would have been if Pas de Calais was the invasion area.[33] But Hitler kept important forces away from Normandy during the critical initial period, so this conclusion seems rather doubtful. The secrecy around D-Day was rigorous, and it is very doubtful that more exact information was given to the Resistance, with well-known problems with security.

Finally, British tax-payers did not have to pay for the Double-Cross system. The Germans brought over money to their agents during the war years. A lot of money; a total sum of £85,000 was provided which funded the entire operation.[34]

When Masterman decided to reveal the operations of the Double-Cross system after the war, it caused some consternation. The morale in the British Security organisation was low after the debacle with the Cambridge spy ring and the escape of Burgess, MacLean and Philby, and Masterman thought there was a need for something more positive. But he was forbidden several times by the security authorities, and therefore decided to publish it in the USA in 1970. This was not popular in Britain and he was even threatened with legal action. Many of his previous colleagues felt that it was wrong to disclose this secret. It was finally published in Britain in 1972, but he was not allowed to mention ULTRA, which was not revealed until 1974.

3

Great Britain During the First Years of the War

When Wulf Schmidt landed in Britain, he found himself in a country whose people lived with the tangible effects of the war, although it was far from the chaos and famine the Germans hoped for, and stated in their propaganda. Most of the European continent had been conquered by the Germans. By a miracle, most of the British army had been rescued at Dunkirk. The Battle of Britain, when the German Luftwaffe tried to achieve air supremacy to make an invasion possible, was reaching the final stage, but the Luftwaffe never reached their goal, and a bombing campaign, called the Blitz by the British, started instead.

The evacuation of several million people from vulnerable coastal areas had already begun in the summer of 1939. When war broke out, 800,000 children and 500,000 mothers with small children were evacuated, sometimes leading to cultural clashes between evacuees and their hosts, as the class system was well entrenched in society. Many of the evacuees soon moved back home again, often retrieved by their parents. The school system went into a long period of chaos. New attempts to evacuate the children, when the Blitz was most intense, were less successful.[1]

General blackout was introduced on 1 September 1939, which 'transformed conditions of life more thoroughly than any other single feature of the war'.[2] Every night, windows were covered with dark material and not the least glimmer of light was allowed. In 1940, 300,000 people ended up in court because of insufficient blackout. At the same time it became increasingly dark indoors, because energy companies decreased the electrical power in the grid. Buses, cars, trams and other vehicles had covered headlights with little slits to spread a small amount of light. Although a speed limit of 20 mph was introduced, traffic still claimed victims. Accidents increased by 100 per cent, and during the first four months, as many as 4,133 people were killed on the roads, mostly pedestrians.[3] Casualties also occurred when people fell into canals or other watercourses, or fell from station platforms, or stairways. All streetlights were of course turned off and a walk home became a health hazard: collisions with trees, lampposts, stacked sandbags, tripping on curbs, or collisions with other people. To make it a bit easier the white centre line on roads was introduced, and pavements were also sometimes painted. Torches could be used, but should be well covered with double layers of tissue. However, batteries were soon difficult to find.

When war broke out in Britain, there were approximately 70,000 foreigners from enemy countries. All Germans and Austrians over sixteen years of age were called before special tribunals and then classified into categories. Category A (nearly 600) were considered as high security risks and were detained immediately. Category B (about 6,500) were 'doubtful cases' and were monitored and subjected to certain restrictions, but they were not allowed to own a car, bicycle, boat or aeroplane [sic], and could not travel more than five miles from their home without police permission. Cameras, guns and homing pigeons should be handed in, and they were not allowed outdoors after 10.30 p.m.[4] Finally, category C (about 64,000 of whom 55,000 had fled Nazi terror, mostly Jews), who were assessed as no security hazard and could live in freedom. As the war progressed, more and more Germans and Austrians, as well as 19,000 Italians, were interned, mostly on the Isle of Man. Furthermore, around 750 British fascists were interned.

Sabotage occurred, but no major damage was achieved because the British controlled all German agents. The head of MI5 was rather unimpressed: 'I am greatly disappointed in what the Germans have managed to do, they are not in the same class as in the last war.'[5] The IRA conducted, during 1939, an extensive bombing campaign, but it was virtually over when the war began in September. German agents in Ireland planned an attack on Britain with bombs concealed in chocolate, cans, coal, soap, pens, etc., which would be placed in the shops, and they also had plans to bring explosive cans of peas into Buckingham Palace.[6] Isolated incidents of minor acts of sabotage were reported. In a delivery of brand-new Blenheim aircraft, lubricating oil was discovered in the oxygen lines, which would have caught fire or exploded on contact with oxygen.[7] Sugar was found in the fuel tanks of several Swordfish aircraft stationed in Scotland, leading to at least one crash.[8] A woman in Birmingham was convicted of sabotage of munitions for aircraft in 1942 – the ammunition could have exploded immediately on firing.[9] On the Isle of Wight another woman was sentenced to death for having cut military telephone lines, but the sentence was reduced to fourteen years in prison; one man got seven years for destroying telephone boxes. A teacher was jailed for having spread defeatist opinions to his students.[10]

RATIONING

Petrol rationing was implemented immediately on the outbreak of war, the ration allowance being equivalent to about 2,000 miles per year. After 1942, however, it became impossible for civilians to get hold of petrol.[11] The price of a small family car, such as an Austin 7, was £125. Most of the country's two million private cars were soon stored in garages. But even buses and taxis were hit by rationing; the petrol allocation for buses was reduced by 25 per cent, and 800 daily tours in London were cancelled, and a third of all taxis were confiscated by the Auxiliary Fire Service (AFS). The streets became emptier, but trains became more and more crowded,[12] and were often delayed; travelling was arduous.

Other forms of rationing were soon introduced, and those who were financially worse off thought it was a good idea, making the allocation fairer. But the scheme came to favour those with large families with many children. The calorie requirements, of course, varied with the work people had.[13] Before the war, approximately 50 per cent of all meat, 90 per cent of grain and fat, and 70 per cent of all the sugar and cheese were imported.[14] By May 1940 the availability of consumer goods dropped to around one third compared with September 1939. Farmers had to be paid to plough up more and more land for cultivation. At the same time parks, recreational areas, and soccer pitches were made to serve as allotments. There were soon half a million people with allotments, which produced 10 per cent of all food in Britain.[15] The food was expensive, partly in order to produce tax revenue, but also to reduce demand; a sales duty of between 16 to 33 per cent was introduced on different products in October 1940.[16] Few households had refrigerators, and freezers did not exist. A system of ration coupons was introduced which also included children.

From 8 January 1940, butter (110 grams), sugar (340 grams), bacon and ham (about 110 grams) and two eggs, were allowed per person per week. An additional allocation of sugar for jam making was sometimes available in the summer. Margarine was introduced as a moderately popular substitute; there was also egg powder as a replacement product – a jar corresponding to twelve eggs was available every other month. In spring 1940 came the rationing of meat (not counted by the weight but by value, 1s 2d, equivalent to 2 lb of meat) and even jam. Fish and poultry were not rationed but were difficult to get hold of, while rabbits suddenly became popular. Another meat product that was not rationed was the legendary tinned Spam – chopped pork in jelly. In 1941, coal, cheese, and the indispensable tea (about 50 grams, a tea bag today contain 2 grams for comparison) were rationed, and in 1942 sweets, chocolate and soap (about 60 grams of toilet soap every month), as well as gas and electricity. The authorities tried to introduce a kind of standard tea, but this aroused great opposition, so diversity was allowed again. Young children and pregnant or breast-feeding women received supplementary allocation of orange juice, eggs, cod liver oil and milk (seven extra pints per week). The portions of the rations varied during the war, but the system actually remained long after the war, for some goods into the early 1950s.

Something that was never rationed was vegetables and neither was tobacco. The state received big money from the tax on tobacco. But there was a shortage of tobacco and cigarettes, and also beer as the grain was needed for bread production. Beer, six pence a pint before the war, doubled in price by 1944 and became diluted and watery. But consumption rose during the war and often the beer ran out before evening closing time in the pubs. The distillation of the favourite drink whisky was reduced. Alcohol became a coveted luxury item and the price of a bottle of whisky varied depending on where it was offered. Tobacco was part of the Lend Lease programme with the USA, but it was supplemented by Turkish tobacco (one variety named Pasha[17]), which was not as popular as Virginia tobacco. There was a shortage of the sought-after cigarettes, with queues in the shops which allocated cigarettes by the number instead of whole packs.

The British had to abstain from ordinary white bread, instead the 'National Loaf' was introduced, which had a greyish colour because the flour contained most of the grain milled. In the state-subsidised bread 85 per cent of the ground flour was used. Thus proper wholemeal bread was supplied and, though not a very popular replacement, people soon got used to it. In fact, the diet was healthy as it was well balanced and nutritious. Vegetables and potatoes were grown increasingly in people's own gardens or on the soil-covered Anderson shelters and the familiar slogan was 'Dig For Victory'. Newspapers, booklets and radio broadcasts were used extensively, to convey hints of how best to use the allocated rations, and all sorts of recipes were published, sometimes with some unusual ingredients. Of course, a lively black market flourished, in addition to the regular allowance. One could also cheat, by 'losing' the ration books and getting new replacements.

At restaurants, there was initially no rationing. This brought protests from the majority of the population, who never could afford such extravagance. Therefore, in 1942, rules were introduced that the food could cost a maximum of five shillings, no more than three courses, and never both meat and fish. For 'ordinary' people 'British Restaurants' were established in 1941, and became very common in Greater London where there were 200. They became very popular and a meal with soup, main course and dessert could be obtained for nine pence. Not gourmet food, but enough to give a full and contented stomach.

In June 1941, clothes rationing was introduced and every adult was given sixty-six coupons per year (from 1943 thirty-six coupons per year). That was enough for a full set of new clothes, for example, a pair of pants or a skirt cost eight coupons, a shirt/blouse four to five coupons, a pair of shoes five to seven coupons, and a pair of socks two coupons. A standard collection of new designs, so-called Utility Clothes, were introduced, which in 1942 could be found in thirty-two different varieties. Most people were very pleased with the design of these clothes – a typical suit cost £3 5s, and ten coupons. Prices of used clothing and shoes were regulated by a complex system. Even shoes were included in Utility Clothes. Rubber for boots and similar things were, however, unobtainable.

A similar system was introduced for furniture, Utility Furniture, because of the shortage of wood. Each year there were about half a million new marriages, and of course the newlywed pair wanted to have new furniture rather than second hand. There was a system of price regulation on both new and used furniture. In 1941 there were about twenty types of furniture of various models to choose from, rustic and functional. For this, another system with coupons was introduced in 1943, starting with sixty coupons that went to the newlyweds and those who had their homes bombed out in the Blitz. A chair required one coupon, a wardrobe eight. For about £55 a set of oak furniture for a household could be bought: one double bed, a wardrobe, a secretaire, a bureau, a dinner table, sideboard, and four chairs. The supply of furniture was reduced later in the war, and the number of coupons was later halved. Plywood disappeared as a material for furniture as it became necessary for Mosquito aircraft.[18] For houses damaged by bombing, the owners were encouraged to repair as best they could, or with the help of craftsmen, for whose services, however, there was a long queue. Nothing could be wasted and reusing things as much as possible was a necessity. Window glass was extremely difficult to obtain. For demolished houses a full refund could be expected only at the end of the war.[19]

In 1942 rationing of bathing water was introduced and a depth of no more than five inches (12.5 cm) once a week was the rule. Often several people took a bath in the same water. The people thus became a little less elegant with the war years, with worn-out old clothes, lack of soap and a bath only once a week. The allocation of paper fell, which was felt by the avid British newspaper readers. Newspapers decreased from eighteen to twenty-four pages to six or eight pages. It was news that was important and many other subjects were neglected. There was also a shortage of journalists as many were called up into the forces. Sports pages disappeared almost completely, as hardly any sport existed for security reasons – large gatherings of people were risky with the potential threat of air raids. But the newspapers were still popular despite the BBC's excellent news broadcasts; four out of five men and two out of three women read a newspaper every day.[20]

THE BLITZ

The most tangible reminder that there actually was a war going on was, of course, the Blitz, which is considered to have lasted from approximately 7 September 1940 to 10 May 1941. It was going to cost about 43,000 lives, half of them in London, where more than a million houses were damaged or destroyed. London was subjected to bombing fifty-seven nights in a row (or seventy-six according to some) between mid-September and November. The invasion, Operation *Seelöwe* (*Sealion*), was postponed, and the probable aim of the bombing was mainly to persuade the British to surrender, but after the failure to defeat the RAF, capitulation was not likely to happen.

At first, London was bombed night and day, but on 15 October it was the turn of Birmingham and Bristol, attacked by unusually large forces – more than 400 aircraft. Between November 1940 and February 1941, bombing spread to most coastal cities, or those with key industries, such as the infamous attack on Coventry on the night of 15 November, with a death toll of 558. By that time, bombing raids took place mostly at night. Large portions of the city of Coventry were razed to the ground, and a new word was added to the German language, *Coventrieren*, meaning to bomb enemy cities, and thereby eliminate both essential functions and population resistance.

When the Blitz started it was increasingly possible to read German and Luftwaffe Enigma-coded radio traffic at Bletchley Park but not always quickly enough to make a difference. The German bombers were guided to their targets by radio beams which could be 'bent' making the Luftwaffe bombers miss their target. It was known that a major attack would come on 15 November, and the target was 'Korn'. The problem was that the British did not know what city this was. But there are conspiracy theories (which even some staff at Bletchley Park believed) that argue that Churchill knew, but could not put this into action, as it would have risked the secret of ULTRA, the ability to read Enigma-coded messages, being exposed. The irony was that most of the aircraft factories and other industries fared rather well in Coventry – it was the centre that was hit. Another week, 1,353 people died in a night attack against Birmingham.[21]

As an example of how the war went on, we can study the activities of a typical week. The number of aircraft listed are those which actually reached the target:

Saturday 30 November: During the day attacks on London and south-east by 185 fighter-bombers. During the night a large-scale attack on Southampton by 147 bombers, between the hours of 6.18 p.m. and 00.55 a.m.

Sunday 1 December: Fog during the day. Once again, Southampton, a raid by 129 bombers, between the hours of 6.15 p.m. and 10.55 p.m. A smaller raid with 17 bombers over London.

Monday 2 December: During the day, a 'fighter sweep' with 70 Me 109s in the south-east, but no bombs. A large raid on Bristol in the evening by 132 bombers; the city received the greatest damage so far.

Tuesday 3 December: Bad weather, but about 60 aircraft in single missions during the day. During the evening, a large attack on Birmingham by 69 bombers. Smaller groups attacked London between 6.25 p.m. and 10.00 p.m. and between 00.24 a.m. and 06.28 a.m.

Wednesday 4 December: Bad weather during the day. Birmingham was attacked during the evening with 62 bombers, London and Southampton with a smaller force of 42 aircraft.

Thursday 5 December: During the day two attack 'sweeps' by fighter-bombers. During the evening Portsmouth was attacked by 74 bombers and London by 29 aircraft.

Friday 6 December: A dozen fighter aircraft appeared during the day. Bristol was attacked by 80 bombers during the evening.[22]

The most serious attack on London occurred on 29 December 1940, with huge fires, and it is sometimes called 'The Second Great Fire of London'. During 1941, bombing was increasingly concentrated on coastal cities, to facilitate Admiral Dönitz's *Kriegsmarine*, which hunted in the Atlantic with their U-boats. Almost all major cities in England were affected at some time including Glasgow's harbour Clydebank in Scotland, Swansea in Wales and Belfast in Northern Ireland, which was hit hard in Easter 1941 with the most loss of life outside London, during a raid.

Defence against bomber aircraft at night was ineffective to begin with. Only in 1941 did efficiency increase with greater numbers of radar-controlled anti-aircraft artillery and searchlights, as well as more effective night fighter radar. The people took refuge in the limited number of public shelters. Anderson shelters (named after the Home Secretary John Anderson) were introduced, which people built in their gardens. These had U-shaped roofs made of corrugated iron and were covered with a thick layer of soil (in which vegetables were often grown). In London, about 80 of the 270 underground stations were used as shelters, where almost 180,000 inhabitants took refuge (i.e., about 4 per cent of the population), but you had to buy a ticket for 1½*d*. Not all tube stations were safe as a German bomb could penetrate 50 feet through solid ground. Marble Arch, Balham and Bank underground stations were some of the stations hit with many casualties. Major, and often heroic, efforts, were made by organisations such as the ARP (Air Raid Precaution Service), AFS (Auxiliary Fire Service), Home Guard and the women's voluntary organisations. In May 1941, the Germans had their eyes directed against Russia and the air raids ceased. Birmingham, which of course had undergone several previous attacks, was the last city to be hit on 16 May when 111 bombers attacked.

Much has been written about the Blitz and Britain's heroic struggle. Comparing the number of aircraft involved, people killed and property damaged, what hit Germany from 1942 onwards was of a different order of magnitude. Nazi Germany never built up an effective bomber force with heavy bombers, as Britain and the USA did. Their workhorse, the He 111, could carry up to 4,500-lb bomb load, not much more than a Mosquito later in the war, and the Lancaster could carry one 22,000-lb bomb or 14,000 lb of smaller bombs. But, of course, it is often said that the victors write the history. The terms 'Battle of Britain' and 'the Blitz' hardly exist in German historical terminology of the Second World War.

OPERATION SEELÖWE

The idea of a German invasion of Britain went back to the autumn of 1939, when Grand Admiral Erich Raeder was awarded the task of developing a plan for such an operation. Without much enthusiasm, he appointed his chief of staff, Vice-Admiral Otto Schniewind, as the leader of a project. On 20 November Schniewind presented the results of his study, '*Fall Rot*'.[23] In this original and concise study he examined the possibilities of a landing along a stretch of around sixty miles of coast west of the Isle of Wight, an area suitable because of its many ports. The conclusion was that what Raeder wanted, a blockade of Britain, was preferable to a direct invasion. The study also identified the four basic requirements, which had to be met before an invasion could take place: the Royal Navy should not be able to intervene, the RAF should be defeated so that German air supremacy could be provided, the British coastal defences should have been destroyed, and the sea routes should be swept of mines but the approach to Dover should be mined. In agreement with the findings of this study, Hitler on 29 November 1939 chose the option of blocking and isolating Britain; an invasion was so far not on the agenda.

Thus, Raeder expected that the invasion plans would be shelved, but in December this decision to blockade rather than invade was reconsidered. Raeder's team then received a memo from the Army's operational commander, Colonel Heinrich von Stülpnagel, who had conducted his own invasion study, called *Fall Nord West*. Stülpnagel had proposed a landing in north-eastern Britain, and now requested comments from the Navy, the Air Force, and others that would be involved, but their comments were anything but positive. The Navy said it would take at least a year before the ships were available, and that air landings were a necessity for an invasion to succeed. At the same time Goering's Luftwaffe said that air landings were feasible only after an invasion was made from the sea. The result was thus status quo; an invasion was not an alternative at the moment.

The situation would be changed and updated in connection with the German advance westward during the spring of 1940. After the French capitulation, the German army in June was at the English Channel coast at Calais, only twenty-five miles from Britain. Despite attempts by Raeder to mitigate Hitler's newly emerging enthusiasm and willingness to invade Britain, direct orders were given to prepare operations starting on 2 July. One important reason for the reluctance of the German Navy was the severe loss of destroyers they had been subjected to in the battle of Narvik in May 1940. Hitler's written order, however, stressed that the invasion was not definitive, and in its initial wording said: 'An invasion of Britain is possible under certain circumstances by which air supremacy is the key. At present, therefore, the time of when this will be, is an open question.' Wilhelm Keitel, head of the army high command (OKW), closed the same order with the words: 'All preparations must be made with regard to fact that the planning of the landing in Great Britain is not fully elaborated, and therefore only a question of preparation for a possible event.'[24]

So from July 1940, the German armed forces worked on the detailed planning of the operation, which soon was named *Seelöwe* (*Sealion*), a cover name which is said to have referred to the lions in the British royal coat of arms, and the fact that the invasion would take place over the sea. The landing area was specified as between Ramsgate and the area west of the Isle of Wight. To build up the Army's invasion force, the number of divisions in Germany was reduced. The Luftwaffe was at the same time escalating their operations against British targets, which evolved into the part of the war later called the Battle of Britain. From 10 July British convoys in the Channel were attacked, which were easy targets, and simultaneously strained the RAF's resources. The constant patrols over the Channel tired both the British pilots, and decreased the country's fuel supply.[25] The attacks escalated on 13 August into the *Adlerangriff* (the eagle attack), the main German attack against the RAF, which was directed against a series of targets on the mainland. These targets were mainly airfields, aircraft factories and radar stations, after Hitler had ordered that: 'The German Air Force shall with all available forces destroy the British air force as soon as possible.' After ten days of heavy fighting, Goering ordered a focus on the British airfields, which were to be destroyed in order to create total German air supremacy. Attacks came, however, to be exhausting for both parties. The lost aircraft could be replaced, but with the shortage of trained pilots, there were problems for both Britain and Germany.

With a severely damaged but not defeated RAF, the Luftwaffe on 7 September changed to the bombing of British cities with massive attacks on the port areas in London's East End. The transition was not entirely without criticism. The British airfields recovered quickly, and due to lack of fuel the German fighters were often forced to leave unprotected bomber formations for long periods of time over British cities. This change of target to British cities was a blessing for the RAF as this gave them some respite and a much-needed opportunity to build up their strength again. With the increasing German losses, even Hitler was considering stopping all invasion preparations, but this, however, did not happen until much later in the autumn.

While the Luftwaffe, during the late summer of 1940, fought hard battles against the RAF, preparations for the invasion in detail continued in the German army leadership. Maps, military intelligence and equipment had been developed, while the invasion plan began to take shape. The operation was supposed to be a main strike, carried out by Army Group A commanded by Field Marshal Gerd von Rundstedt, in the form of a landing where the English Channel was at its narrowest, on the coast of Ramsgate–Dover–Portsmouth. This part of the operation would also be supported by parachute troops, which would be dropped around Brighton and Dover. Further west, simultaneously, Army Group C, commanded by Field Marshal Wilhelm Ritter von Leeb, would land at Lyme Regis, and then move to Bristol. With a secure bridgehead, army groups would then attack London, Gloucester, Oxford and Maldon. If those cities fell, the Germans expected that the rest of the country would soon be forced to surrender.[26]

Those plans were, however, in late summer becoming more and more limited. In a decision on 27 August, the landing area at the coast was reduced to between Beachy Head and Deal, the stretch where the Channel is narrowest. A week later, on 3 September, the earliest date for the invasion was moved from 15 to 21 September, at the request of the Navy, which needed more time for their preparations. In September, it was obvious that the Battle of Britain was lost for the Germans. The British had resisted the Luftwaffe's attacks and the Germans did not achieve air supremacy. On 17 September Hitler decided, after conferring with the army high command (OKW), that the operation should be postponed indefinitely. Some preparations as well as some military operations continued during the autumn. Not until 9 January 1941 were the preparations suspended altogether; Hitler had other plans and his eyes were directed eastward. Britain had resisted the German attacks but they were never entirely abandoned, with bombers and later the German rocket weapons continuing to cause death and destruction in the country.

DEFENCE

The war obviously made necessary a huge increase in the armed forces and conscription was introduced in September 1939 with about one million men being drafted into the army which, in June 1940, numbered almost 1.7 million. England has about 400 miles of coastline facing the continent on the south coast. After Dunkirk, a German invasion was expected before long. In June 1940, there were fifteen infantry divisions and one armoured division available for the defence of southern England. The infantry divisions were roughly halved in strength and they had only one sixth of the artillery that was needed, most of it outdated.[27] Transport vehicles were in short supply and the huge losses of equipment at Dunkirk were severely felt.

Clearly, defence had to become a priority. On 24 May, there was a radio broadcast by Anthony Eden,[28] Secretary of State for War, appealing for more men. The volunteers were soon available, and organised into a corps called the Local Defence Volunteers (LDV, malicious tongues said that it stood for 'Look, Duck and Vanish'); in July it was re-named the Home Guard. Eden was opposed to the name change, not least for the one million new armbands that now had to be replaced.[29] At the end of June there were 1½ million men enlisted, of which half had been in the First World War.[30] The enthusiasm and spirit was high, but there were big problems with the supply of weapons and uniforms, and the training was substandard. They had to produce their own weapons, such as Molotov cocktails, and 'sticky bombs', filled with a mixture containing nitroglycerine. Armament was improved when the Home Guard received half a million First World War rifles from the USA.

One member, John Hastings, remembers that he had his rifle in the bedroom, together with the single cartridge he was equipped with. Later, when he became a corporal, he received a Sten gun; today he cannot understand how they could issue these terribly dangerous weapons.[31] The aim of their mission was also unclear. The War Office and the Army troops saw them as an armed police force with a passive role, which would conduct reconnaissance of German invasion troops, manage security services and liaise with the army. Such a role was ill-suited to the image of the leaders and members of the Home Guard – they thought that their organisation was best suited for an active role in direct attacks against the Germans, and engaging in a guerrilla war.

The presence of former military officers and veterans raised the aims of the units and they considered themselves well trained for military service with their experience of twenty years before. If the invasion had come, it would have meant a bloodbath for the untrained and poorly equipped 'Dad's Army' against the experienced German forces. It would take many years before the corps was a reasonably effective force, but they would soon be useful. Interestingly, the Home Guard was demobilised in 1945, at the time when the Germans were building up their Home Guard against the expected Russian attack on Berlin.

Fear of parachutists was a reality, and if an attack by parachute troops was coming, the codeword CROMWELL would be used. The church bells fell silent, but they would ring when the Home Guard needed to be mustered to resist a German attack. Protecting anti-aircraft artillery and searchlights was important and approximately 142,000 volunteers from the Home Guard were involved in this task. Other tasks for the Home Guard included guarding airports, waterways, railway stations, factories, coastal areas, rescue and emergency services after bombardment, the placement of obstacles for airborne troops and tanks, construction of bunkers and the dismantling of road signs and station names. The Home Guard at times were too zealous with their road block checks: ARP guards were delayed on their way to their posts, the fire service was stopped during call-outs, and a man wrote in the *Daily Express* that he was stopped twenty times for inspection during a journey of six miles. In addition, some were 'trigger happy'; several cases of accidental fatal shooting of innocent travellers occurred, as well as the shooting of a Hurricane pilot who parachuted from his aircraft, which had been damaged in combat.[32] Far down the list came guerrilla tactics or battle along with regular troops. There was a trained corps of 6,000 'scallywags', men with ordinary jobs who would act as a guerrilla resistance movement, if the invasion came.[33] For the RAF, the Royal Observer Corps was an important force which tracked German aircraft once they had crossed the coast during the Battle of Britain and the Blitz. Furthermore, the defence of the coast needed Home Guard patrols and the manning of coastal artillery. Extensive systems of bunkers, fortifications, tank obstacles and barbed wire barriers were built, and beaches and bridges were mined, mostly of course on the south coast.

During the summer of 1940, with fuel supplies replenished, the idea of using petroleum products for defensive purposes was brought forward. Under the direction of the Petroleum Warfare Department (PWD) systems were introduced, such as filling lakes with fuel, which would be set on fire if parachute troops were landing, or fire-traps filled with fuel in low parts of roads, which would be set on fire when German transports drove by. At major intersections, there were also several so-called 'Flame Fougasse' which were manned by the Home Guard. A Flame Fougasse consisted of a 100-litre barrel of fuel, gunpowder and amatol, which exploded and fired off 25-yard-long flames. Eventually there were 50,000 fougasses deployed. A system for setting fire to the sea was developed, where twelve tonnes of fuel per hour could flow out through tubes onto the surface of a reasonably calm sea and cause an inferno.[34]

Women had their own organisations such as the WVS (War Voluntary Service), military organisations, like the 'WRENS', 'ATS' and 'WAAF', or as workers in factories or Land Girls in agriculture (with wages of £1 10s per week), which engaged 1.3 million women. Many typically male occupations were increasingly being taken over by the female workforce. Industry, particularly the large defence industries, became increasingly dependent on female labour, with salaries of up to £2 per week. At one factory which manufactured Lancaster bombers, for example, 60 per cent of the workforce were women.[35]

There were other major voluntary organisations, such as the eager and zealous ARP (Air Raid Precautions) wardens, who, among other things, went around and checked the blackout. This corps of 1.4 million men would come to play an important role in the Blitz, often with heroic efforts, just as the volunteers in the AFS (Auxiliary Fire Service). It was later merged with the regular fire service, and around 370,000 people served, including 80,000 women. With the invasion threat, a large part of the civilian population, who were not needed for defence purposes, were evacuated from the coastal regions; in

Kent 40 per cent and in East Anglia 50 per cent of the population were moved.

There was a widespread fear that a 'fifth column' would emerge if the invasion came. Therefore, 1,600 British fascist were arrested in 1940,[36] of whom 740 were interned.[37] The authorities did everything to dampen rumours, but the fear was still there. A contributing factor was an exaggerated description of what had happened in the Netherlands, from a report on the 'Fifth Column Menace', written by the British ambassador in that country, Sir Neville Bland. Also the military contributed to the flow of rumours. General 'Tiny' Ironside[38] claimed that there were examples of people who definitely had reconnoitred airfields around the country for the enemy, and that on telephone poles and walls markings and signs had been found, exactly of the same kind seen in France before the Dunkirk evacuation.[39] A vice-admiral, who was responsible for the port of Dover, reported that several acts of sabotage had been performed, leaks had occurred in communications, and used cars were bought for high prices and left in various car parks.[40] At the time, all sorts of rumours were circulating about disguised German paratroopers. Just as in the First World War, bearded nuns with hairy arms and remarkably large shoes were still seen here and there. On the arm of one nun in the Underground, a tattoo of Hitler had actually been seen. In May and June there were so many reports of parachutists, that the authorities had to publish an official denial.[41] People who walked close to airfields with cameras were arrested. A teacher, who was obsessed with gangsters, accused a colleague of being a secret agent.[42]

A popular radio voice was Lord Haw Haw, or William Joyce, in radio broadcasts from Germany,[43] but he was mostly regarded as a joke. He could make use of various known facts (often taken from British newspapers), to give the impression that the Germans knew most things, and to make general threats to the British people. One of the more famous anecdotes is that he allegedly announced that a public clock was fifteen minutes slow in Banstead.[44] A propaganda campaign was launched by the British using posters by the illustrator

Fougasse, including the famous words 'Careless talk costs lives'. The BBC launched a series of popular lectures, 'Postscripts', by the writer J. B. Priestley, as a counter-attack against the German propaganda. Several brochures were produced with information on what to do if the invasion came. People were equipped with gas masks, which were soon, however, often left behind at home. Suitcases were packed ready for an evacuation, and a few even made suicide pacts.

The fear of spies was widespread, especially after the arrest of Tyler Kent,[45] a clerk at the American Embassy, who provided the Germans with copies of secret documents. There was, as in the First World War, a dislike of people of German and Italian descent, even those who came as refugees from Hitler, and Jews were not always immune from prejudice. In 1941, Irma Stapleton, of German origin and former member of the German Embassy in London, was arrested. She worked in a munitions factory and was tempted by MI5 to smuggle out samples of the ammunition and important documents.[46] The police received plenty of calls about suspicious strangers and odd behaviour. One mysterious man who stood with a map for a long time in front of Westminster Abbey was reported.[47] In Cardiff someone reported that he had heard his neighbour send Morse messages (which proved to be a leaking tank);[48] a man visiting a small village in northern England was accused of drawing a sketch of the village when he was sitting down and writing postcards;[49] a priest's daughter reported that a lodging officer was in the bathroom at night, but did not flush after him, and he was making signals with a flashlight.[50] RAF aircrew on patrol noticed suspicious marks on the ground which were often caused by farmers who ploughed or harvested a field in a certain way, or plantings of flowers that looked like an arrow seen from the sky.[51]

Rumours of unsuccessful invasion attempts were very common, with a peak in August–September 1940. There were rumours that an invasion attempt or an exercise had been made, but had been successfully defeated in the Channel. Bodies dressed in German uniforms had washed up on beaches in the south and east coast of England, often claimed to be severely burnt. The rumours were spread in the United States and in occupied Europe; many had 'spoken' with survivors, and several British people had 'seen' invasion attempts. From the Free French Information Service Office, it was reported that 30,000 Germans had drowned, a story which had to be suppressed by British authorities.[52] *The New York Times* reported from Oslo that a number of trucks loaded with tied-up German troops had been seen, on their way to Akershus for execution. They had refused to participate in a second landing attempt after 40-50,000 were killed or wounded in the first attempt. All hospitals along the west coast of the European continent were filled with wounded Germans.[53] Bodies found on the beaches might as well have been British. On 31 August, RAF aircraft saw a large German convoy off the Dutch coast, and five British destroyers were sent out. They sailed straight into an unknown minefield outside the Dutch island of Texel. Two destroyers, *Esk* and *Ivanhoe*, were sunk and 300 of the crews were killed.[54] It later turned out that only thirty-six bodies in German uniform had been washed up on the beaches, many of whom had been dead for several weeks.[55] A story that still mystifies, and where there are still closed secret files, is the story of Shingle Street, a village near Harwich, late in August 1940. It is possible that a small German force attempted a landing there, but fell victim to the RAF and burning oil, or perhaps it was all arranged by the British as a propaganda display.

On 7 September 1940 the codeword CROMWELL really was sent out, after the massive bomb attack on London, and because a fleet of large ships off the French coastline was observed from Dover. The regular army forces were put on high alert, the church bells rang, the Home Guard was mobilised,[56] and a few bridges were even blown up. CROMWELL was finally cancelled after about ten days, when it became increasingly certain that no immediate threat of invasion existed.

4

TATE Starts His Work

It was in this environment that TATE would now begin his work as a double agent. Although his objectives would, of course, be changed several times during the war, his mission from the beginning was to report on:

1. The effects of the bombing.
2. The morale and general state of the Army, but not where forces were located.
3. The evacuation of civilians.
4. Obstacles near airfields.
5. The location of air defences, and the calibre of their artillery.

Having managed to start his transmissions after the nights of 16 and 17 October, TATE began his reporting, and during the remaining three months of the year he sent at least thirty-eight reports.[1] Mostly these were weather reports, but also included misleading information about the production of aircraft, number of aircraft at the bases, and information on air defence. He also warned of drifting mines, anti-panzer barriers, and oil pipe lines which could start large fires on the sea off the south coast, and similar arrangements which would impede an invasion by the Germans.[2]

The Germans were also curious about how TATE's identity card had worked. On 13 November 1940, they asked if he could use his identity card, or if there were any problems with it. They needed a quick reply, as this was extremely important information for the Abwehr for the future delivery of agents to Britain (though they, of course, had no idea that MI5 was aware of the information including addresses that SNOW had delivered to the Germans). TATE replied on 14 November that there was no problem with the identity card, but he had not dared to use the ration book supplied by Abwehr because it was of doubtful quality.[3] So the forgers in the Abwehr were certainly ordered to sort this out. He had hidden his Danish passport, because he now presented himself as a British citizen who had grown up in Denmark.

A month later came the question of whether identity cards were also needed in the Republic of Ireland. After an appropriate number of weeks, TATE replied that ration cards and identity cards were not needed in 'the Free State', the Republic of Ireland. This was a very important piece of information for the Abwehr, which saw Ireland as an excellent base in the west, with easy access to Great Britain for espionage by German agents.[4]

After working for only six weeks, TATE was recommended by Nikolaus Ritter to receive the Iron Cross second class for his valuable contributions; he was the first agent to receive this coveted award. To be able to receive this award, he was also naturalised as a German citizen.[5] There was a reference to this award in a message from Germany on 5 January 1941, regarding technical problems with the transmission of message number thirty-seven from TATE on 30 December 1940.[6]

At that time the W Board, which was a precursor of the Double-Cross Committee, decided that the extent of bomb damage could be reported fairly accurately and the nation's morale could also be reported truthfully. It was considered desirable to encourage the enemy to spread their attacks as much as possible. No reports should, however, be given on differences in reactions to the bombing between rich and poor parts of cities, in which the Germans had a curious interest. The British tried later to deflect the interest in London and other cities, and instead get attacks against the RAF airfields, with reports that there were plenty of aircraft there, but they were inadequately defended by anti-aircraft artillery. But the Germans were still mostly interested in the effects on the large cities.[7] However, there were other areas of interest, and in January TATE was also requested to supply information regarding troop movements associated with Greece and the surrounding area.

TATE became one of the main sources for the Abwehr in terms of the effect of the bombing raids,[8] and he participated with great interest in the decisions about what information should be provided, and criticised things that he feared could expose his double game. Once, his superiors were reluctant to reveal that several buildings had been damaged in the De Havilland aircraft factory in Hatfield, but TATE managed to persuade his handlers that this should be mentioned, because it could so obviously be seen from the air. As an example of what he reported, we can see that in February 1941 bombs hit Borehamwood, approximately two miles from TATE's (fictional) home in Barnet. He sent a list of plants destroyed in that raid: Standard Telephones & Cables Ltd, Serum Laboratories Ltd, Smith & Sons Ltd, etc.[9]

In a discussion with MI5, after some time, TATE argued that information from his neighbourhood was now exhausted. He was becoming tired, and he wondered if they could arrange a helper for him, someone either local or from Germany. At that moment this was considered inappropriate, so TATE was asked to deliver a radio transmission to Hamburg in which he complained and stated that he was now fully capable of handling more important tasks, and expanding his geographical area. Probably as a result of this appeal, he received orders to travel around in England and report on airfields and factories. But all the travel was, of course, only fictitious, and Wulf Schmidt must have felt rather bored at times. As an example of his new activity: 'Many bombers are said to be stationed in the Oxford area, mainly in Abington, Besone [Benson] and Breazenorton [Brize Norton]. Reconnaissance follows.' On 25 February he had reached Brize Norton,[10] and could announce: 'New especially large grass-covered mounds of earth, supposedly underground hangars, about 200 x 75 metres in size.' Hamburg thought this seemed strange, but they merely noted that they were not marked on Sheet No. 104 of their maps of the airfields in England. On 26 February, TATE continued:

Further observation of the Brize Norton airfield. The six mounds reported yesterday are in fact underground hangars. I personally saw how two Defiants were pushed into one of these underground hangars on the north-west side. They had the markings N 3446 and N 3479. The exact position of the hangars is as follows: two hangars lie in north-south direction 100 metres west of the village of Brize Norton and north of the road from Brize Norton to Carterton, two further in the same direction but south of the road and 150 metres distant from the road to Bampton; two further lie 1,800 metres south of Carterton and 350 metres west of the road. Observed anti-aircraft positions, one about 750 metres east of Carterton and one 100 metres south of Carterton.[11]

The following month, TATE travelled around near Salisbury to study airfields, and in April in the suburbs of West London. Sometimes his reports contained misspellings or errors in transmission, which probably annoyed the Abwehr, when they searched in their atlases to find 'Heathron Airfield' (Heathrow) or 'Roading' (Reading).[12] MI5 also tried to get the Germans to bomb a bogus munitions store, the coordinates of which TATE sent to Hamburg in March, but no raid was carried out by the Luftwaffe.[13]

During the first part of 1941, espionage activity was mainly concentrated on issues concerning the air war. TATE's reports were of a high standard. As he, in the eyes of the Germans, could travel around freely, he had little difficulty answering the questions coming from the Abwehr. According to later testimony from the captured agent Karel Richter, he stood in high regard among the Germans and was considered a 'gem'. On 6 May 1941, the following message is recorded: 'Have just learnt that you have been decorated in the name of the Führer with the Iron Cross, First and Second Class. We all most heartily congratulate you and our thoughts are with you.'[14] In the end, he actually received his two Iron Crosses from his brother Kai after the war, but to his rage, MI5 laid hands on them.[15] On 6 June he received several questions:

Adjoining the aerodrome at Hawarden west of Chester, there lies at the SW corner 1 Km north of Broughton, the Vickers Armstrong Factory on the surface. Where is the underground factory? Are the works in operation?

West of Chester there is an aerodrome. Is the aerodrome called Hawarden or Broughton? Or are there two aerodromes and where are they, exactly?

Is there an ammunition factory near Chester? We do not mean the factory called Schotten Summer.

In 'Breston' there is an incendiary bomb factory which has 2-3000 employees. We want the name and exact position of this factory. In the port area of 'Breston' there are said to be two General Electrics factories and also a General Electric factory in Salmesbury, which we are told was previously making Spitfire parts.

As weather reports are very important, please tell us how long [before] these will be sent due to your trip. Heartiest greetings.

TATE answered the day after, that his trip would take at least five days but it was difficult to be precise. He requested: 'Please give exact location of the place called "Salmesbury". Further should it be "Preston" and not "Breston"?'[16]

On 26 June, questions were asked about the exact positions of some searchlights. There were two 'Inns', probably pubs close to Hawarden airfield near Chester, and searchlights could be found near one of these places but which one? They also asked about some of the boxes seen at Aintree railway station, and about a plant in Ribbleton, where the tower construction, called 'wohl-cooling-station', was located. What did it produce? TATE could, of course, respond to most of the questions (but it is not revealed in his files what the 'wohl-cooling-station' was). In Radlett, where TATE lived, there was a Handley Page aircraft factory with an airfield, and in July 1941 he was asked for an accurate description. Apparently the production of aircraft engines had decreased from 1,250 in March to 950 in April, and they also wanted details about this.[17]

The Germans obviously had a rudimentary knowledge of the geography of Britain and they must have had only a very vague understanding of the situation in Britain. They had aerial reconnaissance, newspapers, other written material from neutral countries, and their agents in Britain, who were all giving them disinformation. On the other hand, Britain had hardly any agents in place in Germany.

One place that they knew the position of was Coventry. TATE was asked to go there and snoop and report several months after the devastating bomb attack.[18] This was a delicate issue for the Double-Cross Committee. Was there a risk of another major attack on Coventry? It was decided to create a fictional visit to Coventry for TATE, where police activity prevented him from gaining more than a sketchy impression. But even this aroused concerns for the Committee. There was a draft for transmission of a fairly detailed report, but it ended up with TATE giving a report which consisted mostly of rumours. He was carefully unspecific about the damage he saw and tried (indirectly) to advise against further attack, by stating that the key remaining plants were scattered.[19]

WORK ON THE FARM

Those who controlled TATE as a double agent, TAR Robertson, William Luke, Russell Lee and the radio operator Ronnie Reed, of course, had regular briefings to discuss the agent TATE they had created, and to analyse his previous activities. All the time, the risk of disclosure to the German side was a dark cloud hanging over the business. They realised that they had built him into a first-class agent, but of 'low grade' – that is, all the information originated from him, and it consisted almost entirely of material he himself had collected. Therefore, it was impossible for him to be involved in any larger operations of deception. TATE was useful in catching other newly arrived agents, and he provided the enemy with plenty of material, but obtained rather poor information in exchange. To improve the situation they must convert TATE from a low-grade to a high-grade agent. This could not be done by suddenly providing him with high-level contacts, as they had done with BALLOON (or Dickie Metcalf, a sub-agent for TRICYCLE, a former army officer, a bit of a playboy who socialised in high-level circles). Any such attempt would be met with suspicion from the enemy. He could be potentially useful in the role of an agent who collected information that other agents had obtained. TATE, however, should in that case have very little direct contact with them. The reasons why they never built up a spy ring around TATE with several sub-agents are not discussed in his files. This would have been useful during 1943 and 1944 when there was a reduction in how much the Germans used him.

One way to accomplish this was to place TATE in a position where it was physically impossible for him to gather the wide-ranging information he had managed so far. This could be achieved by getting TATE into a role where he was either too nervous, or in a permanent position in industry, or by making him a soldier. His biography was that he was a British citizen but was born and raised in Denmark, and came as a refugee after the German invasion of Denmark. His age group should have registered for military service in July the year before, i.e., before he even arrived in the country. If someone asked why he was not in the army, he must come up with the excuse that he had actually signed up, but somehow had got lost in the system. He could inform the Germans that he, as a result of a general search, had been forced to undergo a medical examination but been classified as C3, which meant that it was unlikely he would be drafted, but he would have to commit to full-time employment. The idea was to arrange a job for TATE at a nearby farm, where he could operate radio transmissions in the evenings, and sometimes get a day off, but it would then be impossible to undertake longer journeys, or have the opportunity to conduct observations of nearby air bases. But he would feel safe in his new situation, with first-class opportunities to communicate, and he would be eager to continue his work. Did the Germans have agents, perhaps unknown to MI5, who had no possibility of using radio transmissions, and who might need his assistance? If there existed any such person, TATE could agree to see him, give his advice and share his experience on how the work should be managed. It was believed that this was a plan that might succeed.[20]

The decision was that TATE, in his contacts with the Germans, should now show clear signs of nervousness regarding the question of why he was not in military service, which had been raised, and that he was waiting for a medical examination. He would lie low and avoid radio communication for a few weeks. But first they had to wait to see how the Karel Richter case developed (see this chapter). In September 1941 they had polished the plan and decided how to carry it out. TATE would first send a message that he had been forced to register for military service, but in a later message, that he had managed to avoid this, but instead had been forced to work on a farm. TATE himself took an active part in the content of all his radio traffic, and his immediate superiors were very satisfied with his enthusiasm and commitment. TATE was skilled in this and eager to help. This probably brightened up his monotonous existence and boredom. He would be careful with his use of the radio in order to underline the seriousness of his situation, and because of the fear of being intercepted. Any questions about air bases and similar requests for information remained unanswered for the time being. First, there should be a communication with signs of a crisis, later followed by a longer report in the same spirit. The arrangement had been planned for several months and on 12 September it was considered to be ready. At 5.30 p.m. TATE sent the following:

Was caught in a police raid at King's Cross Station. Police asked for Identity Cards of all travellers. On being asked whether I had yet registered for military service, I answered the truth – that is 'no', in order not to arouse suspicion by lying. They took the number of my Identity Card, my name, address, etc. I thought it wiser to give my real address to prevent closer investigation about the authenticity of my Identity Card. I was told to register at once otherwise I would be prosecuted. In order to prevent closer investigation, suspicion, or at the worst arrest and its accompanying investigations, there is nothing else to do but comply with their orders.

But was there any occasion when British police suddenly raided a railway station to check everyone? We do not know the answer, but for the Germans, this was a natural part of everyday life; the Gestapo and other security agencies acted in this way. The answer to TATE's message came exactly one day later:

We are very anxious. Head up. Own safety first. Take into consideration that you may be treated as a deserter as you have not followed the registration instructions. Further dangers are:– Personal particulars, parents; previous whereabouts. Further, over there it is known that just the thing we do is to give false Identity Cards.

Consider whether it would not be better to disappear from your lodgings. Buy false documents. Amount of money is immaterial. Possibly go to Northern Ireland for some time. Do you remember the ink formula? The old address is no longer in force. New one is:– Dr Albert Edouard Beau in Coimbra, Portugal, Rua Dr Bernardo the Albuquerqe.

You might like to give us new transmissions times. Give us a possibility to find you in the event of wireless interruption. Possibly a place where you can be, or send another man every first of the month. In case of extreme urgency put an advertisement in *The Times* every first of the month under Used Clothing Wanted containing the words 'Dinner Jacket', Christian name of advertiser – William and address. Possibly you can make other proposals. Heartiest greetings. Hals und Beinbruch. Bruhns.[21]

It should be noted that TATE had sent information about air bases in Cambridge and in the Lincoln area, which he should have sent before he was caught in the police raid. A lively phone conversation followed between those who controlled TATE's activities (someone overheard this conversation, and a certain Colonel Allan's Department was alarmed). TATE's next message:

Many thanks for sympathies. Do not worry too much. Think will be able to master the situation. I have a good plan. Suspending aerodrome messages; afterwards if everything is all right. I think I can do this, have a good plan. Emergency meeting place remain as arranged in my message 253. Because of special danger, put only good men to listen for me during next few days. I must send fast. Everything else later. Heil und Sieg.

We can note that after one year, TATE had sent at least 253 messages. No more radio messages were sent until 16 September:

Today, I intend to make a dangerous step. As this is most important for the future, please, only for today listen out at every hour for 15 minutes. I ask for your utmost attention. If I do not come on I am in the soup. Touch wood.

And the Germans responded that the address of Beau in Coimbra was cancelled, and he would need a new address. TATE informed at 3.00 p.m. that he would send a message, which he was just about to encipher, at 4.00 p.m. It read:

The following has happened. An acquaintance, the owner of a large farm with modern dairy connected to it, who is of good family with important connections, the daughter of whom I was able to help out of an awkward situation, now recompenses me. After I had told him the story of my registration in highly coloured language and the possible unpleasant developments for me, he gave me a letter stating that I had been working for some time in his business and I had done him indispensable service and that my possible withdrawal would be irreplaceable to his firm and the nation. With this document I went to the local registration office and after showing it to them and first giving my my explanation, they questioned me and my friend about my knowledge of agriculture, livestock, dairy work and machinery. As the officer was not very knowledgeable himself, it was easy for me to convince him of my first-class qualifications.

The consequence of this is that now, I, on no side, am no longer liable for military service as I am now busy on war work, but on the other side, I must really enter in this firm at once as my friend's right-hand man; this is of course very inconvenient but is unavoidable and this must be understood by you for better or for worse. I am convinced that my friend, who possibly sees in me his future son-in-law will give me as much time and as free a hand as possible but the fact is that anyhow during the day I am tied and am unable to travel around. ... my friend of course has not the slightest idea of my double life.

I will remain in my old living-place and can in the future give the messages the same as now. Of course I shall have to change my transmitting times in accordance with my working orders. You know I will use all my power as far as possible for the sake of our cause but in the future must leave it to me and my intelligence how to do it and what to do. Finish.[22]

A bit of high drama was added as an extra touch. During the transmission TATE gave a signal that there was danger, he cut off the transmission for three minutes, but then came back again. They wanted to make him look nervous. On the afternoon of 17 September 1941 came the answer: 'Heartiest congratulations that everything has turned out so well. Nevertheless we recommend you to be on the alert and careful. Hals und Beinbruch. Bruhns.'

Usually, the German messages were signed by Bruhns (or Böckel, which was his real name, whom he knew from training in Hamburg), the radio operator Brandt (who signed with 'Hr. Bra'), or Werner. Once there was a message about technical issues signed by Dr Thiele, which was the alias of Major Trautmann, and once from a Prodehl, an assistant to Trautmann. Probably they all wanted to shine in the reflected glory from TATE, a highly esteemed star at this time.

TATE sent a short message on 18 September, in which he expressed his relief that the Germans were not disappointed in him. He felt much safer now and hoped to be useful again. Now TATE and his steering committee were in high spirits – the Germans had swallowed the whole story.

Masterman's Evaluation

J. C. Masterman, the chairman of the Double-Cross organisation, evaluated the implementation of the plan, and how it would have seemed from the German point of view.[23] He thought that everything had been very ably dealt with, and there were no objections until 12 September, and the police control. The story of working on the farm and the influential friend was not quite convincing, and it was hard to believe. Firstly, how had TATE managed to get off the hook regarding why he had not signed up earlier, and secondly, how had this influential man who was his acquaintance managed to make the authorities accept his declarations about TATE's work.

TATE's identity card was not free from suspicion (no wonder, it was a fake) and that the official was impressed by the letter written by his employer, without investigating the identity card further, was a bit thin.

Now TATE had got his £20,000 (see Chapter 5 'Financial Problems') with instructions to gradually build up an organisation, but he had not been given any suggestions as to how to achieve this, nor been asked for an explanation of his plans, or what attempts he had made to start the build-up. Instead, he had stopped sending the valuable reports he had delivered earlier, and unsatisfactory reports were now submitted, based on articles in the *Daily Mail* and other unimportant sources. This led to a decline in quality, compared to his previous work. For the Germans it must have looked as if he was trying to fob them off with inferior information.

TATE's steering group agreed that there were shaky elements in TATE's story, but they had not received any indication that he had been exposed, and the information he was currently sending had started to improve. He would send messages where it appeared that he had followed the Germans' advice, but it was extremely difficult to acquire useful people. However, he now felt much more at home in London's West End than in the past.

ROUNDBUSH HOUSE

We could suppose that TATE had a boring and restricted, almost prison-like, life. How did he cope with this during the spare time between his work with the radio messages? Reading books, newspapers and enjoying music, which he was fond of, probably helped him endure his situation. Obviously, better facilities were needed, and a suitable house in Letchmore Heath (about four miles east of Watford) in the Round Bush area was found, which they would rent. The house, which had belonged at least initially to a Mr L. W. Philips, was a detached two-storey house with a basement and a large garden.[24] One of the rooms upstairs was an ideal place for the radio equipment. But there was also a darkroom next door, which the owner wanted to use, so it was not included in the rent. This meant that the owner could show up from time to time. It was, therefore, necessary to hide the receiver in a lockable cabinet, while the transmitter was already in a concealed case. The officer who initially would be responsible was Russell Lee, with another two men as guards. Lee would get a room of his own and the guards would, in turn, stay for a week with TATE on the upper floor. A cook/housekeeper was quickly recruited and she would also live in the house. They had wondered if iron grilles were needed for the windows of the room where TATE would live, but found it hardly necessary, as it was enough to secure the windows. With this arrangement the intention was to give the staff and TATE a much more comfortable environment.

There were initially some problems with the radio equipment, which Reed fixed. A water pipe was first used as the earth contact, but when this was changed to a ground wire the problem was solved. TAR Robertson, head of B1(a), and his wife Joan and their little daughter with a nanny, also came to live in the house. Wulf repaid their hospitality by helping with household chores, and he took many beautiful photos of their daughter; it was noticed that he was a skilled photographer. Wulf was a very likeable man, full of humour, and TAR Robertson liked him very much.[25] Once he heard Joan Robertson and the nanny at the dinner table discussing what would happen if the Germans came. The nanny said: 'I wonder what would happen if a German agent fell down from heaven and turned up here?' TATE could not resist pretending to be a nasty agent, who came and abducted the nanny. Mrs Robertson was not amused, but the nanny, who had no idea about TATE's background, thought it was great fun.[26] As this story came from Ladislas Farago it may be of doubtful authenticity. So they enjoyed their time together, and TATE could experience family life, thanks to Robertson's wife and child. TATE's life otherwise would often have been marked by boredom, but now at least he had gardening work, and also looking after poultry (and maybe geese as there is a photo of these, in addition to Roundbush House in one of his files[27]) as leisure activities. The daughter of TAR, would eventually work for MI5 when she was an adult. Russell Lee, who wrote many of TATE's reports with him, also thought it was a pleasant job because of TATE's amiable and convivial personality. Was it possible, at this stage, that he developed his interest and talent for photography? The photos of TAR's daughter impressed the people around him. It is not known if he was ever allowed to use the darkroom in the house.

In November 1941, TATE fell ill with a stomach ulcer which required a one-week hospital stay at St Mary's Hospital. But the radio communication went ahead anyway as one of the British radio operators had learned to mimic the style of TATE's 'fist' in transmissions. After this, TATE did not send any further radio messages himself (although he had previously trained so diligently), but he participated in the wording of the messages and in the process of enciphering all radio traffic. But that same month TATE was able to inform the Abwehr that, through the daughter of the farmer (his employer), he had become acquainted with a girl named Mary, who was employed in the cipher department of one of the ministries, namely the Admiralty, the Navy Headquarters.

It seemed as if German interest in aviation activity cooled slightly from September 1941 while they began increasingly to show an interest in food issues, even more now that TATE was employed in agriculture. They wanted to have regular reports on food prices, rationing, availability of food in the country and where the underground food stores were located. Reports on these issues became more frequent during the first half of the year. Quite often TATE had to answer the same question concerning prices several times, which made him more frustrated. Once he received a question from the Abwehr about how the bread tasted and what it cost. TATE replied irritably: 'Have you nothing more important to ask about? It tastes good.' His reaction was understandable – there was a war going on concerning freedom or enslavement of the human species, and they asked about bread! But German interest in other subjects had not completely disappeared and in December he was ordered to focus on Air Force matters again. He had before that, on 4 November, received several questions concerning parachute troops and regular troops transported by aircraft: how large were these forces, where and how long did the training take, was training also carried out in Canada and Australia, would they be sent to the Middle East, type of aircraft used, organisation, etc. Appropriate answers that TATE could plausibly have found out were sent, but they were vague and general. It was common knowledge that such troops existed and everyone talked about them. In the next year, 1942, the interest in food issues reappeared.[28]

5

Financial Problems

On 14 January 1941, TATE sent a message to the Germans about his precarious financial situation, saying that the issue of where and when he would be able to receive more money could not wait. He was told that £100 would be arranged through SUMMER,[1] but this was prevented because Gösta Caroli had made an escape attempt from Hinxton, and had now been arrested and had finished as a double agent.[2] The Germans explained that SUMMER (or Agent 3719, his German designation) had been sent north for a long period. In December 1941, TATE again asked about Gösta Caroli's fate, and learned from the Abwehr that he had fled the country in February.

On 4 February 1941, TATE was told that the Germans would send him money through a reliable friend. They asked how and where he could receive the money, without personal contact. TATE suggested that the money should be sent by mail to the name he lived under, Harry Williamson, Poste Restante, Radlett. The Germans were a bit hesitant and doubtful about the security of this arrangement, but on 11 February the agent *Johnny* (or SNOW as he was known in Britain as a double agent) sent £100 by post, but it was not revealed to TATE who the sender was. After his last visit to Lisbon in March 1941, SNOW was suspected of being exposed and 'blown' as an agent. He had revealed to the Germans that he had worked for the British during recent months, including the time when he sent the money to TATE. A concern, therefore, arose in MI5 about having sent the fictitious money to TATE's postal address from SNOW, but it did not appear to have caused any negative consequences for TATE as a reliable agent of the Abwehr.

On 24 March, TATE again asked for more money, because his expenses had been considerable during the last few weeks when he had travelled around England to spy, mostly concerned with aviation. He now needed a realistic amount of money, since the timing of the invasion seemed uncertain and the source he had previously received money from might not be available. The Germans replied that a direct way to send over large sums was needed. A few days later they said that he must be patient as this could take several weeks to arrange, and money would now come from the agent RAINBOW. The Germans had been alerted that small amounts of money sent by post to a poste restante address was too risky because post offices were being monitored. They wanted a new address and also asked him, rather generously, for a suggestion about how much money he needed. If an emergency arose, they could drop £500 from an aircraft, and asked TATE to find a suitable place for the delivery. On 18 April, TATE replied:

> Consider the poste restante Watford is safe for sending money. However as I only have 18 pounds left urgently require money by air. Have spent the whole day trying to find a good place. Have found a very large open field about 1,000m west of the village of Chalton. Chalton is about 8km NW of Luton where the railway from Bedford makes a bend to the south-east, near to a large cement works. Caution. Heavy AA in Luton. Also two searchlights and light MGs about 1,000m west of my field; these however cannot interfere with me owing to a hill and a wood in between. Otherwise no AA seen in neighbourhood. Please send at same time a crystal for day frequency. Please give date and full instructions.[3]

But the Germans abandoned the idea and said that they had a different solution. A friend, who was tall, blond, blue-eyed and with a wart above the right eye, who *Leonhard*/TATE knew from the Phoenix Hotel in Hamburg, would at the end of April arrive with £300 and a new crystal for TATE's radio equipment. TATE told MI5 that he could not remember anyone of that description. They would meet at 2.00 p.m. at the Regent Palace Hotel[4] (behind Piccadilly Circus), in the barber's shop, on the 30th, 5th, 10th or 15th, at 5.00 p.m. by the entrance to the café in the Tate Gallery, or at 7.00 p.m. at the main entrance of the British Museum. The password for both of them was 'Hello George'. They had also been considering another plan to send him £300 by post. TATE said that they should send the money to Watford in the same name as to the Radlett address.

Now the Special Branch in London started a major enterprise, under Inspector Hunt's direction, to cover all the different venues at the times indicated. It would require at least three, preferably four people, including two female police officers, for surveillance. One of them would be in the hair salon, and preferably new personnel should be used for the other venues. A photo of TATE was handed out as a precaution. Among the guards, it was decided that one should be busy wiping the floor, but this was changed to a man in overalls repairing a radiator. At the British Museum, two of the guards were sitting outside in a van marked with the name 'Thomas Tillan'. As soon as the man approached TATE, both were going to be arrested, which would strengthen the Germans' belief that TATE was still working for them. TATE was in total agreement with this, and he was fully prepared to cooperate and 'play the game'. Perhaps he even thought it was an exciting disruption of everyday routine. 'Tin-eye' Stephens was spoken to, and informed by TAR Robertson that he might acquire a new prisoner for Camp 020 as a result of this operation. They did not want TATE to stay too long at Camp 020 being visible to other prisoners, so he should quickly be moved away. Now it turned out that the Tate Gallery was closed, but the Germans replied that it was too late to change the comprehensive plan, TATE would have to stick to the main entrance of the gallery instead. On 28 April he was informed that the friend from Phoenix would recognise TATE, and could deliver a Morse key, but it was impossible to bring a camera and binoculars.

On 5 May, TATE received information that the departure of his friend had been postponed due to bad weather, but it was hoped that it could be implemented during the next few days. TATE reiterated his difficult financial situation to the Germans on 9 May:

> If you do not help me immediately, I can be of no further use for Das Vaterland anymore, as without money I am finished. Can you send a little through Gösta or somebody else by air? Meeting with our friend stands in any case but at the moment, owing to the money position, I cannot await his indefinite arrival. Immediate solution and help is most urgently required. Please answer today at 1130 MEZ. Will call you.[5]

The Abwehr responded that another friend would approach him, who could provide the money while the Phoenix-man still waited for his departure. They would also send £200 to the poste restante address in Watford, and a new schedule of meetings was created for the meeting with this new friend, much like the first plan involving the Regent Palace, British Museum and the Tate Gallery, but starting on 15 May. The password, however, was now extended to 'Hello George, how are you?', and each man would have a newspaper and a book in their hands. On 14 May the Germans, however, reported that his friend from the Phoenix had finally departed, and they hoped for a rendezvous the next day. Two days later, as no one had turned up at the first scheduled meeting, TATE sent a plaintive message:

> Carried out all instructions yesterday. Bitterly disappointed no contact made. Have contrived with great difficulty to borrow £3 to carry me on till 25th. If no relief comes by then have no alternative except to surrender myself and hope for mercy. Send money before then or it is all over.

On 17 May he received a new message: the meeting would work next time, the agent was on his way, and also a further friend would help, and within a week money would be sent to Watford. The proposal from TATE that he should contact the RAINBOW was rejected as he had moved, and they did not know his new address. However, the Germans and TATE did not know that the friend from the Phoenix Hotel, who was Karel Richter, had been arrested three days after his landing by parachute. We will return to this man in the next chapter. Now TATE was desperate:

> Once again I have met nobody. Now I should really like to know if you are playing a game with me or what is going on? I am desperate and have not enough money to feed myself properly and can only anticipate the worst, but I will try and eke out to the next meeting and if nobody appears then I shall have to get away and cannot give you any guarantee as regards radio transmissions. Where is our friend with newspaper and book? Is it possible to find him somewhere before the 25th or has he, too, just arrived? Are you able to contact him? I can only presume our Phoenix friend has either been badly hurt or caught. Is it possible to drop money by air immediately?

The Germans therefore planned to drop the money from an aircraft, and they proposed that, on the night of 28 May, four one-metre-long birch branches with the money in the thicker end, would be dropped in Chalton at the previously identified location. As a signal, they would drop two 200 kg bombs near Luton, in the vicinity of Chalton, before the birch wood came whizzing through the air. They asked if he could risk spending the night in Luton to find out where the bombs fell as a landmark, a mile from the money drop. TATE answered on 21 May:

> Many thanks for message. It is at least something. I hope it is not only an 'Aspirin' but that action will follow. I will be at Luton at any cost as soon as you wish. Please arrange this immediately. Urgent await your message concerning this.

But there was again disappointment when he received the news on 28 May that it was not feasible – the aircraft had been badly damaged on take off. As it was specially modified to carry and drop pieces of birch wood instead of bombs, no other plane could replace it. TATE answered that he did not believe any longer in their goodwill, and he could never have imagined that they would leave him in this mess. His faith was severely shaken.[6] But help was coming on a London double-decker.

JAPANESE HELP

After this came the successful meeting with the Japanese person on the bus on 29 May. The entire story would not have looked out of place in a spy novel, and has been described in several books. Through a complex plan, money would be handed over by a Japanese person on a bus. The money would be in an envelope in a copy of *The Times* newspaper, which TATE would borrow from the Japanese man. The Germans sent this message on 22 May 1941:

> Our friend from Phoenix has not yet reported to us. He has probably taken a longer time to get to London. We have specially pointed out to him how urgently you require the money. You have to stick to the arranged meetings with Phoenix-friend without fail. The new friend did not perform his job as he should, therefore, changed to the following events: You will wait on the 26th, 29th and 31st at 16.00 hrs at the terminus of bus No. 11 at Victoria Station. You must enter this bus with a Japanese who carries 'The Times' and a book in his left hand. You must wear a red tie and carry a newspaper and a book in your left hand. At the fifth stop both of you step off the bus and take the next bus with the same number on the same route. You shall stand or sit near the Japanese and ask him: 'Any special news? May I see the paper?' In doing so, The Japanese will give you the paper with an envelope inside. If it is not possible to do, you need to get off the bus along with Japanese and go with him. If bus No. 11 not suitable, report a different bus number to us as soon as possible. Sorry that the meetings could not be arranged earlier. Be precise in every detail. Japanese people are very suspicious.[7]

Now, the problem was that bus No. 11 did not have a terminus at Victoria Station, so TATE therefore suggested bus No. 16 instead, which was more suitable. However, no Japanese man turned up on the 26th, and following the failure of birch wood from the air, TATE felt highly discouraged. He indicated, on 28 May, that his confidence in his German masters was lost. If they did not succeed with the bus plan on the 29th, he was willing to take extreme measures. He had pawned everything he owned, and was becoming desperate. Words of comfort came later that day:

Chins up! In no circumstances give up. Should meeting not be successful tomorrow, go at once to the Japanese Naval attaché at the Japanese embassy and ask for help. To make them receive you, give them an envelope with a note in it reading 'I am friend Victoria Station bus number 16 formerly 11.' We will help you whatever happens.

On 29 May, they managed to implement the bus transaction, carefully monitored by MI5, who even filmed the mysterious Japanese messenger. A little touch of farce accompanied the event. The man from Japan was on schedule for bus No. 16 at 4.00 p.m. at Victoria station, but the bus switch was difficult to manage. He got off when the bus stopped at a traffic jam, in the belief that there was a bus stop. Perplexed, he stood on the sidewalk and saw three No. 16 buses go past, before he discovered his mistake. He went to the nearest bus stop and managed to get on the fourth bus. TATE with his red tie was hanging on, but when the Japanese man was going to pay for the ticket on the second bus he dropped his coins on the floor, which TATE helped to pick up, and thus had a pretext to make contact. After giving the agreed passwords, TATE got *The Times* with an envelope with 200 brand-new pound notes, whose numbers we can find carefully noted in one of the National Archives files on TATE. The Japanese messenger left the bus and immediately went to the office at 30 Portland Square, where the Japanese Naval Attachés had their office. They could now identify him as Lieutenant Commander Mitinori Yosii, one of the assistant Navy attachés. Now TATE felt relieved and grateful:

Long live Japan and the Yellow Peril. I received with many thanks two hundred potatoes as a first instalment. I take back all I said and feel the reverse. The bus meeting was most successful. Now I will have a good 'blind', eat plenty and sleep a lot, then I can go on a trip refreshed and full of energy to be able to give you good stuff.[8]

We may assume that MI5 always took possession of most of the money in all transactions, but according to Masterman's book about the Double-Cross system, the agents used to get some of the money they received from the Third Reich, as a bonus.[9] But the purse was soon empty again. On 26 June, TATE called for more money, and this time a large sum, for it seemed uncertain whether the Japanese could remain neutral much longer. He repeated his request, but was told that they would fix it the same way as earlier, with a Japanese person and buses. Perhaps they could bring a new crystal too. They also asked TATE to suggest an arrangement for regular meetings with a contact once or twice a month, in case radio contact was interrupted. But it would be better if he did not reveal his address. On 3 July, TATE sent his proposal that, at 4.00 p.m. every second and fourth Saturday, he should meet his contact in the Strand Palace Hotel, at a table on the left side of the lounge. In fact, the Germans had no idea where the hotel was and they later asked for the address.[10] If the hotel was closed for any reason, they would meet at Stewart's Restaurant. As usual, the password was 'Hello George' and, yes, TATE should have a red tie. But this would only apply if they were not able to make radio contact with each other during a period of three weeks.

On 20 July, there was suddenly a very generous offer. The war was now going well for Germany and they were well on their way in Russia, a victory being expected before Christmas. They wondered if TATE needed a really large sum of money! In this way he could build a larger organisation. Did he believe that, with more funds, he could recruit more people to work for him? With money he could travel around more and get closer to people who knew more secrets. They wondered how much he would possibly need a month to live such a life, of course, without risking his own safety. In response to this, TATE thanked them for the offer, and yes, he had ideas about a larger operation, but he wondered if that meant that they would send people over, or was the idea that he would recruit locally? He could recruit people to work for him and manage the most dangerous part himself – the radio transmissions. And yes, he could definitely operate in more influential circles. He estimated that a sum of £400 a month, was about right, but it should be understood that larger sums – perhaps thousands – might be necessary for bribes for important information. But he had to be guaranteed that the influx of money would be stable. To suddenly interrupt a financially comfortable and respectable way of life could be dangerous. He ended the statement by asking about his brother Kai (in the Luftwaffe), and if there was any other private news; he assured them that he could cope with the news, good or bad. No answer is recorded.

Later, in a further response, he signalled that he had looked around, and established that the situation was favourable for obtaining information from more senior personnel. Income tax was a heavy burden, and many retired officers and former military men, who were now excluded from the armed forces, could be useful sources of information if they were well paid. But recruitment had its dangers.[11]

OPERATION MIDAS

On 1 August, TATE received a somewhat surprising message by radio:

> Urgent because the giver of the money is about to leave. A smaller amount is not possible – please administrate it. Go at once to the theatre agent Eric Sand, Tea House, Piccadilly House, Piccadilly Circus, name plate is on entrance of teahouse. Introduce yourself as 'Harry' and say, 'How do you do Mr Sand – I am Harry and appreciate very much to meet you.' You will then receive £20,000. Please give acknowledgement of money to us at once, as we have to reimburse at once a similar sum to a friend of Mr Sand. It is better to hide the amount in parts.[12]

But the promised £20,000 did not exist. This was a brilliant scheme introduced by the double agent TRICYCLE, or Dusko Popov, which would give MI5 a great deal of cash, and he himself would also get some of the money.

Dusko Popov was a Yugoslav who came from a wealthy family in Dubrovnik, which had substantial international businesses. He had trained in France for six years and in Germany for two years, until he was deported in 1937, after being arrested and treated roughly by the Gestapo for speaking his mind at an alumni association meeting in Freiburg. Popov's family had contacts in the political world, and with the help of the Yugoslav Foreign Ministry, he managed to return unscathed from Germany.[13] Back in Dubrovnik, he founded a firm specialising in business law, and he returned to the glamorous life of a playboy which he had always lived, and would continue to live for most of his life. His income was substantial, his firm was involved in profitable business, and he soon acquired a luxurious lifestyle and pursued a lifelong interest in having many female 'friends'. He spent time in the office between nine and eleven o'clock; the rest of the time he devoted to amusements. Popov was a convinced anti-Nazi.

He had a good friend from his time in Germany whom he frequently socialised with, Johnny Jebsen, who, like Wulf Schmidt, is also said to have been brought up in Aabenraa in Denmark. Though Jebsen was anti-Nazi, he had joined the Abwehr to avoid the army, and to continue the lavish lifestyle that he had grown accustomed to abroad. He had similar habits and interests to Popov, and they had experienced a lot together in their playboy lifestyle. Jebsen had to prove to the Abwehr that he was useful, and asked Popov for help and, with his knowledge of France, Popov helped to write a report on a French politician who could potentially collaborate with the Germans. He chose the right man, Pierre Laval, who indeed became one of the German vassals in the Vichy government. Furthermore, Jebsen also wanted to run a potential agent for his superiors in the Abwehr. His friend Popov agreed to this, with the ulterior motive of deceiving the Germans and, in fact, working against them. Popov, therefore, made contact with the British Security Service in Belgrade, where he now lived. The Germans accepted him willingly, and Popov was assigned a corrupt Abwehr man – von Karsthoff – as his case officer. They would meet several times over the next few years, and although Dusko Popov always succeeded in fooling him with disinformation, he felt a certain sympathy for the German.

Popov was engaged in serious and big business, in addition to the espionage work, and therefore he needed to travel around the world as best he could during wartime, which was an excellent cover. Lisbon was an important place in terms of travel in Europe during the war – a metropolis which flourished with agents, shady businessmen, arms dealers, smugglers, deserters, and people avoiding war service. The Germans had a strong interest in having him in England as an agent, and the British did not mind at all acquiring a double agent who travelled to Lisbon and had direct contact with the Germans. In fact he was almost the only one of their Double-Cross agents to be able to do this. In December 1940 he travelled for the first time to England in a Dutch KLM plane.

It was not easy to convince MI5 that someone was a genuine candidate as an agent, and not a German sympathiser to be planted into the British Security Service. He was subjected to rigorous checks and questioning before they were convinced that he was a man for MI5. He was given the codename TRICYCLE,[14] not because he, as it was claimed after the war, preferred triangles in bed, but because he had two sub-agents. TRICYCLE became one of the most important agents in the Double-Cross system, and he was equally highly regarded by the Abwehr and the Germans. A lively traffic between England and Lisbon followed during the years, with assignments and questions from the Germans, which Masterman and the XX Committee made every effort to answer with just the right mix of genuine information and pure disinformation. TRICYCLE frequently used messages written in invisible ink on the backs his numerous letters, but he eventually also used a radio operator.

He was extremely expensive to run for the Germans (he did not want to ask for money from the English), who funded the immense cost of his highly luxurious life among jet-set people, businessmen and politicians, and especially women. It is still amazing today when one reads how much money was involved. But he argued to the Germans that it was extremely important for his image that he could mix in the right circles, in order to be able to get information of the highest quality, and the Germans willingly accepted his financial demands. He had great courage, and each time he landed in Lisbon he never knew if they were preparing to arrest him when he was taken to von Karsthoff's residence. He had to be trustworthy in every detail, and everything had to be linked in a logical way.

MI5 once believed that he was setting off on his last trip to Lisbon because they knew through ULTRA that suspicions were high against Popov. This could, of course, not be revealed as the secret of ULTRA was more important than anything else, and a life was a small sacrifice to keep the secret intact. But Popov was a master of talking his way out of tricky situations, and succeeded again.

The German agent net in the USA had earlier been completely rolled up and they began to realise the need to build a new spy organisation there. This should suit Popov very well as he frequented high society circles, and had many contacts among the really important and influential people in the world. So he was sent off on this mission, and MI5 saw it as a great opportunity to set up a double agent operation and perhaps a Double-Cross branch in the United States. On 10 August 1941 TRICYCLE was onboard the Pan American Clipper flying boat *Dixie*.

In his hand luggage he had $70,000 in cash, and some examples of an outstanding new German invention, namely the microdot – which on a page was the size of a full stop, but contained several pages of text that could be read with a microscope – the book *Night and Day* by Virginia Woolf, not for reading but as a tool for his codes, and equipment for secret writing. And last but not least, what would become called 'The Pearl Harbor Questionnaire': a series of questions from the Germans, from which it could easily be concluded that perhaps it was also of great interest to their Japanese friends.

The clever idea of microdots was developed by the chemist Henrik Beck at I. G. Farben. Lenses with an extremely good resolution were constructed, and with help from Agfa a new film was developed with the emulsion built on aniline dye, where light and dark parts were decided on a molecular level instead of in the coarse granules in the silver emulsions. The equipment was, of course, very expensive and a powerful microscope was needed to read the text.[15]

The entire USA trip was a fiasco, not least because of the obstinacy of the FBI and Hoover, who did everything to discourage him. Hoover, who wanted the FBI to be a 'clean' organisation without 'filth' (that he was secretly homosexual and a transvestite was only known after his death), disliked Popov intensely. Popov frequently socialised among movie stars and celebrities, and was often depicted in stories in the gossip columns. The great womaniser managed to initiate an affair with the then hugely popular movie actress Simone Simon. Hoover just could not accept this and, though he was informed by the British of agent Popov's excellent work, still did not trust him. MI5's view of a double-agent activity was completely foreign to him. He had a policeman's brain and his goal was to arrest as many agents as possible – good publicity for the FBI and himself – not least because of the internal struggle with the new organisation, the OSS (the predecessor of the CIA), which was treading on the feet of the FBI. The Pearl Harbor line of enquiry was managed deftly by Popov but Hoover was in an awkward situation for a long time after the attack on 9 December 1941. Meanwhile, Hoover just stole the invention of the microdot technique and presented it as a major step forward in the technological expertise of the USA. The situation was hopeless. Popov got nowhere, and he had no information to send to the Germans so, finally, he returned home on 21 October 1942.

Now, he had to expect a tough grilling from the Germans about where everything had gone wrong. He had again cost huge amounts of money, but had not accomplished anything. With MI5's help, he succeeded in constructing plausible explanations for the most part, and managed to talk his way out of trouble again with von Karsthoff, who really did not have any incentive to reveal Popov as a double agent. His own prestige in the Abwehr depended a great deal on the fact that he was handling one of the big stars among the agents, and, incidentally, was able to engage in a pleasant and not too strenuous lifestyle of black market dealings and foreign exchange transactions. Soon TRICYCLE restored his old status as a star, for both the Germans and the English, and performed once again daring, perilous encounters with the Germans in Lisbon, passing on false, and sometimes true but harmless information, from MI5.

He frequently met his old friend, Johnny Jebsen, who had become increasingly disillusioned about Germany. The two very good friends played a game of pretence. Jebsen was convinced that Popov was working for the English, and Popov knew very well that Jebsen knew, but they kept up the masks without revealing themselves. Eventually the situation became increasingly intolerable for Jebsen and he went over to the British, as a double agent named ARTIST. He had many personal enemies in the Gestapo, especially after some financial irregularities, and there was always a potential threat from the Gestapo, which was after him all the time, but he was protected by his superiors in the Abwehr. When Canaris and the Abwehr collapsed, as the rotten, inefficient organisation it really was, guided by ineffective leaders who thought more of their own prestige in a competitive, corrupted environment, the *Sicherheitsdienst* (SD) took over. Jebsen was now in deep trouble. The Gestapo managed to anaesthetise him and one of his colleagues, and transport them in a box in a car from Lisbon to Berlin.[16] Now he was in the claws of the Gestapo and, after torture and concentration camp, he was eventually executed.

But before that, TRICYCLE, who was well versed in the ways of world business, thought of a brilliant way to fool the Germans and get plenty of money. The scenario was an imagined Jewish businessman living in England, who began to feel some concern over how the war was going. He wanted to move much of his fortune in pounds sterling to the USA, something that was impossible legally. They found a suitable candidate in theatre agent Eric Glass, who acted as a minor character, without having a clue what it was really all about. The idea was that, if the Germans put a large sum of US dollars in a bank in the USA, they could take over his large fortune in pounds in England. The Abwehr could then use this fortune in the UK to fund their agent activity in

Britain. Financing their operations had always been a problem for the Germans and they had only managed to transfer small sums in the past. When TRICYCLE presented this plan to von Karsthoff he became excited. This was not just an opportunity to improve his position in the Abwehr, he also realised it was an opportunity to earn himself some money. After several weeks, he managed to get Martin Töppen, the financial advisor of the Abwehr, to sanction the payment of £20,000 in dollars. TRICYCLE was of course going to earn some money from this, but it was less than the 10 per cent of what he had been promised as a commission – von Karsthoff would get half of that.

When TRICYCLE had persuaded the Germans to agree to his plan, and to pay the money, he would send a telegram to Eric Glass with the message: 'X had a son/daughter yesterday, weighing Y kg. Please inform Z'. The first letter 'X', would inform London of the sum and, as a double safety feature, it would be a boy if the sum raised was $10,000 and a daughter if it was between $10,000 and $20,000. 'Y' would indicate the exchange rate, and 'Z' the name of the completely fictitious German agent to whom the sum would be paid.[17] Officially, the exchange rate was $2.25 for one pound, but TRICYCLE, to MI5's indignation, only got $2 for one pound.

A telegram arrived that read: 'Tilly has got a daughter who weighed 3 kg. Tell Harry when you meet him. Mary Concalves.' In the agreed code with MI5, '3' stood for an exchange rate of two dollars. But now TRICYCLE made a mistake – he addressed the telegram to Eric Sand, not Glass. In the spy business the smallest mistake could have fatal consequences, and if the Germans had searched, they would have noticed that there was no Eric Sand in London. However, it seems that the Germans also used the name Sand in correspondence with TATE. But MI5 forgave TRICYCLE as he had started the whole Operation MIDAS, and had a lot to think about, so mistakes could happen. But they found it difficult to accept the poor exchange rate, but, insisted TRICYCLE, it was the best he could get in the market. Töppen and von Karsthoff had arranged $40,000, which TRICYCLE would take with him on his trip to the USA and deposit in a bank there, except for the commission to von Karsthoff and himself. This meant that Harry, that is TATE, could now collect £20,000 from Eric Glass, but it was all, of course, a fiction. In reality, MI5 had gained $40,000, which originally appeared in a US bank account, all for themselves.

TRICYCLE could not contain himself. He visited the casino in Estoril on the evening before departure, and put up a stake of $38,000 to crack a competitive Lithuanian he was determined to beat. But at least he did not gamble away the money. Everything went well and the money arrived safely in the US bank, and TATE could therefore inform the Germans that he had collected the fortune in pounds sterling from the theatrical agent.[18] So TRICYCLE and the corrupt von Karsthoff also earned their commissions. The Double-Cross organisation now decided that TATE on 3 August would send:

All going splendid. Money troubles are over. Hurried to the Piccadilly House. Met Sand as arranged. He appears to be of the chosen race. He gave me £4,000 and explained that he has the whole sum ready, but it is scattered in different places for safety he will collect it and pay me the balance on Tuesday afternoon. Banks are shut on Monday for Bank Holiday.

The Germans were, of course, also happy and sent on 6 August:

Heartiest congratulations for good work. On no account spend all the money on drinks, for that you can wait until we come. We consider ourselves invited. Heartiest greetings. Bruhns and all comrades.

Later came more good advice:

Hide money reserves in different places. In finding assistance be very careful. Don't give your address away. For the moment work as before, slowly change over. Dress better and go to better class haunts, bars, race courses. We advise you not to contact officers as it is dangerous. Safety first always. Try to watch the stopping places near Ministries and higher Commands. Try to observe the girls and contact them later in bus, swimming pool, cinema. But never ask them questions at the start.[19]

This was advice with a very pathetic touch, as from a manual about how to chat up women. Who wrote it? TATE continued during the next few weeks with reports of how he would become a new man. He bought elegant clothes, made contact with bar owners, hotel workers and the like, in order to be able to meet influential members of society. He did not overdo his new life but he could already see signs of success. He visited London for a few nights, and found a few bars where he met some really interesting and useful contacts. But the system of ration coupons made it difficult for him to maintain his new stylish clothing. He also needed help with contacting women who would be able to introduce him to more fashionable places (obviously, he did still need advice about women). At the same time, he was also treasurer for the other agents in the country. Therefore, during the autumn, he paid out a total of £550 to RAINBOW, and £220 to MUTT (both double agents), fictitious transactions from money that did not really exist.[20] But with TATE, as an affluent and well-dressed man who was moving around where the action was, the expectations of the Abwehr would increase. Now he must soon be in a position where he could deliver much more. It was now time for MI5 to invent something, which would dampen the Germans' expectations and requirements. It was, therefore, the creation of the threat of military service, that provided the escape route into mythical farm work, as we have seen in a previous chapter. We can only speculate why the Double-Cross committee chose to keep him as a lonely low-grade agent, instead of taking the opportunity to build a larger network of spies around him.

6

Karel Richter

As we have seen there were initial problems with the supply of funds to TATE. He was promised that, at the end of April 1941, a man with £300 and a new crystal for his radio equipment would arrive. The Germans said that the man was tall, blond, with blue eyes, and with a wart above his right eye, and that TATE knew him from the Hotel Phoenix. His arrival, however, was cancelled several times, until 14 May, when TATE was at last told that he was on his way. An intricate schedule had been drawn up for TATE to contact him at either the Regent Palace Hotel, the Tate Gallery or the British Museum.[1] An extensive police operation was launched to find the man who never showed up. The man who was supposed to arrive was Karel Richter, who, however, had a much more sinister mission than to deliver money and a crystal – he was going to investigate whether TATE was a double agent.

Karel Richter was a very difficult person to interrogate as he lied and changed his statements all the time. He rambled, was vague and unreliable, and there was a constant suspicion that he was in fact planted by the Gestapo. It was therefore very difficult for MI5 to obtain a true and accurate picture of this man, once they had got hold of him.

Karel Richter was born in 1912 in Kraslice in the Sudetenland in Czechoslovakia. After school he worked as an apprentice at a Citroën factory for some years, then in his father's metal business for a few years.

Richter said that his father was Richard Richter, and it was found later that there was such a man in Kraslice, with a firm that manufactured components for musical instruments. In 1932 he started his own car-rental business in Kraslice but after a few years he gave it up. In 1935 he worked for one year as a machinic on a ship during a trip to Java. From autumn 1936 to summer 1939 he worked as a machinic on ships, on the Hamburg–New York route, including large passenger ships with names like *New York*, *Hamburg* and *Hansa*. A round-trip took twenty-seven days and in one year he made thirteen voyages. He left his last ship without permission in August 1939, because he sensed that the war would come, and he was afraid of being enrolled into the German Navy. The ship was taken over by the Navy and was going to be made into either a hospital ship, or put in dry dock to be prepared as a troop transport. He, therefore, returned to his home town of Kraslice for four weeks. He wished to emigrate to the United States, but, in Hamburg, had vainly sought admission at the US consulate. In October or November 1939 he travelled via war-torn Poland to Libau in Latvia, from where he sailed, in a small Norwegian ship, to Gothenburg, where he hoped to find a ship on which to sign on. However, he did not succeed. He had his Czech passport with him, which was no longer valid, and he had no visa or work permit so in November he went to Stockholm, where he hoped he could get the correct papers. But he dared not go to the German consulate. In Stockholm he was instead arrested by the Swedish police. The passport had been issued, strangely enough, by the Czech consulate in New York, which later aroused suspicion of a forgery by MI5. The Swedish police thought he was a German seaman who had deserted.

The penalty was eight weeks in prison, followed by internment in the Langmora camp in Dalarna, Sweden, from March 1940. At that time there were seventy to eighty people detained there, and it was a peaceful life in a beautiful landscape. He took the opportunity of acquiring a new suit for 120 crowns. In July 1940 he was transferred to the German consulate, where he received a temporary passport and was then escorted by the police to Trelleborg, for departure to Sassnitz. When the ferry reached the halfway point, Richter was arrested by the Gestapo on the ship, because he had illegally absconded from his duties on the ship *Hansa*. A thorough, detailed interrogation began at the Hamburg *Staathaus* and the interrogations were, according to Richter, very rough and violent and took place in the basement or on the fourth floor. He was thereafter transported to the concentration camp Fuhlsbüttel outside Hamburg, where he was put to work.

On 2 November 1940, he was released from the concentration camp after helping to remove unexploded bombs after bombing raids, but he was still detained in prison in Hamburg. In connection with this, the intelligence service, with Dr Bruhns (or Julius Böckel) from the Abwehr, made contact with him in prison and offered him freedom if he was prepared to undertake a dangerous mission. Richter decided to accept the offer in November 1940. He now began his training as a secret agent in Böckel's office at Königsstrasse 11. He trained to use Morse under the guidance of Petersen, who had also taught Gösta Caroli and Wulf Schmidt. He trained together with two agents, one of whom would travel to South Africa. Like other agents, they had lessons in recognising British aircraft, identification of anti-aircraft guns of various calibres, invisible writing, etc. During a trip by car in rural areas, camouflage techniques were studied at an airbase, and during a second outing, when a man named Josef Jakobs also participated, he was taught about balloon barrages and had different kinds of anti-aircraft artillery demonstrated in the vicinity of a reservoir near the Elbe. After a while it became clear that Richter was totally hopeless as a radio operator, and it was impossible to teach him Morse. He managed only 25–30 characters per minute, which was totally inadequate. Bruhns/Böckel declared that he was no longer interested in Richter's services. He had to finish his training, but he discovered that he was being shadowed and watched carefully after this.[2] After just a few days, however, he was re-recruited, but now by another person in the security services, Dr Scholtz, and Richter was back in business again. He also took the opportunity now offered, to sell two American-style suits and a camel-hair coat to Dr Scholtz for 220 Reichmarks. The clothes were possibly going to be used by agents who were planted in the USA, or perhaps

Scholtz took them himself. But radiotelegraphy was still a considerable problem as Richter was hopeless at it and found it impossible to grasp this skill. Dr Scholtz also had to give up, and Richter was told that he must join an agent who was skilled in radiotelegraphy.

In January 1941 the group moved from Hamburg to Amsterdam, where they stayed at the Hotel Victoria. He went a few times, together with a man named Basserman, to Vondelstraat in The Hague. Dr Scholtz went with them and was going to try to get hold of a fishing boat for passage to England. But it was decided that this was not the right time of year for such a journey, and they returned to Hamburg. There, at the Hotel Phoenix, he was instructed by Bierman on a new type of radio transmitter that could draw power from the mains supply so the normal 270-volt battery would not be needed. With a special adapter, he could transform an ordinary radio set into a transmitter, or build a custom version with components that he could buy in a commercial radio shop. Apparently, Richter had been trained in radio construction. There was, however, also a battery version of the transmitter, which was no larger than an ordinary camera case. Crystals were no longer necessary as it was possible to set the desired frequency directly on the transmitter. When he put up the antenna, he had to use a compass to find the right direction towards Hamburg. He also had to learn the cipher he would use. Dr Scholtz and Bierman belonged to the Abwehr Fleet department, while Bruhns/Böckel and Petersen belonged to the Luftwaffe section of the Abwehr.[3]

JOSEF JAKOBS
Another agent, Josef Jakobs, is interesting in this context, since he trained with Karel Richter and knew him. Jakobs, after his arrest, provided information about Richter, and identified him in a confrontation after Richter was caught. Josef Jakobs was born in 1898 in Luxembourg of German parents and, during the First World War, he served as a corporal in the infantry in 1916–18. Since then, Jakobs had worked as a dentist, but then became involved in murky and unsavoury deals. He had been called up again in 1940, but there were doubts

about him, as he had been jailed in Switzerland 1935–37 for trading in stolen gold. Furthermore, he had earned plenty of money by the illegal smuggling of Jewish refugees, which had attracted the interest of the Gestapo.

Jakobs came to Hamburg for the first time on 22 September 1940, and came into contact with Dr Beyer (another cover name for Bruhns, or Böckel). In Hamburg, Jakobs was allowed to see examples of messages by Beyer/Böckel, to help him understand how they wanted them sent. Each message carried the code-number of the V-man (*Vertrauensmann*) who had sent them. The examples he saw were descriptions of buildings and factories in Coventry before the big bombing raid on the city, signed by a 'No. 107'. This was apparently a Swede since it was written with a mixture of English and Swedish. The details were so precise that the Germans could easily plot the positions on a map. The locations of road blocks were described, and there was a description of an air base which the Germans should avoid as there were concealed defences there. Ships which lay in a dry dock were named. He also learned that the Germans had five interception stations along the coast, where the messages were decoded and sent on to Hamburg.[4]

He met Karel Richter for the first time on 22 October 1940. Just how much the agents had joint training is unclear, but, as mentioned before, he once travelled in a car with Richter, Böckel and an *Oberleutnant*. The intention was to train in field reporting and map reading. Jakobs and Richter met sometimes off duty in October or November, and once in company with Dr Scholtz at the Café Dreyer. On one occasion Richter got into trouble for having a fight at this café and was arrested. The Ette Orchestra used to play at the Café Dreyer and Jakobs knew the singer in the orchestra, Clara Beurle, who was conspicuous because of her height. She became his mistress, and they lived together for some time in the Hotel Sorgenfrei, where several other members of Ette Orchestra lived.

Richter and Jakobs again met in The Hague in January 1941, where Richter was staying at the Otel Central under the name Link. They met there twice, once at the Café Piccadilly and once at a tea dance in the Café Central. There was an apartment in the Vondelstraat 131 in The Hague, which Jakobs thought was a cover address for a place where instructions to agents were given and radio transmissions carried out, while the head office was somewhere else. Jakobs believed that Richter was an expert on radio equipment and that he trained agents in Vondelstrasse to build radio transmitters. The training took four to five months. In The Hague, Richter and Jakobs decided that they would pretend not to know each other in the future. Jakobs later pointed out during questioning that he knew that Richter was linked to *Nachrichtendienst* and realised later that it was in the Luftwaffe, but he did not know his real name.

Jakobs' journey to England started from Schipol in Holland on the night of 1 February 1941, as the sole passenger in an aircraft with five crew members. His German cover name was *Julius* and it was intended that he would land in the Peterborough area. While preparing to jump from the aircraft, he injured his ankle in the doorway and this was made significantly worse on landing.

On Saturday 1 February 1941 two farm workers, Charles Baldock and Harry Coulson, were strolling across a field at Dovehouse Farm in Ramsey Hollow, Huntingdonshire. Suddenly, they heard something that sounded like three gun shots. In the field, a man lay on his back with a camouflage-coloured parachute covering him. He had broken his ankle and was unable to get up. He explained that he came from Hamburg and threw his gun into a steel helmet. Baldock stayed while Coulson went to find James Godfrey, who was a member of the Home Guard. They called Sergeant Ernest Pottle at the police station in Ramsey, and went to the field now joined by the Commanding Officer Captain Newton of the Home Guard, and Lieutenant Curedale, who was second-in-command. They bandaged the man's injured right leg and searched through his equipment, where they found £498 in one pound notes (a remarkably large sum compared with what other agents usually had), one attaché case with radio equipment, a torn disk for decryption, a flashlight and a map on which the nearby air base, RAF Upwood,[5] and the satellite airfield at Warboys were marked.

His fake identity cards were unusually clumsily forged, with the prefix letters, which were always before the number, missing (the double agent SNOW had given an ID card to the Abwehr[6]). Under the flight suit he was wearing civilian clothes, and when asked who he was he replied that he had flown solo from Luxembourg. Sergeant Pottle had now arrived with a horse and cart which transported the man to the police station in Ramsey, where Detective Sergeant Mills from the Huntingdonshire County Constabulary waited. The man was passed on to Scotland Yard in London, where Major TAR Robertson and John Marriot were waiting for him. They went through his equipment, which included two identity cards, one blank and one with the name 'James Rymer', and a ration book without a name. The map was a Shell map for travel in England and the gun was a Mauser.[7]

The suspect was then handed over to Lieutenant Colonel Hinchley-Cooke. Because he was completely helpless with his broken ankle, he had used the gun to attract attention. During interrogation at Camp 020, he tried to convince the team that he had undertaken the espionage mission with the approval of his Jewish friends, to obtain funds for their organisation.[8] He had been asked by a certain Dr Burgos to join the Abwehr as an agent of a secret Jewish organisation, and intended to make contact with Jews in Britain.[9] He brought with him the address of a Jewish woman, Mrs Lily Snip, 9 Compayne Gardens, NW 7.[10] He also said that he had agreed to provide weather reports for the Germans, but his real intention was to try to get to the USA and Illinois, where he had relatives. During the questioning at Camp 020 they soon managed, with Jakobs seated in a wheelchair, to get some confessions, names of contacts, and details of his training and missions. The interview was quite short and he was passed on to the hospital and did not come back until 15 April.

This rest had obviously done him good, and strengthened his morale and courage, because when he came back he was more reluctant to talk. He took back some of his earlier confessions, and was generally uncooperative and unwilling to provide any useful information. The team had to drag information out of him, and he eventually reluctantly agreed to cooperate. It was his patriotism that maintained his courage. The interrogators were unable to fully discover what had happened; he spoke vaguely about *Nachrichtendienst* officers in Berlin, Hamburg and The Hague. Apparently two *Stellen* (regional offices) were involved, because they got out of him the names Beyer (or Böckel) in Hamburg and *Zebra*, a radio instructor at The Hague.[11]

RICHTER LANDING IN ENGLAND

Karel Richter travelled to Amsterdam, on 30 April 1941, for his next attempt to get to England. There was a 21-foot-long motorboat with two Dutch crewmen available, and on the evening of 9 May, they aimed for Cromer on the Norfolk coast about twenty miles north of Norwich. With about six miles to go, they had to turn back because of bad weather and sea conditions. The next attempt was therefore made by air. On the night of Monday 12 May at 01.30 a.m., a twin-engine aircraft, with Wolfgang Nebel as pilot and Karl Gartenfeld as observer, took off from Schipol Airport in Amsterdam. It flew at high altitude, about 30,000 feet, and they had to use oxygen masks for the entire journey. Around 3.15 a.m. they descended to 10,000 feet and the crew explained that they were between Cambridge and Bury St Edmunds. Richter jumped out, and the landing went well except that he almost landed on top of a house. Karel Richter had landed in a forest in Tyttenhanger Park, adjacent to the A405 road near London Colney, about eight miles north-east of Watford and eight miles south-west of Hatfield, where the de Havilland aircraft factory was.[12] At this time, the prototype of a fighter version of the Mosquito had just been finished at Salisbury Hall, close to where Richter landed, and test flights were commencing.[13]

He was well dressed, in a tweed overcoat and a suit, with three pairs of long johns and two pairs of socks. He buried his equipment with his shovel,[14] and then spent three days, no further away than 500 feet from where he had landed. He had just a little chocolate to eat and whisky to drink; he had also drunk some water from a stream where he shaved. By mistake he had buried his food parcels, which contained, among other things, salami and brown bread.[15] Richter dared not go to

London, but dehydration and hunger forced him to leave – he had even tried to eat some grass.

He trudged off in the evening of Wednesday 14 May, and met two lorry drivers who asked him the way to London, but Richter only muttered a non-committal reply. The drivers thought he seemed foreign and very suspicious, and when they caught sight of War Reserve Constable 106 Alec Scott, they told him about the strange man. Scott rode away on his bicycle in the direction of the mysterious stranger, whom he eventually found in a phonebox. Richter explained in broken English (for example, he mixed up the 'V' and 'W'), that he had come from Ipswich, and was on his way to Cambridge, but was sick and needed to go to a hospital. Scott called his station, which sent a patrol car, and at about 10.30 p.m. Richter was taken to the Fleetville police station on Tess Road, and then he was transferred to Hatfield police headquarters where he spent the night.[16] It was found that Richter did not have an alien's registration certificate, which was necessary for all foreigners, but had a Czech passport with his own name, an identity card with the name Fred Snyder, address 14 Duckett Street, London E.1. (an address that turned out to be an uninhabitable bombed-out house), and a ration book for travellers which, however, was without his signature. Furthermore, the suspect possessed an unusually large sum of money, £552 and $1,400.

The day after, on Thursday 15 May, he was transferred to Latchmere House and Camp 020. Now a long series of interrogations started, which frustrated the team of interrogators as Richter briskly lied and changed his story at every interview. He was unintimidated and full of bravado, saying that the Germans would come soon and then *he* would be sitting on the interview panel. Eventually, he began to run out of steam. Already on the first day he was confronted with Josef Jakobs, who identified him from the time in Hamburg and The Hague, which put a damper on Richter's optimism and bluster.[17] Jakobs, during an interrogation in April, also revealed that another agent was soon coming. An interesting detail emerged: Richter had the address of an Ingeborg Olsson, Hotel Neptune in Gothenburg, to whom he could write if something went wrong. Later, on 21 May, he prayed that they would actually write to her, and tell her that he had broken his leg.[18]

It took seventeen hours of interrogation before Richter revealed what had happened to his equipment. On 18 May, Richter was taken to the place near London Colney where he had landed, and there dug up his equipment. This was watched with great interest by a group including several officers from Camp 020 who had a picnic near the excavation site.[19] There is actually a series of photographs (discovered by Nigel West) of this event in the photo archive of the Imperial War Museum.

Richter had also been tasked to carry out regular spying missions. His orders were to find out about road conditions and how frequent the checks were, for instance, at railway stations, the frequency of identity card checks, if identity cards were checked at hotels, details about how people were equipped with gas masks, and to give weather reports. The issue of gas masks made the interrogation team anxiously raise their eyebrows. Weather reports should include temperature (he had a thermometer), cloud height, type of clouds, direction and strength of the winds according to the Beaufort Scale, and attempts to assess the coming weather fronts. As a former sailor, Richter had mastered this. The reports were supposed to be delivered in letter form, using invisible writing, or by radio (perhaps Richter had finally learned to master the Morse passably). He would buy an ordinary radio set, and transform it into a transmitter, or build one himself. He was quite capable of doing this, and he demonstrated his capability when he later built a good-quality radio at Camp 020.[20] He wrote a long list of what components he needed, and the idea was considered that TATE should visit a radio shop and buy the components. It was then decided that this would attract undesirable attention and, moreover, TATE had insufficient knowledge to identify the correct components.[21] Richter admitted that one of his tasks was to deliver the money according to a complex plan, with meetings at the Regent Palace Hotel, the British Museum or the Tate Gallery.[22]

TATE followed the rendezvous plan and waited for his money, but repeatedly received messages that the delivery had been postponed. On 17 May, after the the money courier failed to appear at any of the three venues, he received a new message, assuring him that the meeting would work next time – the agent was on his way. On 22 May 1941, he was told:

> Our friend from Phoenix has not yet reported to us. He has probably taken more time to get to London. We have specially pointed out to him how urgently you require the money. You must stick to arranged meetings with Phoenix-friend without fail.

In late May, TATE had orders not even to attempt to communicate with Richter, and as late as on 24 June, the Germans stated that they had heard signals from the Phoenix-Richter, but had not yet established contact. When everything worked according to plan, he would receive more than £400. TATE replied that he had no hope at all of ever seeing any money from the man, with whom he was supposed to be familiar from their time at the Phoenix Hotel.[23] The Germans did not know that Richter had been arrested, and must have wondered what had happened to agent 3526, or *Artist*, as the Germans called him. Although it was pointed out that the courier was an acquaintance from his time in the Phoenix Hotel, TATE did not recognise the description of him, nor Richter's photograph taken at Camp 020. Remarkable muddle and confusion appeared to be ruling the Abwehr organisation in Hamburg, and it was definitely not the Richter who had given him lessons in secret writing.

Richter also had a radio crystal with him, which would cause MI5 nervousness and anxiety. The frequency of the crystal was 7,412 kHz, which could not be used in the transmitter which TATE was operating. Was this another example of the incompetence of the Abwehr in Hamburg? Or, a very unpleasant thought that popped up in MI5, maybe the crystal was supposed to be delivered to another agent, who was free and unknown to MI5.[24]

Eventually it became clear that Richter had another assignment, which was much more serious and threatening for the Double-Cross system – to check whether TATE was indeed genuine and not a double agent. In his orders, Richter was supposed to return to Germany by August at the latest, and deliver his report. Karl Praetorius, one of the senior officers at the Abwehr in Hamburg, had said: 'TATE is our finest pearl. If he is a fake, then the whole necklace is false.'²⁵ The origin of this dangerous mission given to Richter, was supposed to be a radio message sent by TATE on Christmas Eve 1940: 'My warmest Seasons Greetings to all Phönizier, to all the radio operators and to Egward and Nebel: if possible, to my family too.' (Egward was a nickname for Gartenfeld.)²⁶ So he actually mentioned the Phoenix Hotel which, according to Richter, no real German agent would have done, because it was a secret meeting place for *Nachrichtendienst*. But MI5 was not so convinced as this did not seem to be especially compromising. The issue was taken up with TATE on 7 July 1941, and he thought it was absurd that this message should cause such a suspicion. Would the Germans really risk sacrificing the life of the agent they sent if they thought TATE was controlled by the British? They had also paid money to him via the Japanese man on the bus, and all the messages he received from the Germans were friendly and genuine. It was unreasonable that the failure of the expected return of Richter before August should be interpreted as evidence that TATE was a double agent. He might just as well have been killed or captured at the time of the parachute jump into England. Possibly, it was one of Richter's own imaginative schemes in order to improve his position among the Germans.²⁷ But on the other hand, there was also a worrying history with SNOW, who had paid out money to TATE two to three months *after* he admitted to the Germans that he was a double agent.

After Richter had assessed the status of TATE, he had orders to return to Germany as quickly as possible in some way, and give his report. During interrogations, it was obvious that Richter was terrified of anything about him that was written down on paper. He was convinced that a German invasion was under way in July or August, with the risk that the Gestapo would get hold of documents relating to himself. That was one reason why he lied and changed his story so often. The Germans would never carry out an invasion without evidence that chaos, disorder and dissatisfaction with the government prevailed in

Britain, and now they had begun to receive reports about this, according to Richter. In a report from 17 June, it was stated that it was obvious during the questioning of Richter and Jakobs, that both were afraid of being hanged, but handled this in slightly different ways. Jakobs was extremely eager to please, and probably used his imagination, which is why his statements were not entirely reliable. Richter, however, was unwilling to give any answers, but what he said was probably true.

THE TRIAL AND EXECUTION OF JAKOBS
The trial of Josef Jakobs was a court-martial, that is, a military trial. It was held in camera at the Duke of York's Headquarters in Chelsea, on 4–5 August 1941. Military men sat as judges, with Major General Wilson as chairman. Eight witnesses appeared, most of whom were civilians or police officers who participated in the arrest of Jakobs, and some from the War Office, including Lieutenant Colonel Hinchley-Cooke. He had questioned Jakobs at New Scotland Yard on 18 June 1941, and on 24 July announced to Jakobs that he would be prosecuted under Section 1 of the Treachery Act of 1940. Jakobs' defence was based on the mysterious Dr Burgos, which was received with scepticism in the court. He was found guilty and sentenced to death by a firing squad (because he was military – civilians were hanged). Jakobs wrote an appeal for clemency to the King, which was rejected. On the morning of 15 August, Josef Jakobs was taken out to the shooting range at the barracks just outside the wall of the Tower, towards Tower Bridge Road. Since his ankle had not healed, he was sitting on a Windsor-style brown chair. A piece of linen was attached over his heart. At 7.12 a.m., he was shot by a firing squad of eight soldiers led by Major Williams of the Holding Battalion, Scots Guards.[28] An autopsy was performed by the famous pathologist Sir Bernard Spilsbury in the morgue at the Tower, and he found a bullet hole in the head and seven in the cardiac region.[29] Jakobs was then buried in an unmarked grave in a Catholic cemetery in Kensal Green in north-west London. This was the last execution carried out at the Tower of London. Godfrey, Coulson and Baldock were celebrated as heroes, and newspapers announced invitations to

a party at the local pub, 'The Farmer's Boy'. It all ended with a fine of 2*s* 6*d* for the landlord Mr Townsend, and 5*s* for Baldock, as they had violated the 'after-hours drinking' law.[30]

Recently medical prescriptions for Rudolf Hess and Josef Jakobs were discovered. The prescription for Jakobs, dated 14 August, consisted of medication for stomach problems and sodium amytal, a barbiturate with a calming effect, which he then took before his execution. The prescriptions were sold at an auction for £750.[31] The Windsor chair has been preserved and will possibly be exhibited at the Tower.

THE TRIAL AND EXECUTION OF RICHTER

Richter heard the news that Jakobs had been executed, and began to realise that the same fate awaited him. He wrote in the autumn of 1941 a series of long letters to his interrogators, in particular to Major Short, with whom he had much contact. The letters had a desperate tone and contained all sorts of ideas that might save him. Still, it was hard to know what was true and what was invented. He returned to his mission to investigate *Leonhard*/TATE, and insisted that without his help TATE would be lost. He even suggested that he should be released, and have permission to travel to meet Dr Scholtz to save TATE as a double agent for the British. But he had no idea how things really were standing with TATE, and the British did not even respond to his letters, or allow any meetings with Richter which he requested.[32]

On 21 October, the trial began at the Old Bailey behind closed doors, and lasted for four days. On 24 October, he was found guilty and sentenced to death according to the Treachery Act. He wrote a request for clemency, which was dismissed on 24 November. He was put in Wandsworth prison to await execution. The date was set for 10 December 1941.

The day before the hanging, the executioner Albert Pierrepoint had a look at the prisoner, as he always used to do. He needed to assess the prisoner's physique, the thickness of the neck, and by using the height and weight he could work out from a table the length of the rope that was needed. A fall of between five to nine feet was needed to crack the neck between the second and third cervical vertebrae. He then tested the trap doors of the gallows, and chose between two ropes, which had metal loops instead of knots. During the night, he let the rope hang with the weight of a sandbag to ensure that it was really stretched. Usually, an execution was completed very quickly. The executioner with the assistant went into the cell, put the prisoner's arms behind his back, strapped them with a leather belt, the prisoner was taken through a door directly to the gallows in the next room, and put in place on the trapdoor marked with a crayon 'T'. Then a white linen bag was put over the head, the noose around the neck, the legs were tied together, the trap door was opened with a lever, and the prisoner fell to his death. Pierrepoint was a legendary executioner, who executed many convicted murderers, spies, and war criminals after the war, even in Germany.

In his autobiography,[33] Pierrepont described the execution of Karel Richter as a terrible mess, but in the book the prisoner was given a different name. Immediately, when Pierrepoint came into the cell, he saw that something was wrong. Instead of Richter sitting quietly at a table with his back to the executioner, who could quickly draw the leather strap around the arms when the prisoner got up, Richter stood up with a threatening expression and clenched fists. He pushed aside a prison guard and threw himself head first against the stone wall. He passed out for a short while, but rose and shook his head. Two prison guards threw themselves on him, a struggle ensued and two other prison guards had to be called. They had to sit on the prisoner to successfully strap his arms behind his back. When they managed to get hold of him and continue towards the gallows, he managed to tear himself free from the leather strap, and now Richter was fighting with everyone, including his executioner. Pierrepoint managed to tie his arms once again, more tightly this time, and Richter was dragged to the gallows, still struggling for his life. His legs were tied together, the linen bag was put over his head and the rope was around his neck. Just when Pierrepoint opened the trap door with the lever, Richter jumped with his feet bound. The noose began slipping from his head but got stuck under his nose. Richter finally dropped to an instant death.

Before and after the execution, it was discussed how much should be disclosed to the press. MI5 feared that more German agents would show up with the task of investigating *Leonhard*/TATE if news of Richter's fate was released or published and so would be available to the Germans. But it was decided by Lord Swinton and higher authority that a notice of execution should be released to the press in the usual manner. No more agents arrived with the mission to examine the case of TATE.

They told TATE on 10 October that Richter had been hanged, and explained that Richter was convicted as a spy; TATE should know that he had no personal guilt in this. TATE was satisfied with the information, and explained that it was better that he had heard the news in this way, instead of the shock of reading it in the newspaper. But those who supervised him were ordered to be extra vigilant over the next few days.[34]

7

1942

TATE had now been working for more than a year as a double agent deceiving the Germans. Meanwhile, the Germans had reached as far as they ever would on the Eastern Front and were stalled by the severe winter, and the Russians had started their winter counter-offensive. Japan had made their attack on Pearl Harbor on 7 December 1941, and a few days later Germany declared war on the USA. In North Africa the Germans were successful, and the U-boats were prowling in the Atlantic.

The coming year would be busy for TATE, with frequent radio traffic. From the records we can get a good view of this, but we have no information about his mood or how he was feeling. There must have been boring, restless moments in his life of subterfuge for, although he had a certain freedom, the guards were always there in the background. How did he cope when he was not occupied with deciphering reports, sending Morse, or discussing the contents of his deceptions with his case officers? What did he do during his spare time? Was he feeling remorse for what he had done and the situation he was in?

In January 1942, TATE received questions concerning the ability of gliders to transport troops. But he was not satisfied with the answers he was going to send. He didn't feel it was a good idea to provide the same vague information as they had given about parachute troops. Therefore, he wondered if he could mention, for example, how many passengers a glider could take, and where he was supposed to have seen these gliders, and how many? Had they been on the ground or in the air? He was also asked about the guarding of nearby air bases. TATE had submitted a report concerning American pilots who he had encountered in the bar at the Savoy Hotel. They ferried aircraft from the USA to the UK (usually to Prestwick in Scotland).

In a more general report from the same month TATE dealt with the mood of the British people. Way back in 1940 the W Board had decided that questions regarding the morale of the people should be answered reasonably correctly, and TATE would report several times a positive attitude and fighting spirit among the British. But in this transmission he reported that he had seen pessimistic messages scribbled on a wall: 'Hitler will win' and 'The government is bleeding the workers'.[1]

On 19 February 1942, TATE received bad news. His beloved grandmother Helen had died at Skovbølgaard. He had spent so many happy summer holidays there and it certainly had been a secure retreat for him after his mother died when he was eight years old and he was being brought up by his father, who had strange ideas about raising children. The Germans asked for TATE's permission to help, by acting in his place to deal with the property settlement, which of course was a friendly and helpful gesture. The family otherwise was well, and sent their greetings. TATE asked the Germans to express his sympathies to Skovbølgaard, and gave the Germans permission to appoint a representative in his place, who would act to ensure that the estate would remain in the family's possession. He also asked them to send telegrams to his uncle George Bruhn and his family. TATE wanted to know when his grandmother had died (it was on 3 February[2]), where she was buried, and hoped that the Germans would arrange for a wreath.[3] In April TATE announced: 'I cannot deal with the inheritance over here, so leave it to my brother. Send him my regards.'

The group which controlled TATE began to wonder if it would not be possible to create additional agents in the country, who would report to him. TATE was quite sure that the Germans would only agree to this if he explicitly asked for help. But if he did try to arrange 'help' from other agents, would the Germans send someone over, or put him in contact with someone who was already in the country? The risk was that the Germans would again come up with the idea that he should investigate the prospect of building up a larger organisation – especially with his large stock of cash – which was not desirable from the British point of view. They had only recently succeeded in avoiding this escalation by inventing his time-consuming work on a farm. There is no clue as to why his controllers did not use him as an agent, like GARBO, with a network of sub-agents. There was an opportunity to develop him further as an extremely important source for further, large-scale disinformation.

In late March, a new evaluation of TATE's work, and role in the Double-Cross system, was made in a report by D. I. Wilson, one of B1(a)'s 'case-officers'. Again, it was found that it was difficult to engage TATE in any major projects of disinformation. He still worked on his own, and would also, in the near future, deal with more short-term, day-to-day work. The time of his transmissions in the evening should be moved to at least half an hour after dark. The information he passed on would be based primarily on data from the technical press, such as '*Flight*', '*Aeroplane*', and '*Grocer*', and reports would be submitted about orders given to farmers by the Ministry of Agriculture. The volume of TATE's traffic had declined, and it was decided that his information should come mostly from publications in journals. Examples of TATE's submitted information, which were beyond what was published in newspapers and magazines, were listed:

1 February. Russian anti-tank aircraft.
19 and 26 February. Air defence organisation in England.
5 March. American Navy base at Wig Bay.[4]
8 March. On 'Floating Fortresses'.[5]

He had already received questions about air defence in November 1941. There were other questions from the Germans which had not been answered:

1 January. Secret stores of food.

13 January. Forces which were sent out of the country, and the departure times of these shipments.

18 January. The Vickers aircraft factory in Mold.

28 January. Stores of refrigerated food in London.

It seemed reasonable that TATE would not be able to provide information about the second and third subjects. The other questions, he should be able to answer. The only thing he had previously sent was parts of an article on the food supply in the *Daily Sketch*. It was noticed that he was again questioned about the food supply. Recently, new questions had come:

3 February. Gliders which could carry troops or cargo.

10 February. The organisation of regiments which guarded air bases.

5 March. Factories that manufactured tanks with production figures.

13 March. Airborne Divisions, American bases, and arrival of new troops.

It was obvious that TATE, with his work on the farm, could not possibly answer all these questions. But he lived near London, had the weekends and sometimes a week off, and should be able to pick up some information that was worth sending. He could also use his own observations, and visit pubs and mingle among the guards of the local air bases. He was going to try to make a story out of this and information about the Army Air Corps that had been taken from the press and transmitted. TATE's controllers had specifically asked the Germans if they wanted detailed information about the Stirling bomber, but received no reply and therefore postponed this (perhaps understandable as the Stirling was already outdated and suffered from poor performance; now the new Lancaster and Halifax bombers were more interesting).

As a resource for the future, a girl named Mary, employed in a cipher department, had been invented. It was perhaps time to start using her, and the group including TATE together wrote the first message containing information stated to have come from contacts through Mary. In the spring they also invented another farmer, a friend of the farmer near Radlett who employed TATE. This man lived in Wye in Kent, a village about eighteen miles from Dover, where the English Channel was at its narrowest opposite the Pas de Calais. The site was strategically well placed for future observations of fictional movements of troops, and other military information. They were probably already looking ahead a few years, to the day when it would be time to carry out a landing on the European continent. The work of the double agents was likely to be of great significance for this critical operation. TATE would later, during the spring of 1944 when there were more serious invasion preparations, be said to be staying at the farm in Wye to help the other farmer. Of course he was in reality still in the Watford area, but it was vital to ensure that his radio transmissions appeared to be coming from the Wye area.

On 28 April, D. I. Wilson wrote a report complaining that he thought there had been insufficient radio traffic from TATE after his 'visit' to Wye in 1942. An experienced agent could hardly fail to make observations of unit signs, make references to military units, or identify some of the divisions that existed in the area. Quite understandably, it was realised that he could not give too much true information, but they could, as they had with the agent BALLOON earlier, modify and adapt the information, and also make use of the list of fictitious divisional signs planted on the Germans by the double agent GW. If it was not possible to arrange for TATE in the future to give information that seemed to come from his own observations in the neighbourhood of Wye, Wilson found it difficult to see how they could use TATE in a major operation, which justified his stay in southern England.[6]

FOOD ISSUES, RATIONING & AGRICULTURAL INFORMATION
The Germans' interest in food and agriculture continued during spring. As a good example of how useful it was to use press reports in order to obtain information, the group pointed out that TATE sent regular transmissions with food prices, which were gleaned from the

Grocer magazine. But the questions from Germany showed that the men in Hamburg knew little about agriculture. A discussion about terminology arose, where TATE showed, on the other hand, that he possessed extensive knowledge in the field. Some of the Germans' questions were:

Question 23. How big is the area of wintering ('*ausgewintert*') crops in hectares and how large is the percentage of the total harvest of wheat, barley and rye?
Question 24. Are these areas re-seeded ('*neubestellt*')?
Question 25. How large is it estimated that the areas for harvest of wheat, oats, barley, rye, potatoes, sugar beet, and others will be in 1942?
And please leave weather reports.

TATE replied:

Subject 23. Do you mean '*ausgewintert*', '*überwintert*' (sown in autumn and winter resting) or '*über winter brach gelegen*' (lie fallow over the winter)?
Subject 24. What do you mean by '*neubestellt*'? Do you simply mean sowed, sown on fallow land or re-sown?

They would have to study agricultural newspapers and documents to give answers. But it felt as though more information would be needed. From the Ministry of Agriculture they had obtained a limited flow of information, despite requests. Perhaps they should invite an expert on the subject from the Ministry. They had got hold of a brochure on crops for livestock feed from the Ministry of Agriculture, but it was difficult to obtain answers to these very specific questions. Maybe they knew more at the Ministry of Food, so they decided to ask them. But there was no hurry; it could wait until after Harry's vacation. On 2 July TATE announced to the Abwehr that he had just come back from a refreshing holiday in the Lake District (he had not noticed anything of value there). Even though Harry had worked in the agricultural sector during his youth, all these questions must have seemed utterly boring for him and his team of controllers.

Apenrade   Westerstrasse

Above: 1.
Aabenraa was
a German city
from 1864–1920
when Northern
Schleswig, in
agreement with
the Treaty of
Versailles, became
part of Denmark.
Many residents of
the city, however,
considered
themselves to be
Germans. (Leif
Vonge)

Right: 2.
Wulf's parents
William and
Helena Schmidt.
(FamilieJournalen)

3. Wulf Schmidt grew up in a large house on Lindsnakkevej in Aabenraa. (Museum Sønderjylland)

4. Wulf Schmidt as a recruit at Gardehusarregimentet in Copenhagen. If he had continued his career in the Danish cavalry, he would probably have been a senior officer at the outbreak of war. (Nigel West)

5. Wulf Schmidt in 1933, the year he travelled to Argentina.

6. Wulf Schmidt in 1936 when he studied agronomy at the University of Berlin.

7. Gösta Caroli trained together with Schmidt. They would become close friends but their friendship would eventually lead to Schmidt's arrest. (Claes Caroli)

9. Caroli was the first German agent who was delivered to England by parachute. He was, however, almost immediately arrested by the LDV. (Claes Caroli)

8. *Oberleutnant* Karl Gartenfeld, leader of *Staffel Gartenfeld*.

10. Wulf Schmidt landed about 100 yards from a manned searchlight.

11. The first interrogation of TATE was held in the pub 'Three Tuns', the headquarters of the Home Guard in Willingham. (Mike Smith)

12. Latchmere House or Camp 020. (Imperial War Museum, HU66759)

13. Lieutenant Colonel Robert 'Tin-eye' Stephens. (Imperial War Museum, HU66769)

14. Dr Harold Dearden, physician at Camp 020. (Imperial War Museum HU66755)

15. Colonel Thomas Argyll 'TAR' Robertson, later Lieutenant Colonel. (Special Forces Roll of Honour)

16. Building Anderson shelters.

17. TATE sent over 1,100 messages to the Germans. Most were weather reports (over 600) but TATE also reported on troop movements, airfields, and rationing, among many other things. (NARA)

18. TATE's radio equipment, which he brought from Germany. (National Archives)

19. Agent TATE. When TATE became ill in November 1941 a British radio operator continued to send messages to the Germans. (National Archives)

20. Bus No. 16 during the Second World War. (London Transport Museum)

21. At the end of May 1941 TATE received £200 from an unidentified Japanese man on a No. 16 bus in London. MI5 monitored the meeting and later identified the man as Mitinori Yosii, assistant Navy attaché at the Japanese legation in London. This photo is taken from MI5's monitoring of the meeting. (National Archives)

22. The German agent Karel Richter was executed on 10 December 1941 under the Treachery Act. (National Archives)

24. The search for Karel Richter's hidden equipment. Richter (centre) accompanied by members of the interrogation team at Camp 020, (from left to right) Lieutenant Colonel Robert 'Tin-eye' Stephens, Lieutenant Colonel G. Sampson, Major R. Short, Lieutenant Colonel D. B. 'Stimmy' Stimson and Captain E. Goodacre. (Imperial War Museum, HU66766)

23. The German agent Josef Jakobs was executed at the Tower on 15 August 1941 under the Treachery Act. Because of a fractured ankle he was shot sitting on a chair. (After the Battle)

25. Albert Pierrepoint, the executioner. (After the Battle)

26. The country house 'Skovbølgaard' outside Aabenraa, where Wulf Schmidt's grandparents lived and where he spent many summers. Skovbølgaard would later become one of the venues for Schmidt and the German Military Intelligence, Abwehr. (Museum Sønderjylland)

27. The radio operators at Wohldorf worked in shifts around the clock to receive messages from Abwehr agents. (Arthur O. Bauer)

28. Roundbush House, where TATE lived from 1941. (National Archives)

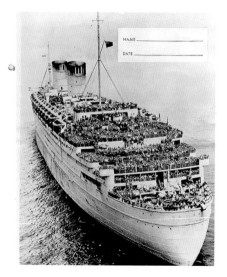

29. RMS *Queen Elizabeth* with soldiers. This is a postcard which was available for the soldiers. (Maurine Harrison)

30. Bletchley Park, fifty miles north of London. The main building was surrounded by several huts, where the important decoding of German Enigma messages was performed. At least 9,000 people worked here in 1944. (Jack Harper)

31. Agent TATE. There are indications that the Germans suspected several times that TATE was a double agent. Despite this, he would provide the Germans with information until the end of the war. (National Archives)

32. American troops on their way to Omaha Beach in a landing craft on D-Day. (National WWII Museum)

33. A difficult landing for a Horsa glider on D-Day. (National WWII Museum)

34. A V1 on its way to the launch site. (Bundesarchiv)

35. A V2 rocket ready for launching. (Bundesarchiv)

36. A German U-boat under attack from a Sunderland aircraft. (Royal Navy Submarine Museum, Gosport)

37. A German Type VIIC U-boat. (Royal Navy Submarine Museum, Gosport)

38. A British Mark XVII Contact Mine. Photo taken at the Valletta National War Museum. (Le Monde 1)

39. For the German Nazis in Denmark Aabenraa was a stronghold, with demonstrations already taking place before 1939. Young Harry (or Wulf Schmidt) took part in one in 1938. (Museum Sønderjylland)

40. The front of Harry Williamson's house at 55 Leggatt Wood Avenue, North Watford. (FamilieJournalen)

41. Harry Williamson in the garden. (FamilieJournalen)

42. Colonel Tommy 'TAR' Robertson in 1991. Nigel West to the left. (After the Battle)

43. Harry Williamson and Nigel West at the field outside Willingham, where Harry landed by parachute on 19 September 1940. The photo was taken in 1991. (After the Battle)

44. Harry Williamson and the radio operator Russell Lee 1991. (After the Battle)

45. As an envoy for Watford, Harry visited Germany in 1959 where he met the Mayor of Mainz.

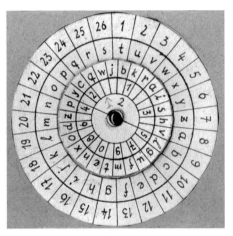

46. TATE's Cipher disk. (National Archives)

47. Greville's Photostudio in Queens Road, Watford. The building is demolished today. (Photo from Bob Nunn)

48. Map of England and occupied Europe.

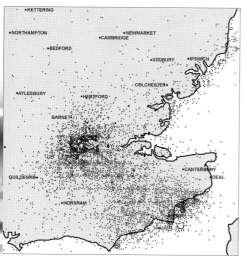
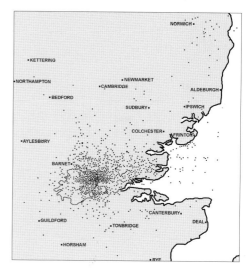

Above left: 49. V1 impact points in England.

Above right: 50. V2 impact points in England.

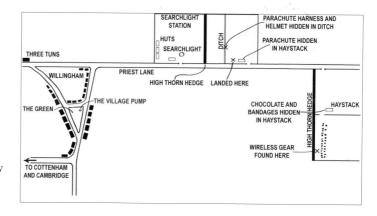

51. A sketch of the surroundings, where Wulf Schmidt landed by parachute on 19 September 1940.

SEARCHLIGHT STATION

PARACHUTE HARNESS AND HELMET HIDDEN IN DITCH

HUTS

SEARCHLIGHT

DITCH

PARACHUTE HIDDEN IN HAYSTACK

THREE TUNS

WILLINGHAM

PRIEST LANE

HIGH THORN HEDGE   LANDED HERE

THE VILLAGE PUMP

THE GREEN

CHOCOLATE AND BANDAGES HIDDEN IN HAYSTACK

HIGH THORN HEDGE

HAYSTACK

WIRELESS GEAR FOUND HERE

TO COTTENHAM AND CAMBRIDGE

52. TATE's fictitious minefield south of Ireland. The filled squares denote AM 8849, 8839, BF 1315, and 1249 on the German grid map.

84	85	86	94	95	96	74
Cork						Bristol
87	88	89	97	98	99	77
Fastnet Rock					St Eval	
11	12	13	21	22	23	31
14	15	16	24	25	26	35
17	18	19	27	28 29		38
				Brest		

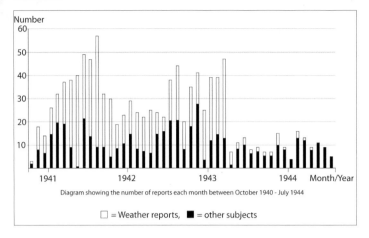

53. The numbers of messages from TATE.

Diagram showing the number of reports each month between October 1940 - July 1944

☐ = Weather reports, ■ = other subjects

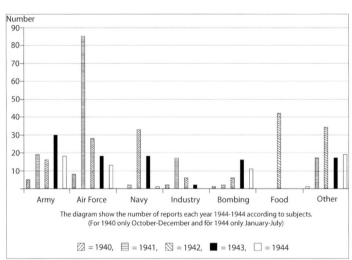

The diagram show the number of reports each year 1944-1944 according to subjects.
(For 1940 only October-December and för 1944 only January-July)

▨ = 1940, ☰ = 1941, ◩ = 1942, ■ = 1943, ☐ = 1944

54. The distribution of reports which were not weather reports (487 in total). During the same time TATE sent 604 weather messages until July 1944, nearly half of these (288) in 1941.

Below: 56. A hedge-hopper version of the flame fougasse (HM Government (1942). Military Training Pamphlet 53 Part I: Barrel Flame Traps. War Office)

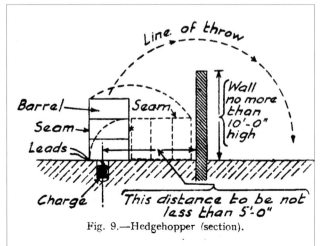

Fig. 9.—Hedgehopper (section).

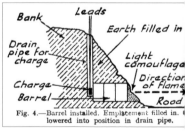

Fig. 4.—Barrel installed. Emplacement filled in. lowered into position in drain pipe.

Above: 55. A safety flame fougasse, the most common version (HM Government (1942). Military Training Pamphlet 53 Part I: Barrel Flame Traps. War Office)

The weather reports were missed because of the long messages, or sometimes they were simply forgotten. TATE in July sent reports on two fictional food stores (he had been out looking for one near Great Gaddesden where it should have been in a forest, but he had not managed to find it), a message that the wheat harvest had increased by 25 per cent, that people had begun to acquire chickens, the gratifying fact that the cheese ration had increased, and that an extra pound of sugar for jam production was distributed.[7] The Germans, of course, wanted general information about the British rationing conditions. When he was asked to report on the quality of the clothes, that the British were able to buy with their meagre ration coupons, TATE replied: 'You can kiss my ass' (and used twenty precious characters for this[8]). In the middle of this he found a personal message that his sister Hilde was on leave, and sent cordial greetings. He decided to interrupt a long report on cattle feed with a return greeting to Hilde. On the whole, TATE was allowed to correspond about familiar things over the years. He had heard about how things were with his brother Kai in the Luftwaffe,[9] and he 'participated' in his sister's wedding by letting Wohldorf give a 'blow to blow' account of it.[10]

He regularly requested the delivery of a new crystal for his transmitter. This was a deliberate move from the British side. His current crystal had a frequency of 6,195 kHz which made effective contact very difficult. The performance using the second crystal of 4,603 kHz was modified to give the impression that it was getting worse. By manipulating the transmitter technology, under the direction of the radio operator Ronnie Reed, the transmitter power was decreased so that broadcasts would be barely audible to the Germans. They also tried to reduce the antenna size, but then the signal was too bad and the Germans heard hardly anything at all. The receiving station was situated in Wohldorf outside Hamburg, but suddenly in March 1942 it was noticed that transmissions from the Germans became much stronger. They had changed the location of their radio station. By direction finding they succeeded in determining that it was now about twenty miles south of Paris.[11] After this, the Germans from time to time moved the location of their radio stations.

IDENTITY DOCUMENTS

The Germans were still worried about his fake identity card. Or rather, they wanted to know how to equip their next agents properly. As early as 19 September 1941, they had asked if TATE still used his old card, or had managed to get a new one. TATE replied that he certainly was not worried as he had used it several times without problems and nobody had questioned it. But the Germans asked again on 21 February 1942 if their fake identity cards from 1940 were still good enough for their new agents, or had changed, and did they now need more documents? No, TATE replied, they would do fine, and no other documents were needed. However, everyone must have a book of ration coupons, which was something new and complicated, and in addition clothing coupons were needed. Evidence that you were registered for military service was also necessary if one was of the right age. He pointed out that for a newcomer it was absolutely essential to have an experienced friend on hand to survive, because of all the changes that had been made. Later, TATE explained further (on 30 May 1942) that a new ration book was obtained by submitting your credentials, and at the same time showing your identity card, and stating your age and occupation, at the 'Local Food Office'. Then you received your book with ration cards by post. Something called the 'Personal Ration Book' was given right away, and it covered food that could be rationed in the future. Of course, in 1941 he had himself managed to get a ration book and clothing coupons.

ASSESSMENT OF TATE

A review of TATE's recent radio transmissions was made in August 1942 by J. H. Marriott, who was secretary of the board of the Double-Cross committee. By employing him at the farm they had achieved their aim of restricting his movements, and the amount of information he could possible get hold of. The information had previously been so plentiful and wide-ranging, that they were afraid it might even make the Germans suspicious. By providing him with £20,000, they had hoped that other agents would show up, to claim financial help. The plan had not succeeded as no unknown agents had appeared, and it seemed from the radio traffic from Germany, that they had no such plans either. It seems somewhat strange that the Germans did not demand more explicit activities now that he had all this money. Perhaps chaos prevailed in the Abwehr organisation, which caused it to be forgotten. Throughout TATE's career as a double agent there were several examples of obvious incompetence and disorganisation in the Abwehr.

The only payments TATE seems to have made during 1941 were £220 to the Norwegian John Moe (MUTT) and £550 to Bernie Kiener (RAINBOW). In August 1942, he was again ordered to pay £120 to MUTT, of which his colleague Tor Glad (JEFF) would have half (of course, they had other cover names with the Germans, *Ja* and *Tege*, during their training in Norway). In their radio transmissions, the word 'Henry' should appear somewhere in the report,[12] and if they had been revealed, the word 'Henry' would be missing from their messages. But TATE did not know who JEFF was, and was going to ask about him when he reported that the money had been paid. The notional amount was sent through the mail.

The Double-Cross organisation began to look ahead. If TATE was going to play a role in larger and more complex operations, and maintain the confidence that the Germans had in him, he had to improve the quality of his information. They went through his service during the previous ten months, and discovered, to their surprise, that he actually had access to several sources which had not really been exploited. Now there was the possibility of real improvement. The report listed the examples thus:

1941

30 September. At the Savoy managed to hear conversations between two American pilots who ferried aircraft.

5 October. Met with an RAF sergeant on leave.

14 October. An RAF officer told me ... (TATE had had a personal conversation with him).

19 October. Ended up in a conversation with some Irish Guards.

14 November. Overheard an interesting conversation between two senior officers.

18 November. The first time he mentions MARY, who is employed in the cipher department of one of the big ministries.

23 November. Have been working my way slowly but surely, into the better circles in London ... now matters well advanced.

25 November. An RAF officer told me.

18 December. The following rumour is current.

21 December. Have heard that ... (information concerning the placement of anti-aircraft divisions, which he had received directly from a conversation).

29 December. At Box Hill[13] so and so is said to be the case.

1942

2 January. Gives information about paratroop training in the Middle East.

11 January. Overheard in a high class bar, which I frequently visit.

18 January. Have heard that the parachute troops, etc.

22 January. An American pilot who ferries planes across the Atlantic told me.

28 January. Have heard that the gliders have been active recently.

29 January. A naval lieutenant told me ... (about tests of a new fast motor-boat).

1 February. It is said that the Russian anti-tank aircraft, etc.

19 February. Mobile anti-aircraft is said to be, etc.

26 February. Mobile anti-aircraft is said to be, etc. (again).

5 March. Heard from someone about Wig Bay (the RAF base for seaplanes).

8 March. Heard from a good source (information about the floating fortress off the East Coast).

4 April. Was introduced to a Norwegian ex-naval officer.

6 April. Overheard a conversation between some naval officers.

19 April. MARY revealed that she had been lent by her ministry to the Americans.

22 April. TATE was ordered to further use MARY and her circle of friends.

1 May. Heard that the railway line at Bath, etc.

8 May. Heard from MARY.

13 May. Met an officer from the RAF regiment.

31 May. MARY reports that ... (Molotov was visiting Britain).

19 June. Met MARY yesterday.

22 July. MARY reports that.

28 July. TATE receives instructions to make more use of MARY.

31 July. At a party with MARY and met an American naval officer.[14]

It was concluded in the report that TATE had managed to acquire good friends in London, from whom he received information in addition to ordinary social conversation, this being the result of several meetings. Through his good upbringing and education, he had succeeded in being accepted by a wide circle of people whom he could meet by appointment. The only person mentioned by name was MARY, of whom he was seeing more and more. It was planned that they should create more fictitious names from among the people of his new social circle. In addition, he should be elected to a club, an environment where opportunities existed for every sort of indiscretion, and the Junior Carlton Club was suggested.[15] How this ended, we do not know as a list of Junior Carlton Club members has never been made public.

TATE should now have become acquainted with the local families where he lived and where some people might be imagined to work in ministries, perhaps at Lloyd's (shipping insurance), or with important war work. Although the questions from the Germans had not really been concerned with important subjects in recent months, his reports seemed to have been treated seriously and in a business-like manner. A gradual improvement in the quality of his information, should also lead to an improvement in the questions from the Germans,[16] which would be of benefit to MI5. Of course, the agents in the Double-Cross organisation were asked numerous questions about all sorts of things. Until the autumn of 1942, questions about 354 different factories and firms had been sent by the Abwehr to their agents.[17]

QUESTIONS ON AIRCRAFT MATTERS AGAIN

Again an increased interest in aircraft matters was noticed from the German side. TATE would respond to this, by reporting, for instance, about air bases in Cranfield and Sywell (two airfields used for training, i.e., rather unimportant from an operational standpoint), giving the impression that he had been on reconnaissance over the weekend. His steering group thought it was good that they now began to get questions about military matters which would make possible future major disinformation projects. This curiosity about food and agricultural issues appeared to be relatively unimportant from a military point of view. The new interest was in an area of military activity where they really did need to deceive the Germans. But the responsible authorities were very cautious in pursuing and developing this new opportunity. Therefore, TATE had to make an additional visit to Cranfield and Sywell, in order to give better and more recent material as the first report was now almost obsolete. Information regarding pilot training at Cranwell, an important training centre for pilots, was, however, delayed for several weeks as it seemed to be a sensitive topic.

The excellent Mustang fighter had now entered RAF service, but TATE was not allowed to give any significant report to the Abwehr until shortly before the news was revealed in the press. This resulted in fears that it would seem too obvious that TATE had given this information only at the same time it was becoming widely known through the press. TATE himself proposed giving more substance to his reports and, if he went to Cranfield, he could just as easily also report on the air raid carried out on 23 July in Bedford, which was next door to Cranfield. He reported that the bombs had fallen about thirty yards from the railway station, which only received slight damage to the roof. Moreover, he had been authorised to send information regarding damage to Denham airfield but, because it was merely a training facility too, it might raise suspicions, so nothing was sent. It was also decided that a question concerning a company in Birmingham, 'Semape', would not be answered because TATE could not have had time to acquire this information. A report about an emergency food stockpile in Chipperfield was also declined; TATE had already given so much false information on the food supply. However, they had approved information suggested by TATE himself, such as about the manufacture of Mosquitoes, the bomber base at Bovingdon near Watford, the American Air Forces headquarters in Bushey Hall Hotel, and an RAF headquarters in Aldenham Lodge Hotel in Radlett. He also took the opportunity of reporting on military camps near Stevenage and Watton-at-Stone.

Now the harvest had been taken in, and TATE had time to smarten up his apartment in London, but he would not disclose the location unless he was asked a direct question. As he now lived in London, it was highly desirable to get a bit of high-quality gossip from MARY and her friends, or from new contacts in London, but the steering group held back for the moment. TATE wanted to send some information about the air defences in Hyde Park, but it was decided to wait until it had been in action and he would then be able to give a more vivid description of their activity. TATE had so far (September 1942) not been involved in 'The General Plan', as they called it – the long-term goal of an invasion. He had only been at Wye on one occasion so far, but when things began to happen, he would be sent there again. There was actually a division, the 46th, stationed around Wye for real. During his previous visit, TATE had made reports of troop movements there, which he could refer to in future radio messages.[18]

The MARY Effect

More frequent contact with MARY now meant that TATE could start to give reports on marine issues, and he was given tips by the Abwehr about how he could make use of her. Ewen Montagu, who was the Navy representative in the Double-Cross team (famous for Operation MINCEMEAT, the dead man in the Mediterranean Sea with important documents, which fooled the Germans about the invasion of Sicily), and TAR Robertson were behind the whole idea. TATE was easy to get along with and possessed natural charm, so he suited the role of a lady's man.[19] They had placed the fictional MARY in the cipher department of the Admiralty, the Fleet's most important office. She was later lent to the US Naval Mission, and eventually also spent some time in Washington in the United States, from where she returned on 23 May 1944, filled with useful information.[20] She was created as an extremely indiscreet person when it came to passing on information to her friend TATE. Through her circle of friends he came into contact with Navy men, both Britons and Americans, thanks to the idea of MARY's time spent working for the United States. Occasionally, officers stayed overnight in his flat, and they were of course talkative concerning secrets.[21]

The Commander-in-Chief of the Navy demanded an improvement in protection for the stricken Arctic convoys bound for Russia. This was managed by, firstly, exaggerating the number of ships, and reporting that the newly arrived American ships filled the gaps between convoys. Secondly, it was reported that the escort ships, which looked few and far between from the air, were reinforced by a large escort of submarines. It was established that TATE primarily would deliver these messages to the Germans.[22] During the successful German U-boat period in December 1942, TATE, along with other double agents, took part in reporting that an increasing number of escort ships had been moved from the Mediterranean, to reinforce the convoys across the Atlantic.

Questions about the planned convoy routes were commonly asked by the Germans – a delicate thing to answer for the Double-Cross committee. TATE accounted for his lack of such information by claiming, very reasonably, that it was extremely difficult to obtain as no sailor would risk his own life. However, TATE on one occasion reported the exact route (from information received from MARY) of a convoy, which conveniently had to be cancelled.[23] The U-boat war and the Battle of the Atlantic were of great concern, and according to Churchill were the greatest threat throughout the war, until effective counter-weapons were developed.

The Germans had invented a new method of protecting their U-boats when they were trapped by an escort with Asdic (a signal that was sent, and bounced back from the U-boat, which thus could be located by the echoes). They used *Bold*, sonar decoy device, which ejected capsules from the U-boat's stern through around 10-cm-diameter tubes. The capsules contained metallic zinc and calcium which reacted on contact with water to create hydrogen. The hydrogen bubbles lasted for about fifteen to twenty minutes, and they caused echoes on Asdic equipment resembling those from a U-boat. This was often enough to allow the U-boat to sneak away undetected.[24] TATE claimed that he had managed with the use of alcohol to thoroughly loosen the tongue of an officer from a new frigate. Under the influence, he had bragged that they had sunk a U-boat with help of this new device: 'The bloody fools didn't

realise that they were helping us by blowing their bloody bubbles.'
TATE managed to match his report with a U-boat that had actually
been sunk despite the bubble-blowing.[25]

The Allies were especially worried about the safety of the fast,
large passenger ships, like *Queen Elizabeth* and *Queen Mary*, which
transported huge numbers of soldiers from the USA. The vessels could
take up to 15,000 troops, and a total of nearly five million American
soldiers were transported by the 'Queens' and other large passenger
ships. The ships were ocean greyhounds; both *Queen Mary* and *Queen
Elizabeth* had a cruising speed of 28.5 knots, much faster than a U-
boat with a surface speed of 17 knots. The escort ships were informed
about the position of U-boats as a result of regular decrypts of Enigma
messages at Bletchley Park, or via radio location.[26] On one occasion on
15 April 1944, Captain Valentine of *U-385* stated that he had sighted
Queen Mary and fired three torpedoes, two of which hit the ship. But in
fact they had not hit *Queen Mary*, which reported that they had heard
underwater explosions, probably torpedoes, which for some reason
had exploded short of their target.[27] The Double-Cross operation could
make a difference in this part of the war, by spreading rumours about
the latest type of excellent anti-U-boat armament mounted on escort
ships. None of these large passenger ships, packed with soldiers, were
ever sunk.

TATE was even involved in the war against Japan. In December
1942, the British had only one aircraft carrier, HMS *Illustrious*,[28] in
service while another aircraft carrier, HMS *Indefatigable*[29] was not
yet completed. TATE passed on the information that *Indefatigable*
was already on active service, and he reported that the two aircraft
carriers had left for the East, which the Germans, of course, forwarded
to the Japanese. The illusion was kept alive by fictional radio traffic
during their voyage.[30] Faith in TATE's credibility was now strong and
the Abwehr asked him to obtain specific charts, but he was forced to
point out that this was absolutely too dangerous and impractical a
task.[31]

Operation TORCH

On 8 November 1942 just over 70,000 American and British soldiers landed in French North Africa – Operation TORCH. The landings took place at Casablanca, Oran and Algiers. The intention was to remove the Germans from Africa, take command in the Mediterranean, and then carry out an invasion of southern Europe. This was the first major, organised, and complex strategic deception carried out by the Double-Cross system. In order to deceive over the main objective, two major plans were drawn up in July, where many agents were involved. The first disinformation operation was called OVERTHROW, and had the north coast of France as the target. The second was called SOLO 1, where an intended landing in Norway was presented. There were also a series of plans, where the accumulation of forces in Gibraltar before the invasion was presented as a manoeuvre to strengthen Malta.[32] Originally, the Double-Cross organisation wanted to present Dakar in Senegal as the fictional landing area, but this plan was stopped in the planning stage.[33] Various rumours were circulating, however, and the Germans were still quite convinced about a landing at Dakar.

The Double-Cross system was governed now as a part of a new organisation, the London Controlling Section (LCS), which was directly under the Allied Chiefs of Staff, who now realised the importance of deception. But the beginning was slow, with increased bureaucracy and LCS did not have much freedom of action. Trying to deceive the Germans about an invasion of Norway, instead of North Africa was a bit far-fetched. But it was decided that parts of the Allied naval force should actually sail away in a north-easterly direction, but someone had to give a clearer hint to the Germans and this became TATE's contribution to Operation TORCH. He reported to the Abwehr that he had met at a dinner a few British officers from HMS *Anson* and some American officers from the USS *Alabama* and the USS *South Dakota*. They told him that their group of five destroyers had been given orders, at short notice, to equip with full winter clothes and cold weather equipment.[34]

It is believed that the OVERTHROW and SOLO 1 operations did make a contribution to the success of TORCH. It was likely, however, that the Germans' growing belief and wishful thinking that Dakar was the target was the most important factor. The Navy force, with 334 landing vessels, remained completely undetected by the German U-boats, with only one ship being attacked, probably by chance while Dönitz had stationed the bulk of his U-boats off Dakar.[35] The large convoy from the USA to North Africa was, however, very close to being detected which would have caused the loss of the element of surprise. Through ULTRA, a message was received concerning a Portuguese, de Freitas Ferrez, on board a fishing boat outside Newfoundland. He was a German spy, equipped with a transmitter, with a mission to spy on convoys. The fishing boat was searching for the convoy, and if successful, he could then have followed it and reported the course to the Germans. But a British Navy escort ship stopped the fishing boat in time, and took care of Ferrez, who finally ended up in Camp 020.[36]

8

1943

In January 1943, TATE sent a message which worried TAR Robertson. The Abwehr had proposed that TATE should set off on a reconnaissance trip. The answer was:

> Best thanks for message. My boss here has already proposed a holiday for me as I look worn out. It will perhaps therefore be possible for me to travel for one or two days now and again. Let me know what you want to know and then I will do my best.

Robertson wrote in his report that they actually had arranged the farm job for TATE in order to deal with the fact that he now had a large sum of money, which could lead the Germans to demand much better results. The idea was that selected requests could not be answered, because his ability to travel was limited by the work on the farm. Robertson did not like the phrase 'now and again'. It would be better to alter the arrangement to allow him to go on one trip only. In this way the Germans would be forced to limit their questions, and in this way MI5 could discover what was most important and interesting to them – what information was, in fact, vital to them.

One wonders how much freedom they had now given TATE, who seemed to be able to convey information without direction from his controllers. The Double-Cross operation needed, of course, to approve of all communication before it was sent. But the radio operator, Ronnie Reed, who was part of TATE's steering committee, thought that for TATE to get just four days off in a year was rather harsh. On 16 January it appeared that Ewen Montagu had proposed that TATE should send information that 30,000 Americans had arrived the previous week, but by mistake only 3,000 troops were mentioned in his report. It was decided that TATE should send a new message, with details of what kind of troops had come and state that the number of 3,000 had been a mistake, perhaps in the encoding. This was, however, never sent. Instead TATE reported on 23 January that after checking his notes he had discovered that the reported number was wrong.[1]

A few months later the steering group suggested that TATE should make it clear that he was worn out and unhappy. It would be interesting to see the German reaction to TATE's completely understandable and natural reaction after three years of living on his wits in a hostile country, and perhaps it might provide an opportunity to develop additional aspects of *Leonhard*/TATE's fictional character. No response from the German side is, however, preserved. In the spring, there is a report of a meeting between TATE and his case-officers TAR Robertson and Russell Lee, in which the question was raised about whether they should either end his activities, or expand the organisation with some sub-agents. The result was a compromise: TATE would henceforth send only once a week and in this way the Abwehr would not get their frequent weather reports.

It was pointed out to TATE that Abwehr agents regarded as the best by the Germans were those who had built up their own organisation. The Abwehr did not seem to care about their agent's feelings or mental state. Perhaps those who managed him in the beginning had ended up on the Eastern Front, and others, who did not personally know TATE, had taken over. He agreed, but he was not prepared to start recruiting sub-agents as they would cost money, and if the money ran out, he ran the risk of being blackmailed. This sounds strange, because everything was actually just a game, including the financial transactions. It was decided that, as an insurance policy for TATE, if the Germans won the war (he thought the chances were fifty-fifty, which Robertson thought was slightly excessive), he would continue his reporting to the Germans, but less frequently. He would announce that he would now send only once a week. The group from MI5 were interested in discovering how long the transmissions could be before the Germans thought the risk of detection and discovery would become too great, and he was going to ask for their opinion on this.

At the end of June 1943, Masterman, Liddell and Reed discussed the fact that TATE's life, with its never-ending monitoring, had begun to make him and the guards nervous and twitchy. It had been agreed that TATE should have the freedom to roam in Radlett, and he could easily have escaped if he had wished. However, it was reasoned that if he went back to the Abwehr, he could scarcely explain away his activities to the Germans, and he might be accused of being responsible for the arrest and execution of Karel Richter followed swiftly by a death sentence from the Germans. There was work available at a photographers in Watford, Greville's Photography on Queens Road,[2] and this job would increase his range of movement by five miles. Taking extra precautions, by informing the Chief Constable and distributing photos of TATE, would make a successful escape attempt highly unlikely. They gave permission for his work, and on 9 July he began his employment.[3] We can assume that it must have been a very positive move for, after years of boring routine, he had finally found a 'real' job which interested him.

At the conference in Casablanca in January 1943, Churchill and Roosevelt decided that an invasion of France across the English Channel would be launched in the spring of 1944. The British Major General Frederick Morgan was appointed head of staff at COSSAC (Chief of Staff to the Supreme Allied Commander) in April 1943, and was commissioned to develop a plan for a full-scale invasion, which was codenamed OVERLORD. In July 1943 it was decided that the invasion would take place in Normandy. There, the beaches were protected from wind, there were plenty of suitable exits from the beaches in order to push swiftly inland, and it would be possible to gain access quickly to the deep water ports of Cherbourg, Lorient, Saint Nazaire and Brest. The plans would include various forms of cover operations used in the same way as OVERTHROW and SOLO 1, which had assisted the landings in North Africa. They wanted to include threats of action against northern France and Norway, to persuade the Germans to reduce their forces in the Mediterranean area and on the Russian front, and to entice the Luftwaffe into the air for a war of attrition across the English Channel. This initiated a series of different operations with these objectives, in the autumn of 1943. The General Plan was named COCKADE, and consisted of sub-operations like STARKEY, an Allied landing in the Boulogne area in northern France on 9 September 1943, followed by WADHAM, an American attack on Brest in Brittany. In the big plan, STARKEY and WADHAM would then be called off, and instead be succeeded by a fake invasion of Norway by five divisions, which was code named TINDALL.

In July 1943, the issue of how best to use TATE in Operation STARKEY was considered. For this TATE was instructed to report on military exercises held on the south coast of Wales, but supplemented a few days later with information that it had only been an exercise. It was decided that TATE would now stay with some friends in Kent, leaving on 11 August. He, therefore, asked if there were any specific instructions about what information he should try to find out. The leave would continue until 22 August, and during this time he would be able to take a look at the fake air base, which had been built near Hawkinge, and observe troop movements in the Dover area.

In September, there was a worried report from TAR Robertson. During the last six months there had only been fourteen recorded messages to TATE from the Germans. Most dealt with his codes in the future, or were about his family. There were only two that were interesting: one question about British night fighters, and one about the Victoria Bridge (rebuilt and renamed Chelsea Bridge in 1937) in London. It was obvious that they were not using TATE for observations of troop movements, or for other information from the area around London. It was decided that TATE should break off radio communication for fourteen days, and if the Abwehr wondered why, he would state that he had been ill. Robertson concluded that TATE's time as a counter-espionage agent was coming to an end, but the Admiralty wanted to continue to keep him going.

Since there was no reaction from the Germans, it was difficult to evaluate what confidence the enemy actually had in TATE. The concern over what the Germans really thought about him persisted throughout the autumn. It was decided to allow him to continue, but with not too frequent transmissions. They tried to find events that would arouse a bit more commitment and interest from the Germans. So, TATE stated that he had lost his apartment as it had been requisitioned by the armed forces who had insufficient accommodation. He had difficulty in finding a new home and the proposal that he would sign up for AMGOT (Allied Military Government for Occupied Territories), i.e., the future organisation for the administration of primarily France when it was regained, was presented. In that case he would be away for three months, but no further reports on this subject have been saved. However, the decision to keep TATE/Harry Williamson was unshakable, particularly at high levels in the Admiralty. TATE would be needed for Operation OVERLORD, the landing in France.[4]

Was TATE 'Blown'?

On several occasions the British had reason to fear that TATE had been revealed as a double agent by the Germans, despite all the painstaking work of preparing and checking the content of his radio messages. The first time was when he received his first cash contribution to help cover the cost of his work. This was a payment of £100 sent by the double agent SNOW by post in February 1941. By this time, SNOW himself had probably, about three months before this payment, revealed to the Germans that he was a double agent. All SNOW's British contacts were then, of course, in danger of being under suspicion by the Abwehr. But TATE survived on this occasion and he continued supplying his extensive information which was genuinely appreciated by the Abwehr without any sign of suspicion.

The second occasion was when TRICYCLE came back from his unsuccessful time in the USA between August 1941 and October 1942. Shortly before, he had been the brains behind the skilfully implemented plan MIDAS, which ended with TATE suddenly having £20,000 in his hands. But TRICYCLE had a lot to explain to the Germans about his useless and very expensive time in the USA – he was very expensive to run, often needing five figure dollar amounts in order to maintain the façade of a playboy and jet-setter who moved around in the best circles. He was supposed to have built up a string of agents in the USA, but accomplished absolutely nothing, mostly because of the FBI and Hoover's obstinacy and complete ignorance of the concept of double agents. When TRICYCLE was to return to Europe via Lisbon there was great anxiety – he could now finally be revealed during his inevitable debriefing by the Abwehr. His controllers in the Double-Cross organisation devoted a great deal of time putting together a comprehensive and water-tight story, with explanations covering any potential issues from the Germans. TRICYCLE had to learn these by heart in order not to show the slightest hesitation and he turned in another magnificent performance. As usual, he was a master of talking himself out of tricky situations.[5] His immediate supervisor in the Abwehr, von Karsthoff, was really not very interested in reporting that TRICYCLE was 'blown', for he himself lived well on the reflected glory from TRICYCLE. So the whole transaction involving £20,000 seemed credible and justifiable, and TATE himself was in the clear.

The third risk was probably the most serious. The career of the Norwegian Tor Glad (JEFF) was short and he had been operational for only slightly more than four months. He had worked a little too enthusiastically with the Nazis in Norway before he fled, and had difficulty sticking to the rules. During a pub crawl in Aberdeen, he had begun to question people loudly, making notes in his notebook, which led to his arrest. MI5 became so suspicious of him that, in the autumn of 1941, he was interned in Camp WX on the Isle of Man which was also used for the incarceration of some suspects who had passed through Camp 020. Gösta Caroli had also been held there after his escape attempt in January 1941, until he ended up in Camp 020R in Huntercombe in 1943, a reserve prison for Camp 020.[6] Nearby was another camp, Camp L, which held fifty genuinely ardent German Nazis. But there were leaks and easy communication between these two camps. Most of the prisoners in Camp WX and their stories, were known in the Nazi camp, until the inmates of Camp WX were transferred to Dartmoor in 1942. Soon it emerged that one of these Nazis (Erich Karl, a member of the German War Graves Commission in Belgium and Holland, but probably an Abwehr agent[7]) had been repatriated from Camp L to Germany late in 1943, as part of an exchange deal between Britain and Germany for about fifty civilians. When the former Camp WX inmates (there were 'stool pigeons' or informers there) heard about this in November 1943, it was obvious that they were fully convinced that this German, Erich Karl, had revealed all about the double game played by JEFF, MUTT, and also TATE.[8]

This was confirmed after the war in part of an interrogation of Major Böckel, or Bruhns, as he called himself, about his activities as the trainer of, among others, agents Wulf Schmidt and Gösta Caroli, in Hamburg during the six-week period in 1940 before they were sent to England. He revealed that at Abwehr HQ in Berlin they were unsure whether TATE, Agent 3725, was indeed genuine, and not being manipulated by the British. But Böckel, however, continued to maintain contact with A3725, or *Leonhard*, TATE's German cover name.[9] The Abwehr was a fragmented organisation with local stations or *stellen* in each military district, which seemed to work fairly independently. An assessment was also made by the Double-Cross committee in December 1943 at a meeting in Dartmoor, as the situation seemed serious. It seemed certain that JEFF (Tor Glad) had been unmasked, and they could not rule out that TATE also was 'blown'. Possibly the Germans only partially believed in the disclosure. In the Abwehr there was a reluctance in some quarters to pass on any possibly damaging revelations, as several officers were living very well on their agents' successes. There was never the slightest trace of distrust by the Abwehr in their continued communication with TATE.[10]

A conclusive piece of evidence indicating the Germans' continuing faith in TATE was that he was given a new code by them. This contributed to the decision to continue using TATE as a double agent during Operation FORTITUDE.[11] The Germans continued to trust his reports, in spring 1944, about the forthcoming invasion (even if TATE had a minor role there), the effects of the V1 and V2 campaign, and the anti-U-boat minefields.

When TATE sent his 1,000th message, announced on 21 September 1944 (i.e., well after the invasion), the Abwehr made exceptional efforts to establish his bona fides. A special committee was set up, with General Maurer as chairman, regarded as the most scrupulous and careful of judges, and composed of the most hard-boiled intelligence experts, communications experts, and even a psychiatrist. Their conclusion was that he had indeed transmitted valuable messages, and had done a good job. Captain Wichmann, head of the Abwehr in Hamburg, apparently reported this to Canaris, and TATE was recommended for the 'German Gold Cross'.[12] But this can hardly be the whole truth as Canaris had been dismissed in February 1944.

But the evaluation of TATE from the German side seems to have been extremely variable. In an interrogation document from 22 April 1945, with a captured Major Brede who had worked with the Abwehr in March 1941, it was stated that he remembered an agent, who was called Lena Six (or probably *sechs* in German). From the description it is clear that this was TATE. He argued that the information from this agent was of little value; it was mostly about airports around London, and Abwehr I Luft in Hamburg was sceptical. This perhaps is contradicted by the statement of Dr Karl Praetorius, probably in 1941, that *Leonhard* (TATE) was 'a pearl among agents'. Even after Operation MIDAS (the £20,000 windfall), Berlin was apparently convinced that Lena Six was controlled by the British.[13] Still, the German side continued to carry out communications with TATE throughout the entire war, which seems strange and contradictory. German intelligence was significantly fragmented, and eventually reorganised during the war. The staff came and went and were, perhaps, ill-informed about history and continuity.

Parts of their intelligence service were probably a mess, like much of the whole of Nazi society.

The different *Stellen* of the Abwehr seemed to work independently, with poor contact between each other. On 5 April 1941, in a message intercepted from Ast Bremen, it was said: 'Report Lena 3725, military trucks and passenger vehicles of all types and units north of Chausee Slough – Maidenhead, east of Beaconsfield Strasse', but it is obvious from the text that they had no idea who this 3725 (i.e., TATE) was.[14]

THE WEATHER WAR

During his career as a British double agent, TATE sent fairly correct weather reports to the Abwehr and in fact more than half of his reports concerned meteorological data.[15] Already during his training in Hamburg the Germans had pointed out the importance of weather reports, and that he should send them as often as possible, preferably every day. This instruction was given to most of the Abwehr agents sent to Great Britain. The reason was that the shortage of reliable weather reports was a significant disadvantage for the German Headquarters in Berlin as the weather was fundamental to all Air and Navy operations. The weather forecast was, for example, of major importance to those controlling German night fighters in their desperate combat against the Allied bomber armadas over Germany.

When the war started in 1939 all international exchange of meteorological information ceased, and the Germans had to find other ways of collecting the information they needed. Among other things Dönitz's U-boats were expected to transmit regular weather observations in addition to their positions, something which became more difficult as the hunt for the U-boats became increasingly successful, and from 1944 almost no U-boats were present in the Atlantic. Air observations were, of course, used for weather reports, from bases in northern Norway, mostly using Heinkel He111 and Junkers Ju88s.[16] In autumn 1944, these flights, however, had to be cut back because of the shortage of fuel.

Several ships were also used for obtaining meteorological data. In September 1940, the weather trawler *Sachsen* was sent to the Denmark

Straits and the pack ice close to Greenland, but it was sunk in May 1941. The next weather ship to be sunk, the *Lauenburg*, was a lucrative prize in June 1941, as the Allies at the same time managed to capture an Enigma machine. The *Hessen* went out in 1943, but was wrecked, and had to be towed to Tromsø by a U-boat. The *Wuppertal* operated between November 1944 to January 1945, but probably perished in a storm.[17] Several other ships, often trawlers, were used with varying success.

Dr Hans Knospel, one of the senior German meteorologists, realised that weather stations on land were needed. Several German attempts to establish weather bases on Greenland were made, without success, and they were soon destroyed by the US Coastguard. Also a small force of mainly Danes and Norwegians (the Sirius sledge patrol) equipped with dogs and sledges travelled around 500 miles on Greenland searching for German weather observers. The Holzauge weather station, on Sabine island off the east coast of Greenland, transmitted more than 1,500 weather reports before it was discovered by this sledge-patrol, and later destroyed by an American bomber attack in the spring of 1944.

On the western part of Franz Joseph's Land, a group was landed in September 1943, but they were struck down by trichinosis (a parasite infection acquired from raw meat) and had to be evacuated in spring 1944. In September 1944, a new group disembarked on the north-eastern part of Iceland. Jan Mayen had a Norwegian weather station which continued to work after the German occupation of Norway, but they were evacuated in October 1940. In November the same year, a hunted German weather trawler was wrecked against the rocks, when they tried to land meteorologists. In May 1941, a Norwegian weather expedition was established on the island and sent reports every third hour, but were heard by the Germans, and a bomber force was sent out, though it did not manage to destroy the base. Jan Mayen continued to be a thorn in the side of the Germans throughout the whole war.

Svalbard, with the largest island Spitsbergen, was inhabited by some thousands of Norwegians and Russians. Norwegian weather bases were placed on Spitsbergen and Bear Island, which provided the mainland with data, but they were evacuated and everything was destroyed. After that, these islands were uninhabited. In September 1941, a Junkers Ju 52 landed, and the Germans built their own weather station. After a few months four meteorologists started reporting, and were reinforced with another five men, with Dr Knospel, at another station. They worked without interference and were, according to plan, evacuated in August 1942. New personnel arrived, but had to make a quick escape by U-boat in spring 1943. Another station was established on the northern part of Spitsbergen, but ceased to function in June 1944, when Dr Knospel died in an accident. Other stations were set up, but only one, Taaget, remained at the end of the war.

In May 1942, the Allies tried to build a meteorological station on Spitsbergen, but were surprised by a Luftwaffe attack, with great losses of ships and personnel. They were reinforced, and decided to attack the German base on the other side of the island, but when they arrived the Germans had left. After this, the Allies operated a weather station on Spitsbergen which supplied decisive information for D-Day. The Germans tried to destroy it by several attacks; in one of them, Operation *Sicilien*, *Tirpitz* took part on 7 September 1943.

From 1942 the Germans started to use unmanned, automatic weather stations, called *Kröte*. These measured temperature, air pressure and humidity, and then details were then sent by radio. An improved model, WFL, could also measure the direction and velocity of the winds. They were placed on several islands in the North Atlantic, Barents Sea, and also on Greenland and even on Labrador in Canada (it was called 'Kurt'). However, the batteries only had a duration of four to six months.[18]

These stations were, however, widely spaced and the Germans had difficulty in following the weather fronts; their ships and bases on land did not last long. At the same time, the Luftwaffe were short of fuel, and the U-boats had disappeared from the Atlantic. The German coverage of the weather in the Atlantic was thus inadequate.

This is an example of one of the many weather reports sent by TATE: 'Weather yesterday 21.00 hours. Temp 57. Baro 2960. No wind. Clouds six. Light mist. Weather today 07.00 hours. Temp 52. Baro 2950. No wind. Thick mist.

The question whether there was any value in falsifying the weather reports was discussed. In that case, they had to be consistent with the messages from DRAGONFLY, who also gave weather reports. There was a danger that false information could be revealed by German air reconnaissance, or by observation from the Pas de Calais. The decision was that, in the event of a situation where it was clearly very important to falsify the weather reports, they would assess with great care the risk that such a deception might be detected by the enemy.

9

1944 & 1945

At the Tehran conference in November 1943 Churchill uttered his famous words: 'In wartime, truth is so precious that she should always be attended by a bodyguard of lies.' And BODYGUARD became the name of the comprehensive action against Germany with sham operations and disinformation to keep German troops out of France and Russia, and instead focus on Italy, southern Germany, the Balkans including Greece, and Scandinavia. As a cover for OVERLORD (and NEPTUNE, as the crossing of the Channel was called) two major projects were created, which would be full of false information, FORTITUDE NORTH and FORTITUDE SOUTH. The whole operation was led by the organisation known as SHAEF (Supreme Headquarters Allied Expeditionary Force), with Eisenhower as the head. In this work, the double agents of the Double-Cross system were going to play an important part, perhaps the most significant of the war.

In early 1944 TATE made a scoop that impressed his German masters, and strengthened their confidence in him. Early on the morning of 15 January a brief message was sent from him to the Germans: 'Overheard that Eisenhower will arrive in England on 16 January.'

This brief report was his 935th message, and it was received now by a Major Herrman Sandel in Sophien Terrace in Hamburg. The buildings in the street had been hit hard by the bombings in the summer of 1943, but the Abwehr was nonetheless soon continuing their work there. Sandel had lived many years in the USA and was considered as an expert on the Anglo-Saxons. The message brought a certain gloom as it was no secret that an invasion was being prepared, but this indicated that they would soon know when it was going to happen. Eisenhower was appointed Supreme Commander on Christmas Day 1943, but then he seemed to be missing. TATE's report was sent while Ike was in his private railway carriage en route from Prestwick to London, seven hours before he arrived in London, and forty-eight hours before it was announced officially. Major Sandel redirected this vital information by telex to the Abwehr secret headquarters in a Berlin suburb, and transmitted the usual evening message to TATE at 8.30 p.m.:

> Many thanks for the excellent No. 935. Keep us posted on Eisenhower movements in context of invasion preparations.[1]

On 16 January 1944, TATE sent message number 937:

> There are now more than 7,000 American officers and men in London, in addition to those who come here temporarily for their leave. Most of those on duty work at various invasion headquarters, one of which is located on Berkeley Square in Mayfair.[2]

And already, on 17 January, came the next message on Eisenhower:

> The arrival of Eisenhower is by now featured prominently in numerous news items in the press and on the radio ... Another announcing the arrival of Eisenhower's deputy, British Air Chief Marshal Tedder, demonstrating the rapid progress of the Anglo-American command apparatus for the pending operations. As far as the naming of General Bradley as 'Commander of the United States Army' (American Army Group no. 1) is concerned, it is notable that Bradley at one time commanded the 82nd Airborne Division (whose partial transfer to England from Italy had become known from an 'unimpeachable source' ('sichere Quelle'[3]), and was subsequently in command of the 28th Infantry Division, whose arrival in southern England was reported by another agent.[4]

By BODYGUARD it was intended to portray the preparations for the invasion as being worse than expected, and that the invasion would come later than initially planned. There were not enough landing craft, the strength of the Allies was not sufficient, and the formation of the troops was delayed. One way to point out the lack of landing craft was to play on strikes. On 20 January, TATE announced that problems with the workforce in the United States had reduced the production of invasion boats so dramatically that the date of the planned operation would be affected.⁵ Other double agents gave information that the training was so poor that Montgomery would, as he did in Egypt, have to re-train all the troops again. The widening of roads in areas around Portsmouth and Southampton was behind schedule and perhaps they were going to wait for the Russian summer offensive before the invasion was launched. Perhaps the invasion would not come at all, and the outcome of the war relied on the crucial impact of the bombing raids over Germany instead. Eventually, it was necessary to depart from the misinformation about 'postponement', especially when the big rehearsals for Operation TIGER and later, FABIUS, were held in the English Channel in April and May, which the Germans could hardly fail to notice. Such big rehearsals would not have taken place if several months were left before the invasion was carried out. During Operation TIGER, involving a landing exercise in Devon on the south-west coast of England, German E-boats attacked, and sank several landing craft, 749 US soldiers being killed in the attack on 28 April 1944.

The air operations against Germany were widespread and heavy at that time. TATE was, in January 1944, asked to go to Cambridge and report on the build-up of bomber formations for raids. They discussed the matter with TATE, and concluded that it would be a good idea to send a message that he had made enquiries, but they showed that the mission would be extremely difficult to perform. It was impossible to determine from the activity at an air base if a large raid was underway. And it was extremely dangerous for anyone to be near air bases between the hours of 6.00 p.m. to 5.00 a.m. in the morning. The RAF often took over the telephone lines for operational reasons, so they were not available locally, and TATE had not been able to find a reliable colleague in the field. In addition, everything depended on TATE's ability to make nightly radio transmissions, which was impossible with the equipment he now had. In March the request was sent again:

The assembling of the bomber formations near Cambridge, by night English by day American, is of the very great[est] importance. Try by all means to carry out this job. Feign illness or other grounds to take a few weeks leave.[6]

TATE took this as the strongest instruction and order he had ever received from the other side. But he had not received any new batteries for his transmitter which was now running on mains electricity (which he had arranged as instructed by the Germans). He, therefore, needed to stay indoors for transmissions as his equipment was now much larger and more difficult to move. With the radio crystals available to him, the quality of his radio signals was still very poor at night. It was suggested, by the Germans, that he should pretend to be ill, but in that case he would have had to stay at the farm, and could not travel to Cambridge. The mission would only be possible to arrange with help from a collaborator, who was staying outside the air base, and who reported by telephone to TATE. It was not easy to find a reliable person and TATE would take a great risk with that kind of cooperation. He had no candidate, but he would search, or perhaps the Germans had a suitable man who could work as an observer? As for the American raids during daytime, the build-up of the formations was so extensive and widespread that they were hardly any great secret and it could last for an hour before all units were gathered for departure to Germany. The British had on their nightly raids no corresponding mass formation of their forces. Each individual bomber squadron flew over England to reach the right altitude, with a deadline to meet when, from a particular point at the British coast, they would leave for Germany. The Allies did not want an agent giving information about this, but there were so many activities with training exercises and flight testing of aircraft at the air bases that misunderstandings and errors could cause faulty reports of ongoing raids.⁷ The security around air bases against conventional agents like TATE was rigorous, but the electronic possibilities were like an open book. German interception revealed the increased radio traffic when radio equipment was tested, and aircraft made test flights during the day before a major bombing raid. Also, when the armada was on the way, it could easily be followed by radar and with the help of signals from the abundant radio equipment used by the bombers. The German night fighters now had radar, which helped them to locate the bombers, and were often helped by these radio signals streaming from the aircraft. It became clear how extensive the German's ability in the field of electronic intelligence was, when a Junkers Ju88 filled with electronic devices landed by mistake at Woodbridge on 13 July 1944.⁸

On 23 March there had been a story in the *Morning Post* with a picture of a missile, which was a part of British air defence. The Abwehr's Spanish section wanted to know what calibre it was; previously only the 7.62-cm calibre was known, but this looked bigger. On 13 April, therefore, TATE received orders to find out the correct calibre. The British interpreted this as evidence that TATE was still trusted by the Germans, and that they did not consider him a double agent. He had also received requests for reports on the air defence of London. It was therefore decided that TATE would make a round trip to London to find out the facts. He had to prepare a route that seemed logical with the available public transport, and a plan for his journey to London lasting a week was made. It was about places like Richmond Park, Wimbledon Common, Raynes Park, Kingston, Bushey Park, Blacksmith, Shooter's Hill, Woolwich Common, Chigwell, Enfield, Harrow, Willesden and Wormwood Scrubs. He was allowed to provide detailed information about all locations except the final three. It was important that he pointed out that the Bofors guns and the 3.7-inch anti-aircraft guns were mobile. The final report was:

Have visited a large number of A.A. sites in South, South-East, South-West, North-West and North-East London. Very tíring, as travelling by public transport now take a long time and is tedious. Of the total number of A.A. sites visited about 30 percent were rocket gun sites consisting of 64 guns arranged in a square. About 75 percent of the remainder were equipped with six 3.7 inch A.A. guns and the other 25 percent had from two to four 4.5 inch A.A. guns. Every site I saw had one Bofors gun in addition. Mixed crews were seen on nearly every site with a small percentage Home Guard. I have not seen any American A.A. sites. I think some of the 3.7 A.A. and Bofors guns must be mobile ...⁹

The overall objective of FORTITUDE SOUTH was to make the Germans believe that the landings in Normandy 6 June were just a diversion and the main invasion would come later in the Pas de Calais area, where the English Channel was at its narrowest. FORTITUDE SOUTH was fairly complex. Initially it was thought that the vast misinformation could be given via five channels:

1. Physical disinformation. To mislead the Germans about non-existent units through forged infrastructure and equipment, inflatable aircraft, and tanks and artillery built of wood.

2. Simulated radio traffic would reinforce the image of fictional military units.

3. To provide a public image of a highly competent staff linked to the fictitious military forces, like the FUSAG (First US Army Group). Above all, George Patton was involved. He was one of the best-known and experienced Allied commanders.

4. Controlled leaks of information through diplomatic channels in the neutral countries to the Germans.

5. The use of double agents in the Double-Cross system to send false information to the German intelligence.

General Patton, dressed in a tailored uniform, riding boots and polished helmet, had fallen rather out of favour after making some strange observations, and slapping two soldiers in hospitals in Sicily, who were probably suffering from post-traumatic stress symptoms. But they knew that he would be required in an operational role later on, when landings were completed.

Since the Germans had no practical means of aerial reconnaissance and had no real agents in Britain, the physical deception was soon considered quite irrelevant. The diplomatic leaks became too unreliable and this campaign was paused. So the misinformation that was having the greatest effect was the radio traffic from the fictitious military forces, and, above all, by the double agents' reports sent by radio and written communications or physical meetings (mainly in Lisbon). The examples of TATE's radio transmissions contained in this chapter were only a fraction of all the messages that flowed from double agents in the Double-Cross system. TATE was not even a main character in this campaign of disinformation. As an agent acting without a network of sub-agents, maybe the Germans regarded his opportunities of uncovering information as limited.

There were a few agents who would become the most important, namely GARBO (the Spaniard Juan Pujol, with a network of sub-agents. He was called *Arabel* or *Cato* by the Germans), BRUTUS (the Polish officer Roman Czerniawski, named *Hubert* by the Germans, liaison officer for the Poles at General Omar Bradley's staff) and TRICYCLE (the Serb Dusko Popov), and partly TREASURE (the Frenchwoman Lily Sergueiew, called *Tramp* by the Germans), who conducted a voluminous traffic. It was, of course, GARBO who had such an important status among the Germans, that his reports were crucial in making the Germans delay the deployment of all available forces, including an armoured division, against the bridgehead in Normandy, in anticipation of the 'real' invasion in the Pas de Calais.

An attempt was made by the Allies, as we shall see, to use TATE, but he did not seem to have been particularly highly regarded among the German military command. TATE's reports were, however, appreciated by the Abwehr, one of whose men considered that TATE's report might 'even decide the outcome of the war'.[10] The Abwehr, however, was a dying organisation now working for the *Sicherheitsdienst* (SD), and the German military seemed to have a different opinion. Few of TATE's messages were even included in the reports of the *Fremde Heere West* (Fhw), the army's intelligence service in Western Europe, with Colonel von Roenne as head.[11] Von Roenne's work was frustrating as there was not enough information to determine where and when the invasion would come, and his faith in the Abwehr was not great; they had accomplished too little. The Abwehr was abolished in February 1944, and their place was taken by *Sicherheitsdienst* under Schellenberg, but most of their personnel carried on as usual.

FORTITUDE NORTH was a diversion to make the Germans expect an invasion of Norway. A fictional British Fourth Army would be stationed in Scotland, and TATE had a small role in this operation. On 25 March 1944 he informed the Germans that the British ambassador to Sweden, Victor Mallet, was in London for consultations.[12] This was part of the plan GRAFFHAM, which was supposed to fool the Germans into believing that Sweden would be drawn into war. When Mallet returned to Stockholm, he began trying to get permission from Sweden to use airfields, and persuade the Swedish army to be prepared to take Trondheim in case of an Allied invasion of Norway. It also sought, through other double agents, to give the impression that Denmark was threatened. There were meetings between the former British air attaché in Sweden, Wing Commander Thornton, and the head of the Swedish Air Force, General Bengt Nordenskiold. The British wanted the right for all civilian aircraft to be able to land at Swedish airfields in order to avoid German fighters, and Allied reconnaissance flights over Sweden should also be allowed.[13] Discussions between experts in logistics, concerning the supply of goods to Sweden and Norway if the Germans pulled back would be addressed. Sweden should be willing to accept Norwegians at risk of German victimisation during an Allied invasion, but they would obviously not be able to cope with a mass influx.

Present at the meetings was a 'pro-German Chief of Police' who reported to Berlin. This was partly the writer Dennis Wheatley's creation (he was part of the staff which was involved in disinformation[14]), but according to German records, it was a leak from the British Embassy. In a speech that Mallet made after returning to Stockholm, he said that good relations with the Swedes would now be exposed to a test, and that it would halt shipments of ball bearings and iron ore. The use of Swedish air bases was also raised in the German report, but it said that only minor operations were planned in Scandinavia. Hitler was furious, but he was already obsessed with the strategic importance of Norway, and had already placed seventeen divisions there, with a quarter of a million men at the time of D-Day. Operations FORTITUDE NORTH and GRAFFHAM strengthened their grip, and Hitler's fears for Norway caused one further division to be placed there.[15]

Operation IRONSIDE was designed to deceive the Germans that a landing on the French coast in the Bay of Biscay was planned. Misinformation about the south of France was rather neglected and the area was not included in FORTITUDE SOUTH. Bordeaux would be taken by forces which sailed out from ports on the west coast of Britain. Subsequently, troops which sailed directly from the USA would come to support the operation. TATE gave reports built on information from MARY, who had just returned from Washington after having temporarily worked there for the US Navy. On 23 May:

Saw Mary for the first time for a long while. She was sent on a special mission to Washington. She says she worked on preparations for an independent expeditionary force which will leave U.S. for Europe. That is all I have found out so far.

Four days later:

Saw Mary. Found out that the before mentioned expeditionary force consists of six divisions. Its commander is General Friedenhall. The objective for this army, in Mary's opinion, is South France, but I do believe that Mary herself does not know much on this point.[16]

The fictional Mary worked as a secretary at invasion headquarters in Norfolk House. TATE could not resist asking:

Well, what do you think of Mary? Isn't she quite a gal?[17]

False reports were given by other agents concerning actions from the Mediterranean coast in southern France. There was a General

Fredendall,[18] who TATE wrongly named Friedenhall, and he used this misspelling consistently in all his reports. The General was in the USA, but the press was subjected to secrecy concerning him, and not allowed to mention him.[19]

The fictional farmer who had employed TATE in Radlett, had his farmer friend at Wye in Kent in south-east England, where TATE would work sometimes. TATE was, in April 1944, ordered to stay in the area and gather information about the coming invasion, which everyone now was expecting. There were restrictions on civilian travel, but TATE was needed for work on the farm, and therefore he had a special permit. On 25 May he sent:

> Farmer friend in Wye is being called upon to do practically full-time Home Guard duties as he is an officer ... Owing to this my boss has agreed to lend me to his friend to help him out.

To emphasise the safety aspect, he added:

> I am going to refuse to go unless I can get lodgings where I know I can take my transmitter.

Three days later came the news:

> Have found first-class lodging with elderly couple in Wye. So far as I can see, ideal for radio purposes perfect for radio broadcasting.[20]

On 1 June, he could report that he had moved in. He now moved his transmitter there (fictional of course) and they had to arrange that his Morse transmissions were linked to Kent by cable before they went out on air, in case the Germans took bearings of his signals.[21] Since he had demanding agricultural work to do, his ability to gather information would be limited. But the Germans evidently did not appreciate this, because on 31 May, he was ordered to investigate troop concentrations, movements and preparations in the areas around London, Southampton, Plymouth, Bristol and Oxford.[22]

The Germans had always shown great interest in fighter squadron bases in England. The British Second Tactical Air Force and US IX Tactical Air Command were designed to support the invasion and were located in Hampshire and Kent. This was not possible to hide, but it was as far from Normandy as from the Pas de Calais. However, it was felt that a big build-up in Hampshire, being due north of Normandy, could give the enemy an important clue as to where the invasion would be. Therefore, a large imaginary air exercise using sixty-six squadrons took place with an apparent focus on the Pas de Calais. This exercise was reported by TATE on 2 June, but also by BRUTUS and GARBO's sub-agent No. 7. All three revealed the fictitious target as the Pas de Calais. If the Germans had been alert, they would have suspected something was wrong. How could a farmhand, a Polish staff officer and a Welshman who lived in Dover have a clue about the objective of this exercise?[23] According to Farago, whose book was based on German sources, TATE gave daily reports of troop concentrations where there were few, of a general identified as 'Ashland' who existed only in the imagination, and sent an entirely fictional 'Order of Battle'. He described a visit to 'the restricted' Dover area, where he claimed to have seen 20,000 Canadians, and to Ashford, where he discovered the 83rd US Infantry Division, and to Folkestone, which he described as 'the city of the US headquarters', where he saw overcrowded trains with new arrivals from the United States. He went to Newmarket, Thetford, Cromer, and Norwich, where he identified division after division. He crossed into the 'restricted areas' (*Sperrgebiet*) without difficulty and had, of course, arranged all the documents needed to enter these restricted areas. His sources, he stated, were an Air Chief Marshal, a captain in the Royal Navy, and a highly placed RAF officer, who he identified as 'Spekeman'. No one in Germany seemed to question how TATE, an insignificant Dane, could gain the confidence of such prominent British professionals who would reveal the innermost secrets of OVERLORD to him. The source for this information is Farago's *The Game of the Foxes*, which was based on German sources whose reliability could be questioned. According to Kahn's book, which was also based on German sources, TATE reported on large groups of English, Canadian and American troops stationed in the forests of south-east Kent.[24]

From January 1944, GARBO had sent about 500, always long, reports from Madrid to Germany. On D-Day +3, i.e., 9 June, GARBO sent his main message, perhaps the most significant report of the entire period of the Double-Cross system. The lengthy report was sent in several parts, and was based on a fictitious conference he had held with all his sub-agents. GARBO pleaded that it should immediately be sent to the German High Command. The report contained a summary of what had been sent for months before, and was based on the concept of FORTITUDE. It said that there were seventy-five divisions in the UK. The landings in Normandy had been carried out by forces which had recently returned from the Mediterranean region, reinforced by Canadian and American troops. None of the FUSAG forces had participated as they were still in southern and south-eastern England. They consisted of two armies of six army corps, two attack divisions, five armoured divisions and twelve infantry divisions, units that the agents previously had reported on. There were over 100 landing craft gathered on the East Coast (they existed for 'real', as inflatable dummy craft). GARBO concluded that in his opinion the attack in Normandy was a large-scale diversion to establish a strong bridgehead, to entice the maximum of German reserve forces to the area, and keep them there, to enable the success of a second attack. He explained why the second attack would come in the Pas de Calais area. This was followed up by lengthy daily reports, which would substantiate the claim that the landings in Normandy were merely a diversion.[25]

When the invasion of Normandy began, several other double agents revealed that this came as a completely unexpected surprise. TATE signalled on 7 June that the date of the invasion had been completely unknown to him, because everything in his district seemed completely unchanged. No departures of troops had been observed, instead more and more were coming every day.[26] A fictitious acquaintance with a clerk at Ashford railway station enabled him to receive information concerning the fictitious FUSAG's movement to embarkation harbours, which he could then transmit to reinforce the fictional threat to the Pas de Calais). On 8 and 9 June he sent:

The Special Trains section of the Southern Railways (a railway company) has opened an advanced office at Ashford Junction. This section is part of the London East Division of the Southern Railway ... and all important troop movements are dealt with by this. A friendly clerk in the Ashford office billeted here tells me that the advance control office has been opened to cope with the increased troop movements in that area.[27]

And on 14 June:

Railway clerk friend has been very busy working out adjustments to timetables. Was able to see at his place a railway notice called 'Special Working Arrangements in Connection with Movements of Troops'. Unfortunately, no dates given. Dates also unknown to friend. On the cover, there were several instructions. The first part dealt with 23 trains to Tilbury from Tenterden on a date described as 'J minus 11'. Thirteen of them were for tracked vehicles and the rest were passenger trains, each with about 500 seats for men and 30 or so for officers. There were about six pages in all but had not much time to get much detail of the others. They covered a period from J minus five or six. The places of departure include Heathfield, Ashford, Elham. The destinations were mainly Gravesend, Tilbury and Dover. Every timetable carried a list of trains to carry tracked with vehicles ... One included eight to ten 'warflats', which I was told were for tanks or other big vehicles. There were only 12 trains in this timetable. There were frequent references to connections with the LMSR-line. On the last page of timetable, there was a list of hospital trains destined for Birmingham but no times for the movement was shown.[28]

But the Germans did not wake up. On 21 June, TATE received orders:

Do everything possible to investigate the troop formations which pass through your place or in the district. If there are no troops there try to get information on the concentration areas and reserve areas, either from your own travels or from third parties. Especially now such messages are of colossal importance.[29]

Nothing was, however, asked about his friend at the railway in Ashford. On 23 June, he was able to announce that a convoy of US Infantry 83rd Division crossed Wye in a westerly direction. One driver said that they came from Elham and that many had gone before him. After the invasion had started he continued to deliver reports:

28 July. At Cambridge station a train for troop transports, one with a U.S. division. The sign a circle with a white diagonal cross with red and blue light.

31 July. In Leicester troops from a U.S. Airborne Division. Their character is a white circle with blue light, this vertical flash in yellow.

31 July. Orders from Germany: Information concerning troops is more important than the flying bombs (TATE had at that time an important role regarding misinformation on the V1 which had now begun to plague London).[30]

6 August. I think it was 9th Airborne Division.

8 August. French army corps has arrived in England.[31]

27 August. Recent days large U.S. convoys have passed between Hatfield and Watford in the direction to the west. Division Brand black snake on a circular blue background. Saw other vehicles on the road in the same direction. He describes their mark, a complex subject with many triangles.

September 10. Saw a large British convoy on the road in a northerly direction through London on September 8.[32]

September 30. Question from Germany. Where are the anchoring sites for bases or aircraft carriers at the East Coast between the Thames and Scapa Flow? Can you find out where on the English and Scottish east coast invasion preparations are going on? Do they gather material for the invasion?[33]

5 October. Heard from a good source that an American corps is on their way from New York to Marseilles. It consists of an armoured division and two infantry divisions.

20 November. Have been in Spalding in Lincolnshire a few days. Saw a large British convoy passing through town toward Boston. They had the sign of the 5th

American Division. At the station were British troops with the yellow sign on a blue square cartridge.[34]

According to Kahn, TATE reported that he had seen the US 11th Infantry Division move east along the main road through Cambridge. At the railway station he saw the XXth Army Corps on their way west and the 25th Armoured Division moving south with tanks on railway wagons. He later saw the personnel from this unit in Norwich (these two units did not exist at all).[35] On 21 September 1944, he sent his 1,000th message:

> At a time like this, my 1,000th message, I ask you to submit my humble greetings to the Führer, and the hope of a speedy victory to fully end the war.[36]

In November 1944, they stopped using TATE in FORTITUDE and instead he was going to concentrate on the Navy and the war at sea. Unfortunately, he had not received as much attention from the Germans concerning the invasion as had been anticipated. Until April 1945, communications about the FORTITUDE imaginary armies continued to be sent to the Germans by other agents.[37] In early 1945, there were fears among Germans that a new landing was under way in northern Germany or Denmark. As part of this concern came questions to TATE on 31 January 1945: 'Can you travel in the areas around Bristol, Reading, Southampton and possibly also in the area of the Humber?'[38]

On 4 February 1945, a request came from SHAEF to use TATE for misinformation concerning the Western Front. In a message to the Germans it would appear that Major General Guingand, Chief of Staff of Field Marshal Montgomery, lay ill in a 'nursing home' in London, and that Montgomery had come over to visit him. TATE was the best possible source as GARBO could not make any radio transmission until several days later, and could not deliver the message in time. The Double-Cross leadership responded that the message certainly seemed innocent, but was potentially dangerous. They did not want to risk TATE's credibility, which must be preserved at all costs, because of the deception which the Admiralty was engaged in. It also added that the statement seemed a bit silly because the Germans would not have time to change the disposition of their forces if they were informed to expect an American attack instead of a British when Montgomery was away. But this disinformation was regarded as so important by SHAEF that they were prepared to go to higher authority to ensure that it was given to the Germans. Finally, under protest, Double-Cross gave in, but explained that only this message was going to be sent. Masterman pointed out that it showed that there were too few double agents and their numbers must be strengthened.[39]

In the last message to TATE on 2 May 1945 the Germans were grateful for reports of the mining of the entrance to the Kola Peninsula and, in addition, they answered a question from TATE about his suitcase with personal papers and valuables (including the 2,600 Reichmarks which he exchanged for his pounds brought from the Cameroons), which he left in Hamburg in 1940. He was told that they had given it to his sister in September 1944 after the destruction of all incriminating documents.[40] After more than four and a half years the double life was over for Wulf Schmidt, A3725, *Leonhard*, TATE, or Harry Williamson.

10

New Threats From the Sky

The British urban population had, during the Blitz of 1940–41, endured nearly daily bomb attacks by the Luftwaffe, which claimed the lives of countless victims. Since May 1941, however, these raids were becoming more sporadic, and the population experienced a relatively quiet life, while the cities recovered. During 1943 and in February 1944 the Luftwaffe had carried out a number of major attacks on British cities, but despite extensive damage these never reached the level achieved from September 1940 to May 1941. The D-Day landings in Normandy on 6 June 1944 had also given people greater security and hope for a rapid end to the war. Five long years of war, rationing, and suffering had been extremely exhausting, but in London and other major cities, people could feel relieved when the frontline had moved from the British cities.

All this changed during the night of 13 June 1944, when Londoners were woken by a strange sound from the sky. The sound was later described as a motorcycle without a silencer, or a worn-out steam engine struggling up a hill. Several civilians, who saw the monster that night, have said that they saw something they thought was a burning aircraft with a long trail of flame and smoke behind. At 4.25 a.m. the monster fell and hit the ground on Grove Street in Hackney, East London, with a huge explosion. Six people died in the blast, several houses were destroyed, and a railway bridge was seriously damaged, but what hit the site would remain unknown to the civilian population for a while. To the British Secret Service, it was clear that the first German *Vergeltungswaffe* (retaliation weapon) had reached Britain. For one year, British intelligence had conducted a war against these German retaliatory weapons, which the British had code named DIVER, but today is better known under the German name V1 or *Vergeltungswaffe* one. Among ordinary people they would be called 'Doodlebugs'.

The Royal Air Force had for a long time been engaged in an ongoing campaign of bombing the launch sites in northern France, and Allied aircraft had delayed the launching of the first V1 rocket by nearly six months. Two days later, on 15 June, the attacks by V1 rockets took off in earnest, and during the weekend of 17–18 June about sixty V1 rockets reached London daily. The population was now going to suffer a new threat, and it would not disappear until the final months of the war.

German Rocket Research

The development of rocket guns, which led to the V1, goes back to the early 1930s and the *Verein für Raumschiffahrt* (VfR), which consisted of amateur researchers interested in rockets. VfR had been founded in 1927, and among its members were people like Max Vali, Hermann Oberth, Willy Ley and Wernher von Braun whose research later contributed to the development of German rocket weapons.[1] In the early 1930s, the German Army, *Reichswehr*, showed a growing interest in the research conducted by VfR. Under the Versailles Treaty, Germany was prohibited from any development of offensive weapons, such as artillery and aircraft, but neither rockets nor gliders were specifically mentioned in the Treaty. The development could, therefore, focus on rockets. In 1930, the German armed forces financially supported rocket research in VfR, and the club was given permission to use the Army's land in Reinickendorf outside Berlin.[2] The armed forces were carrying out their own rocket research simultaneously, under the direction of Walter Dornberger at *Waffenamt Prüfwesen*, a division of the army's weapons department. Wernher von Braun was soon recruited to Dornberger's team of about ninety employees, and research was conducted until May 1937, at the Army training area at Kummersdorf, south of Berlin. Rocket research was then moved to the Army's new research area, *Heeresversuchsanstalt* Peenemünde (HVP), in northern Germany.

On the same site *Erprobungsstelle der Luftwaffe* was established in April 1938, i.e., an Air Force Research Area, which became Peenemünde-West, while the Army area was named Peenemünde-East. Rocket research was carried out in parallel by the Army and Air Force, and over the years a range of projects was developed by both, but completely separately. However, the A4 rocket of the Army and the 'flying bomb' Fi 103 of the Air Force were going to become best known as the V2 and the V1. While work on the A4 rocket was headed by Dornberger and von Braun, the foundation of Fi 103 had been developed primarily by Robert Saffron at the Fieseler Company, and Fritz Gosslau at the Argus Company. At the beginning of the war, however, the German armed forces had gone from victory to victory, and there was no need for missiles. Only when the first setbacks affected the armed forces were more resources allocated to rocket science. Test firings began in March 1942, and later that year successful launches were made in October with the V2 rocket, and in December with the V1 rocket. The success of the missiles indicated that mass production of the V1 and V2 should be expected in the near future, and in September 1942, Dornberger was given the task of coordinating the V1 and V2 programmes. Eventually, Himmler and the SS would take over the whole enterprise.

Operation CROSSBOW

Disturbing details of the German rocket research had already reached the UK in autumn 1939, this by an anonymous report, which shortly after the outbreak of war was posted to the British Embassy in Oslo. The so-called Oslo Report was met, however, with scepticism from MI6, who felt that the data described unrealistic dreams, and possibly could be a deliberate deception from the German armed forces. Only much later would it emerge that the author of the report was Hans Ferdinand Mayer, head of Siemens' research laboratory in Berlin, and more than familiar with the German development of new weapons systems. Mayer was an opponent of the Nazi regime, and had authored the report during a business trip in Scandinavia, a fact that did not emerge until Professor R. V. Jones, MI6's wartime scientific adviser, revealed Mayer's name in 1989.[3]

Dismissed as utopian, however, the Oslo Report was shelved in 1939, but was rediscovered in May 1942, when the British again had reason to investigate the allegation about German rocket research. The RAF carried out air reconnaissance over Peenemünde, but because of different opinions concerning interpretations of aerial photographs, no action was taken.

In the autumn of 1942, however, it became increasingly difficult for the Germans to keep things secret, when they expanded their activities in Peenemünde. This expansion led to the recruitment of workers from the whole of German-controlled Europe to the site, and leaks were inevitable. In the intelligence reports from Allied agents, Peenemünde was more frequently mentioned, and on 12 April 1943, Winston Churchill was informed of the matter. Despite an uncertain intelligence position, the same month Operation BODYLINE was initiated, which later, on 15 November, would get the code name CROSSBOW.[4] The aim of the operation was to prevent the development of German rocket weapons, which in the initial stages involved the British aerial photography unit, the Central Interpretation Unit (CIU) at the RAF base at Medmenham, which in June 1943 on four occasions conducted flights over Peenemünde. Analyses and interpretations of the photographs, however, gave no definite information, even though the outline of the later V1 rocket was visible on these.[5] However, the issue was raised on 29 June, at a meeting with the Defence Committee, the Operations Department of the Cabinet War Room, which took a decision to bomb Peenemünde. The order, number 176, was submitted on 9 July to Bomber Command under the code name Operation HYDRA. On the night of 17 August 1943, 596 heavy bombers, led by Group Captain John Searby of 83 Squadron, took off on a mission to attack Peenemünde. The attack was devastating for the Germans; at least 733 people, unfortunately mainly foreign workers but only a few scientists, died. Large parts of the plant were damaged, but several of the important production buildings survived unscathed. The main part of the bomb load fell a short distance south of the main target. At the same time Bomber Command paid a high price with forty bombers being lost. The result of the attack was a reorganisation of activity, with research continuing in Peenemünde while the production of rockets was moved underground into caves, such as Mittelwerk at Nordhausen in Tyringen.[6]

No follow-up of the bombing of Peenemünde was carried out for almost a year and instead the air attacks were directed at the launch sites, which the Germans had built in Western Europe. Of the more than 100 launch sites the Germans had established, 74 had been identified by November 1943, mostly as a result of intelligence from the French Resistance, which was subsequently confirmed by aerial reconnaissance. CROSSBOW operations against them began on 5 December 1943, and were given high priority during the following nine months. The primary attack target then changed to oil production. No attacks against V1 depots were implemented although, in February, eight such terminals had been identified but, because of their extensive protection by anti-aircraft artillery, attacks were considered too risky.[7] At the request of the British War Cabinet, Dwight Eisenhower on 19 April 1944 ordered that CROSSBOW attacks would take precedence over everything else, and at the end of that month all launch sites should have been neutralised. It was soon discovered, however, that the Germans, in the meantime, had built new 'modified' launch sites which were more difficult to identify.

The culmination of the war against the German rocket weapons came shortly after the Allied landings in Normandy in mid-1944. A Belgian agent reported on 10 June, that he had seen a train with thirty-three wagons rolling through Ghent, each wagon laden with three 'rockets'.[8] No verification of this information had been possible, because since 4 June no air reconnaissance was feasible due to bad weather. When it was resumed on 11 June, great activity, particularly at the new launch sites, was noticed. The result of this activity became obvious during the night of 12/13 June, when the first V1 rocket crashed into Grove Road in Hackney. A few days later, starting at 10.30 a.m. on 15 June, more than 200 V1 rockets were fired against Britain in one day. Of these, 144 reached the mainland, of which 73 reached the intended target, London. Eisenhower, therefore, on 16 June, reiterated his orders that CROSSBOW attacks would take precedence over everything else; only essential operations for the fighting in Normandy were exempt. During the weekend of 17–18 June, V1 rockets continued to reach London in greater numbers. In an attempt to reduce the threat of the V1, US aircraft bombed the development facilities at Peenemünde the same weekend. The result of the bombing was modest, despite the fact that 921 tons of bombs were dropped. There was little damage, and production had long since moved from the site.

AGENT REPORTS FROM LONDON

On 13 June, the day when the first V1 rocket reached London, interest in the BBC radio news was intense among the Germans involved in the rocket projects. Now they were waiting with bated breath for what would be reported. They were to be disappointed as the BBC only briefly mentioned 'Hitler's new weapons' as the last item of the news. The effect was described as 'insignificant', and was said to have resulted in 'few losses'. The news from the BBC was dismissed, quite correctly, as propaganda by the Germans. The British had deliberately toned down the reports of the incident. With this arose the question of how the Germans could evaluate the results of the V1 attacks. The British reports were, of course, not to be trusted, and the best outcome would be for the crash sites of the V1s to be verified on site by a credible and reliable source.[9]

It was not long before the Abwehr's agents in the country, in reality double agents for the British, received messages in which the Abwehr asked specifically for information regarding the V1 attacks. The agents would act as target observers and damage assessors, which would help the Germans to improve their accuracy. The Germans called on their agents to report the time and place of the V1 hits, which left MI5 facing a dilemma. If they, through their double agents, reported accurate information, it would be helpful for the Germans, while false information would threaten to expose double agents.[10] The V1 crash sites in and around London could be observed by German air reconnaissance, at least in theory. The fact that the Germans actually did not carry out any kind of air reconnaissance over London between January 1941 and September 1944 would emerge only after the war.[11]

The solution to the dilemma was that agents' reports would exaggerate the number of rockets which hit London's northern and western parts, while the number of rockets which hit south and east London were minimised in the same manner. Based on these manipulated reports the Germans should conclude that the V1 rockets flew too far, and therefore reduce the range, which they did. R. V. Jones proposed another method of deception which the agents then included in their reports: it was to indicate the correct time a V1 rocket arrived over London (which the Germans had control of), but to give the wrong landing site. Instead of the real crash site, often a little south of the central parts of London, they used the site of an earlier detonation in north London. This was sent to the Germans, who now changed their aim even further south of London.[12] The solution was politically sensitive, as it meant that bombs were guided to areas south of London, where different people would suffer. 'Who are we to act as God?' asked one of those who were opposed to the idea, the Labour politician Herbert Morrison. By this method it was estimated that 2,750 fewer people were killed and 8,000 fewer injured. This was obviously difficult to calculate exactly, but they would have been happy if they had achieved a tenth of these figures.[13] Eventually the invasion forces reached the headquarters of Colonel Max Wachtel (the German officer in charge of the V1 campaign), and found to their surprise that some V1s were fitted with radio transmitters, which enabled a precise plot of the crash site of each bomb. But a report was found, where it was stated that the Germans relied more on the information from their agents, and assumed that something was wrong with the method of estimating the impact point by radio signals.[14]

One of the double agents who was involved early on in the new German weapon and retaliatory countermeasures by the Operation CROSSBOW team was the Spaniard Juan Pujol, who the British called GARBO and the Germans *Arabel* or *Cato*. Pujol, in mid-December 1943, received a message from the Abwehr in which he was asked, for safety reasons, to move from London, because of the coming violent attacks.[15] That this statement referred to the new German retaliation weapon was beyond reasonable doubt, and throughout the spring of 1944, Pujol was involved in a radio game, in which the British tried to find out when the first V1 attack would be carried out. However, it was on 16 June that the Abwehr first asked him specifically about the V1 attacks. The Abwehr then wanted him to note dates and locations of the impact points using a map grid available to both Pujol and the Abwehr.[16] The Abwehr added, however:

> The forgoing is only intended for your guidance with the knowledge that it will be almost impossible for you to obtain those details ... your primary objective is not to endanger or take risks with the rest of the Service which continues to be of primordial importance.[17]

The uncertainty about how this request should be answered required that GARBO should try to delay the Germans until a plan had been prepared. On 18 June he sent a longer message in which he praised the new weapon and also sowed seeds of disinformation:

> ... I am proud that you have been able to prove the fantastic weapons, the creation by German geniuses. Although I have not personally seen the apparatus in flight, from what I have heard said it must be an object of marvel and when the present trials have finished, and when the scale on which it is used is increased, I am certain that you will manage to terrify this pusillanimous people who will never admit they are beaten. I am also proud that my services may be of use in obtaining this objective. Although I have not got the plan of London which you suggest, I shall send the Widow to buy one tomorrow ... The work will nevertheless be

difficult as according to rumours current in the Ministry of Information, the area is so extensive that it embraces a semicircle from Harwich to Portsmouth, circling London to the north and west. But nevertheless I repeat, we will do all in our power to assist in the work which my agents, like myself, will find pleasure in realising.[18]

In the message GARBO implied that the retaliation weapon was far more effective than British propaganda would admit, and also added that it was the north and west of London that was hit; therefore, the rockets had flown too far. Concrete information on crash sites was reported by Pujol for the first time on 22 June, when he sent a message about a couple of crash sites in the West End, which in all likelihood had already become known to the Germans via the foreign press.[19] Further reports were to be sent during the month, until 30 June, when GARBO received new instructions from the Abwehr; they urged him to fully concentrate on information about troop movements. Unfortunately, this request coincided with genuine major troop movements, and the Headquarters Allied Forces in Western Europe, SHAEF, had ordered a minimisation of the military intelligence which was to be sent to the Germans. In a clever plan, the Germans received reports in early July that Pujol had been arrested by the British police. After a week it was reported that he had been released, but he did not send any further reports concerning the V1.[20]

Since the British could not use GARBO for further deception on V1 attacks, three possible double agents remained: TREASURE, ZIGZAG and TATE. The first, TREASURE or Nathalie Sergueiew, which was her real name, had at that particular time lost confidence in the British, and her career as a double agent was interrupted abruptly (she was upset because her dog had died in British quarantine). In the case of TATE, almost all traces of his activity are missing. All communications concerning current V1 attacks from the time around the summer of 1944 have been destroyed, and in his file at the National Archives in Kew there is an unfortunately large gap.[21] By contrast, the activities carried out by ZIGZAG are documented. ZIGZAG, or Eddie Chapman, which was his real name, had been imprisoned on the German-occupied island of Jersey. Recruited as a German agent, he had in December 1942 parachuted into Britain, where he promptly surrendered to the police, and offered his services as a double agent. But in June 1944, Chapman was in Norway, where he was an instructor in a German training school for agents. However, it was with the mandate to report on the V1, that the Germans in the same month once again delivered him by parachute to Britain, where he immediately contacted his British handlers. From 1 July, Chapman sent a steady stream of rigged reports on the V1 and Guy Liddell, head of MI5's counter-espionage, noted in his diary that 'ZIGZAG has started his transmissions. Currently it is planned that he will be based in London and work with deception in connection with rockets.'[22]

The whole operation became impossible on 25 July, when the British tabloids began publishing maps which showed where the V1 rockets had struck.[23] The risk that the Germans would get hold of some of these maps was too big to allow the misinformation to continue. But at that time radar-controlled anti-aircraft batteries supplied by the United States had begun to shoot down V1 rockets in large numbers, while several other countermeasures were taking effect, including the use of high-speed fighter aircraft capable of matching the speed of the rockets.[24] V1 rockets would arrive in Britain right up until 29 March 1945, but the big V1 campaign culminated in the autumn of 1944. As the Allied forces advanced, the Germans began, from 18 August 1944, to dismantle their launching ramps in northern France. During the night of 30/31 August the last V1 rockets were fired from France, nine of which reached London.[25] The CROSSBOW attacks on the launch sites were ended on 3 September, and priority was instead given to German oil production targets.

WITHOUT WARNING

From 13 June 1944 to 29 March 1945, 9,521 V1 rockets were launched against Britain, of which 2,419 reached London. This resulted in at least 17,981 injured and 6,184 dead, but as the V1 rockets flew at a speed of 400 mph, and were clearly visible and could be heard, civilians were often warned before the impact. Repeated air-raid sirens also disrupted the work of the civilian population, who spent much time in the nearest shelter waiting for the 'all clear'. Indirectly, the V1 rockets caused disruption of production and work in general, in some ways more detrimental to the war effort than the actual civilian and material losses. It was not only Britain that was the target for the V1 rockets. Antwerp, which was a very important port for the allied forces, became the target for another 2,500 rockets, and 9,000 more were aimed at other targets on the Continent, such as Paris, Lille, Mons, Maastricht and Liege, but it has been estimated that only 25 per cent hit their target.

No such warning was given when in the evening of 8 September 1944, a violent explosion suddenly shook Staveley Road, Chiswick, in London. The result was three dead and twenty-two wounded, while eleven houses were demolished, and a further twenty-seven seriously damaged. What caused the explosion was known only to a few.[26] The first V2 rocket to land in Britain would not be announced by Winston Churchill until 10 November, after the Germans two days earlier had openly talked about their new V-weapon. Over the following months a total of 1,402 V2 rockets reached Britain, of which 1,358 reached London, forty-three Norwich and one Ipswich. In London the attacks led to at least 2,754 dead and 6,523 injured. As the rockets had a speed of 3,500 mph on impact, after reaching the altitude of fifty miles, and reached its target in less than three minutes, civilians were never forewarned (because of the speed it was actually impossible to see the rocket before impact), and most countermeasures used against the V1 were ineffective against the V2. Antwerp was also a target and 1,700 V2 rockets were aimed against Antwerp, of which, however, only 30 per cent hit the city.

As a countermeasure, CROSSBOW resumed attacks against the launch sites shortly after the first V2 attack. However, the V2 launch sites were mobile and almost impossible to pinpoint, and it was mostly the continuing V1 activity that was attacked. On 17 September, Dutch targets were bombed which were suspected of being bases for modified

Heinkel He111 bombers used for firing V1 rockets from the air. They also bombed several launch sites in the Netherlands, with mixed results. One of the targets was Haagse Bos outside The Hague, from where more than 100 V2 rockets were fired. On 3 March 1945, in a CROSSBOW attack against Haagse Bos, the bombs were dropped by mistake on residential Bezuidenhout, with 486 civilian casualties. The most effective measure against the V2 rockets was, in fact, the use of British double agents, in the same way as against the V1 rockets. Due to report to the Germans that the range of the V2 rockets was too long, the flight distance was shortened, with the result that the V2 rockets struck less populated areas. The agents who were present in this case were ZIGZAG and TATE, but ZIGZAG had now ended up out of favour with the British. After he had, on more than one occasion, discussed his role as a double agent with friends, ZIGZAG's career was ended, and the only agent left standing was TATE.[27] He would, however, in the autumn of 1944 share this task with a new double agent, with code name ROVER, a Polish naval officer, who was sent as an agent by the Germans to Britain in May 1944, but who immediately became a British double agent. A certain confirmation of TATE and ROVER's deception work came in February 1945, when MI5 reported to Churchill on their activities during the month of January. MI5 noted then that:

TATE and ROVER have been successfully supplying misleading information about the fall of V1 and V2, and there is some reason to believe that their messages are having an effect on the places where these missiles are falling.[28]

This conclusion was also revealed in a message TATE received from the Abwehr, on 22 February:

Very pleased with your message. As it is extremely important, please work on the following task at once. V2 messages, procedure as before. V1 messages: how many hits, observed or reported, in a given period of time, e.g. from the 25th to 12.00 hours to 27th 12.00 hours. Part of the town affected, extent of damages; how many V1 shot down by the opponents; extent of the defence. Fighters, types of A.A., balloon barrages. If possible the number, location and height of the balloons.[29]

The Abwehr's confidence and interest in TATE's reports on the V1 and V2 was also confirmed a month later on 21 March when he received this message:

Requests for the present all other observations take second place, and that first priority is given to the V1 and V2 matters.[30]

At this time, the German army was retreating and the rocket campaign against Britain was approaching its end. On 27 March, the last two V2 rockets hit the country and two days later the last V1 rocket. One more time V1 and V2 rockets were used against other targets in Europe, but success was lacking, and finally, on 2 May 1945, Operation CROSSBOW was suspended altogether.

As a V1 could be seen and heard, it was psychologically a more feared and threatening weapon. When it appeared, everyone waited with bated breath for the engine to cut out, and then for the explosion (the strange sound of the rocket was because it was powered by a pulse jet engine). The V2 rockets were neither seen nor heard; they were actually only noticed by the terrific explosion. There were no warning signs with psychological effects on the citizens of London. The V1 was cheap to produce, but the considerable resources needed for developing the V2 could probably have been used more effectively for other military purposes.

11

The Minefield that Never Existed

The messages that TATE had sent to the German intelligence service had, until 1944, mostly concerned military, industrial, and civil affairs in Great Britain. The initial task entrusted to him had been to report on airfields, air defences, the effects of German bombing, evacuation of civilians, and the general mood in the Army[1] from the area between London, Cambridge, and Birmingham.[2] Likewise, his friend SUMMER was given the task of reporting on the same issues, from the area between Birmingham, Oxford, and Northampton.[3] The two German agents had thus been assigned different areas which would give the Germans a comprehensive picture of the situation in the country. A number of other agents had been assigned to other tasks, and among these was TRICYCLE, who arrived in Britain in December 1940 and, among other things, intended to infiltrate the circle of people around Sir John Tovey, Commander of the Home Fleet. On the initiative of Rear Admiral John Godfrey, director of the British marine intelligence, and with the help of Lieutenant Commander Ewen Montagu, his representative in the XX committee, TRICYCLE was for a long time to be Britain's main double agent for marine deception operations against the Germans.[4] In August 1941, when TRICYCLE left Britain and went to the United States, that role was taken over by his sub-agent BALLOON (Dickie Metcalf), who, as a fictitious businessman with connections in military circles, could provide the Germans with intelligence on ships and new weapons of the Royal Navy.[5]

Some marine intelligence information would be sent by TATE, in particular in connection with his fictional friendship with MARY, who was claimed not only to work for the British Admiralty, but also for the United States Naval Mission. On 18 November 1941, TATE mentioned MARY to the Germans for the first time, and indicated that she worked for the 'cipher department of one of the major departments' (actually the Admiralty[6]). A number of communications with marine intelligence followed, in which he stated that the information came from officers in the Navy he had met. However, it was only after TATE, on 19 April 1942, announced that MARY had been transferred to the US mission in Britain, that the Germans seriously began to show interest in her. Three days after TATE's message, there was a direct call for him to infiltrate the circle of friends around her, which was later followed on 28 July by a call to make more use of her and her contacts. The Germans thus showed a keen interest in TATE's liaison with the fictional MARY, and the XX Committee was not slow to exploit the situation. In response to the Germans' second request TATE stated, on 31 July, that he had been to a 'party with Mary and met an American Naval Officer'.[7] On this basis, a plan was developed in the late summer and autumn of 1942, known as the Carter-Paterson Plan.

The Carter-Paterson Plan

The idea of further developing TATE's fictional relationship with MARY during the autumn of 1942 was twofold: firstly, to try to create new ways for the British to supply the Germans with false documents, and secondly, to convince the Germans that a minefield off the Faroe Islands consisted of more mines than were really there. The first objective was a request from MI5 Division B1(a), who felt that this was of great value for the Double-Cross committee, while the other, concerning the minefield, was a request from the Admiralty Operational Department.[8]

In the developed plan, TATE, who was considered appropriate for this deception, should inform the Germans that he had been visited by a British Naval officer, who stayed overnight. The Naval officer had just returned from Scotland, where he participated in an operation in which the fleet had planted mines, and at TATE's home he had kept an unlocked bag in TATE's living room during the night. According to this concocted scenario, TATE searched the bag, and found a chart and notes, which he assumed were for a report. The note that TATE read stated:

Sailed 31.10.2230. Started laying 1400/1/11. Finished laying 1530/1/11. Home and dry 0830/2/11. Line A SOUTHERN PRINCE 550 mines MENESTHEUS 420 mines. Depth 10 feet. Line B PORT QUEBEC 520 mines AGAMEMNON 520 mines. Depth 90 feet. Eight prematures and five married failures in Line A. Two prematures and seven married failures in Line B. Laid in company.[9]

The title of the notes would be 'Operation 3D', and the chart would show an area which TATE suspected was the Faroe Islands, marked with two lines, 'Line A' and 'Line B'. To meet the first objective of this intelligence game, trying to create new ways for the British to send false information to the Germans, TATE would say that he had made a copy of the chart, and that he wanted to send it to them.[10] After a discussion between Ronnie Reed and Lieutenant Commander Ewen Montagu, the operation was approved on 8 December 1942, and after that the first message was sent. TATE ended his message with: 'There is no doubt that this map would be of great value to you. How can I send it to you?'[11]

An answer to his question was, however, not given at once. On the evening of 8 December instead, a greeting was included: 'Congratulations and greetings from Hilda, parents, brothers and sisters and all Phönizier.' TATE's birthday was the day before, and the fact that the Germans remembered and recognised this was, according to Reed, a good sign as it showed that they still believed he was a free agent. Had they suspected that he was controlled by the British authorities, they would never have sent such a message.[12] Not until 18 December did the Germans answer TATE's query about how he could send the chart to them, but the response was not what they had wished for, because the idea of sending it was rejected. The Germans wrote:

> Sending of the parchment copy wastes too much time. Forwarding by radio is of utmost value. First. Buy at J.D. Potter, or E. Stanford Ltd, or Siston Praed & Co. Ltd Admiralty charts numbers 117 and 245. Compare tracing with these charts. If it fits forward number of chart. Second. Try to insert the lines A and B in the charts which fits. Communicate geographic beginning and ending points of the line.[13]

The reply gave the British two options: either to accept that the Germans probably had no effective channel for receiving documents or, alternatively, to force them to create such a channel. If they accepted that the Germans could not accept the chart, but instead were forced to send the information by radio, another two options were possible: that TATE managed to get the charts, and then send the information the Germans demanded, or that TATE informed the Germans that such charts could only be procured after he had first applied for permission from the British authorities, which he considered to be too risky. The British security services were well aware that there was a German agent who was able to pass on the chart, the double agent GARBO, but involving him could also be very inconvenient and risky, for both the British and the Germans.[14]

The following morning a rather serious attempt was made by TATE to acquire those charts. Together with Reed, TATE visited the firm of Ryman at 43 Whitehall, which only had an ordinary map of East Kent. After having specified that he wanted an Admiralty chart, the clerk suggested that he should go to Stanfords[15] on 15–16 Longacre, which was one of the places the Germans had proposed. Stanfords, however, could not give him the Admiralty chart as they too only stocked an ordinary map of East Kent, but if he submitted an application, they could order the correct chart, if the request was approved by the authorities. Obtaining it would be impossible for TATE as he would have to file an application and state the reason why it was needed. The authorities would almost certainly have denied him a permit and that was also what he transmitted to the Germans. He reported that to seek permission to acquire the chart would be too great a risk, and would surely be unsuccessful.[16] Whether the Germans accepted the false information on the false minefield in the Faroe Islands is unconfirmed, but with TATE's statement that he was unable to secure charts, the plan died without achieving the objective of forcing them to open a new channel for delivery of documents. In the autumn of 1944 a similar operation would begin, but this time with confirmed results.

TATE's Irish Minefield

The German U-boat force would, during the second half of the war, suffer setbacks which increasingly limited their operational capabilities. In July 1943, while the Royal Navy's cipher, which the Germans had for a long time been able to decrypt, was replaced by a new secure one, the German Enigma ciphers continued to be broken one by one by the Allies. The exception was the 'black' period between February and November 1942 when the German Navy had added a fourth rotor to their Enigma machines. With this intelligence advantage, the Allies launched a strategic war of extermination against the supply and maintenance U-boats in the Atlantic. These had made possible the range of the U-boats' hunting operations against the Allied convoys. During a short time in summer and late summer of 1943, seven of the eight supply U-boats (or 'milk cows'[17]) which the Germans had in operational service were sunk. This was a tactical strike but also a risk as the Allies feared that the German navy might have realised that their cipher communications had been broken.

This concern was fortunately not justified as the German navy did not replace their ciphers. Instead the Germans had increasing hopes for new technology for their U-boat force. New, more advanced torpedoes and U-boat types were developed, and to meet the threat from enemy aircraft, U-boats were equipped with more effective anti-aircraft defences. Also important were the countermeasures against new Allied technology, including 'Aphrodite' and 'Thets', which consisted of continuous aluminum strips as a decoy for Allied radar. This countermeasure misled the Allies, who, in the belief that they had found a German U-boat, sent out flights against fictitious targets. They also developed 'Bold' and 'Pillenwerfer', which produced a cloud of air bubbles to confuse Allied sonar devices (Asdic). Most important for the German U-boat force was the development of the U-boat schnorkel which was a Dutch invention refined by the Germans and gave U-boats the ability to stay underwater for longer periods, and to use the diesel engines while submerged. The speed submerged was moderate compared with the speed achieved on the surface but with a schnorkel a U-boat could get enough air for its powerful diesel engines while submerged, and recharge their batteries without the need to be on the surface with all the attendant dangers of being spotted by aircraft.

All these technological advances were features of a revolutionary U-boat which Germany produced from the autumn of 1944. Perhaps this development could have affected the war, if it had been possible to use it much earlier. The previous U-boat models, VII and IX, had in reality been ships which could submerge. The new, so-called Electro Boat models XXI and XXIII could travel at high speed under water, did not have to surface for weeks, and could carry out attacks totally submerged. Although the first Electro-Boats were launched more than six months before the capitulation in 1945, very few entered operational service, and they never had time to carry out more extensive missions. However, the older models would still continue to be a threat to the Allies, even after the landing in France on 6 June 1944.

Despite several setbacks for the German U-boat force, and although the Germans in 1944 lost their very important bases in France, a number of U-boats operated against Allied targets in the Atlantic and around Britain even after the summer of 1944. During and after the invasion in June, and up to 30 August, a number of U-boats operated in the English Channel, and sank or damaged thirty-four Allied ships. Following the loss of the important French U-boat bases, they were in September transferred to Norway, where they were based as three squadrons, and continued to operate. To carry out missions from Norway gave the Germans new headaches, especially when the ships which supplied the bases with maintenance equipment from Germany were constantly attacked by Allied aircraft. Furthermore, it took twenty-eight days each way for a U-boat to reach the English Channel from Norway, which considerably shortened their operating time. Constant attacks by Allied aircraft and ships made the trips very slow. Journeys to and from the Channel were made submerged for twenty hours a day, thanks to schnorkel technology. This was exhausting for the crews, and the speed submerged was only one third of the speed on the surface.[18] That German U-boats continued to sink Allied ships off the British coast was obviously disturbing, but it was also a serious threat. Although the Allies had landed in France and victory was in sight, the forces were still dependent on vital war supplies which were carried from the USA by ships of the Atlantic convoys to Britain, and any loss of this materiel could have a direct impact on the units that fought against the Germans.

It was to obstruct and prevent possible attacks on convoys which sailed to Britain by a route to the south of Ireland, that TATE again in autumn 1944 was involved in marine issues. The Allies met the U-boat threat at the time by laying minefields which were deep enough for convoys to sail above them, while they caused problems for the U-boats. In total, the British Navy laid 10,043 Mk XVII mines in 1944–45, usually as contact mines or proximity mines (with sensors which activated the mine when a U-boat was passing close to it), and these minefields caused the loss of at least three German U-boats.[19] Lack of both mines and suitable ships prevented a more substantial minefield system. In TATE's reports to the Abwehr, the same fictitious Navy officer who figured in the Carter-Paterson Plan was mentioned in November 1944. This time the Navy officer talked about extensive minefields around Britain, using a new type of mine, which was laid out in small groups near the seabed. TATE reported that they were positioned outside officially mined areas, and in otherwise mine-safe sea lanes, but especially concentrated in the area around Fastnet Rock, a small rock island four miles from the coast of south-west Ireland.[20]

The reporting continued in the spring of 1945, and the final report about existing minefields was sent four days before the German capitulation, when TATE reported that the same type of mine was now laid in the English Channel and north of Norway.

That TATE's reporting produced results is reflected not least in the German U-boat force's war diaries of the time. On 17 November 1944 there was a reference for the first time to one of TATE's reports, concerning a type VIIC submarine *U-1006* with *Oberleutnant* Voigt as commander, which on 16 October was sunk south-east of the Faroe Islands by depth charges from a Canadian frigate. The U-boat's fate was unknown to the German U-boat force, but on 15 November, TATE reported that he had talked to a crewman of a British combat ship who said that the U-boat sank in a minefield south of Ireland. TATE had in the same report indicated that forty-four survivors from the U-boat were taken as prisoners of war, and that this new type of minefield against U-boats had been placed both south and north of Ireland.[21] The only thing that was true in the report, was that forty-four crew members survived the sinking, and had been taken as prisoners of war, otherwise he misled the Germans about where and how the U-boat had been destroyed.

The impact of that report was confirmed the next day, when *U-991* and *U-1202*, operating in the area, were ordered to stay out of the 'minefield' area which TATE had reported.[22] More false reports of minefields continued to be sent to the Germans, and on 24 November the German U-boat force once again referred to TATE's reports. He had sent his message about the new type of mine laid close to the seabed, and U-boat Headquarters quoted TATE's report, which stated that the minelayers *Plover* and *Apollo* in September had laid 2,000 mines north of Ireland. In later reports he also mentioned similar minefields created south of Ireland. However, the U-Boat force had on 24 November recorded:

The report is doubtful since there is no evidence that the agent is still credible. He has already spent three years in England. He is also suspected of working for the enemy.[23]

The same doubt appeared when the U-boat force, one month later on 29 December, reported that *U-1006* was probably sunk by depth charges off the Faroe Islands, something that totally contradicted TATE's report.[24] In spite of this, a warning in the U-boat force's war diary was recorded two days later, which cited a report from TATE on 28 December. This time TATE specified a minefield covering an area fifty-five kilometres south-east of Fastnet Rock in Southern Ireland.[25]

The Misdirection is Confirmed

Although information about the imaginary minefield had reached the German U-boat forces, it was not until after 1 January 1945, that the Allies learned that the deception had succeeded. That day the Allies intercepted a warning of a minefield, decrypted by ULTRA, and sent to all German U-boats:

> An agent reports a deep-set minefield southeast of Fastnet Rock Ireland. Size not known. Avoid this area. Channel boats would do best to haul off to southward.[26]

This confirmed, therefore, that the Abwehr still relied on TATE's reports.[27] The British Government Code and Cipher School, better known as Bletchley Park or Station X, was working at the time with a staff of 9,000 people, and German messages sent using the Enigma cipher were usually decrypted in one or two days. In September 1944, they read daily about 2,200 Enigma messages from the German Navy.[28] During the last five months of the war, further German messages were decrypted with references to TATE's minefield. On 9 January yet another message to the U-boats was intercepted, with a correction of the position of the minefield:

> Correction to standing war orders: According to agent's report, a deep-set minefield is said to have been laid out 30 miles southeast of Fastnet Rock, Ireland (R). Further information concerning extent etc, not at hand.[29]

The Abwehr in Hamburg had previously asked TATE for more details, but this correction was sent out before he even had time to answer. The U-boat force, a few days later on 14 January, forwarded another report from TATE about a new minefield in the North Channel between Britain and Ireland.[30] TATE's data this time had a direct impact on four German U-boats which operated in the area. *U-1009*, which was north of Ireland and on its way to the Irish Sea, was ordered not to cross the North Channel, but instead continue in a south-westerly direction. At the same time *U-285*, *U-1055*, and *U-1172*, positioned in the Irish Sea, received orders to return to their home base, the 11th Flotilla in Bergen, rather than follow previous orders to go to Ireland's southern tip.[31] The next day, *U-1009* was ordered to patrol off Inishtrahull island, later to proceed to the Irish Sea,[32] but the U-boat would never pass through the North Channel; after sixty days at sea, *U-1009* arrived in Trondheim on 8 February. The cause of that submarine's new orders was unknown, but clearly shows a degree of uncertainty in the U-boat force's current reports about minefields.

On 8 February, yet another message was sent out to the U-boats, referring to TATE's fictitious minefield south of Ireland, with the information that this minefield was probably closer to the coast, with the addition of 'if ever there are mines there'.

Correction to standing war order 481 section D
1. If possible pass southwestern corner of Ireland at periscope depth at high water or at greatest possible depth. As pencil note made in section D of the above order about mine report southeast of Fastnet rock probably is closer to the coast.
2. Observations of a boat in this area about sinking noises similar to falling, non-exploding depth charges may be connected with agent's report.
3. If there at all mines are presumed to be in 30-50 metres. Effectiveness of shallow mines in seaway and current conditions there is regarded as slight.[33]

However, it is not certain that the U-boat force had doubts about TATE's reporting; it may well have been a matter of some uncertainty concerning the location of the minefield. All possible doubts concerning

TATE would eventually be dismissed when a German U-boat was sunk by a mine near TATE's false minefields.

A U-BOAT IS SUNK

The fact that a German U-boat actually would be sunk in the area reported as mined by TATE was not something the Allies had expected. When this happened in March 1945, all possible German doubts about TATE must have disappeared. Commanded by *Oberleutnant zur See* Klaus Becker, and with a crew of forty-eight, *U-260* had on 18 February left Horten in Oslo Fiord, for a mission in the North Atlantic, around Britain and then south of Ireland. The *U-260* never had any major success during the war with only one British ship being sunk by it in December 1942, nor during this mission would the U-boat sink any ship. However, at 10.30 p.m. on 12 March, *U-260* managed to end up in a British minefield which was just outside the area identified by TATE as being mined. The minefield, called CF-2 (A), had been laid by the minelayer HMS *Apollo*, which TATE had mentioned in his reports, and consisted of 156 Mark XVII mines laid at 200 feet. This type of mine, one of the most common British contact mines during the war, damaged the U-boat and, after surfacing, a message reporting the incident was sent from the U-boat. However, the damage was so serious that the U-boat could not possibly return to base, and the only option for the Captain was to scuttle the U-boat. The crew reached shore in inflatable boats at Galley Head on the Irish coast, where they were interned. Following the message sent by *U-260*, the German U-boat headquarters next day sent out a warning to all its U-boats:

(officer cipher)

A boat reports being mined in naval grid square AM 8883 at depth 'A'. Hereby confirmation of agent's report concerning suspected mining southeast of Ireland. From now on:

1. Avoid the area inside grid squares AM 8849, 8839, BF 1315, 1249.[34] If boat gets into this area proceed at shallower depth than 20 metres.

2. Passage to the Irish Sea:

A. either close (as far as navigational practicably) under the southcoast, by night or at shallower depth than 20 metres.

B. or: hauling off south off the area mentioned in para 1.

3. Pass the old declared minefield area as in standing order 481 or 451 (St George's Channel) as previously ordered, on northern route or likewise close under the coast.

Additional: the war orders referred to are to be corrected accordingly.[35]

The result of this order was that the German U-boat operational capacity was restricted, and that the Allies in practice had a major U-boat-free area for the convoys on the last part of their voyage to Britain. Despite this, the German U-boats carried out 113 patrols in British waters from 1 January to 31 April 1945,[36] but with heavy losses of fifty-six U-boats sunk. During this period the U-boats sank sixty-three ships totalling 284,000 tons,[37] a poor result compared with the German U-boats' 'golden era' at the beginning of the war, when, for example, the U-boat ace Otto Kretschmer, as an individual commander of *U-13* and *U-99*, nearly reached the same sunk tonnage (forty-four ships sunk with a tonnage of 262,203) before 1941, until he was captured and interned in Canada.

How many ships and lives TATE's deception saved is incalculable. It is only possible to conclude that Allied ships were able to enter a U-boat-free area south of Ireland on their way to and from Britain. By the time this was the case, however, only a few months of the war were left. When the war ended, German U-boats were ordered to cancel all operations against Allied shipping. Most U-boats returned to bases in Germany and Norway; 174 U-boats surrendered and 222 were sunk or otherwise destroyed by their commanders.[38] The U-boat campaign had claimed the life of 31,000 sailors and in the process 28,000 U-boat crew had perished.

12

After the War

How could we summarise Harry Williamson, TATE's, work during the war? He arrived with the intention of serving his German masters well but, partly because of his friend Gösta Caroli's testimony, soon turned into a double agent. After the war, Harry/TATE commented upon why he had switched his allegiance:

> Nobody ever asked me why I changed my mind, but the reason was really very straightforward. It was simply a matter of survival. Self-preservation must be the strongest instinct in man.[1]

TATE reached the peak of his career early in the war, in 1941 and 1942. He was the main agent for the Germans in terms of reporting the effects of the Blitz and gave important disinformation concerning defences against a coming invasion. He helped extract large amounts of money paid out by the Abwehr, and gave important disinformation about shipping, during the critical years of the success of Dönitz's U-boats. That he used radio transmissions was a major advantage as this resulted in rapid communication, compared with letters written in invisible ink, or personal meetings with the Abwehr in neutral countries like Portugal. On some occasions, he was in fact the only agent who had a working radio communicating with the Germans. Furthermore, his work resulted in the arrest of other Abwehr agents. After his modest contribution to Operation TORCH, it seemed as though his star faded. Between March and September in 1943, only fourteen messages were sent to him by the Germans. MI5 actually considered at several meetings ending his career, but they were ordered to keep him going.

TATE was a loner and he never (in consultation with his steering group) built up any large organisation with sub-agents, as for example GARBO and BRUTUS did, who therefore became the most important double agents for the implementation of Operation FORTITUDE, as well as TRICYCLE, before he had to end his career some months before D-Day. TATE had a modest role in this deception, although he had almost exclusive access to a radio. But a single agent could not collect large amounts of information from different parts of the country. The reports from the farm in Wye during spring 1944 were, however, characterised by an Abwehr agent as being able to 'even decide the outcome of the war'.[2] TATE had an important role in the disinformation about the V1 and V2 campaign. Then in 1945, he carried out what was considered to be one of his most important deceptions of the war. This was the notional minefield, a deception which had a decisive effect on the important convoy traffic in the final stages of the war. TATE was the double agent who worked for the longest period during the war, from September 1940 to May 1945, and – according to Masterman in his book *The Double-Cross System* – was to end up being regarded as a 'pearl among agents' by the Germans.[3] He had probably received this information from the interrogation of the unfortunate Karel Richter.[4]

It was very difficult for MI5 to assess how TATE was evaluated by the Germans, unlike some other double agents. He was mostly transmitting to Wohldorf in Hamburg, and all reports on him were sent by cable within Germany out of reach of the British. Perhaps the Germans suspected him of being a double agent, but there is evidence that contradicts this, for example, the evaluation made by the Abwehr committee under General Maurer, when TATE delivered message No. 1,000 in September 1944.

Ladislas Farago – who seems to have simply collected numerous documents from the Abwehr – probably had a good insight into how TATE's character and personality appeared in his radio traffic with the Germans, characterised in his 1971 book *The Game of the Foxes*:

Salty no-nonsense messages of nothing but hard facts when reporting intelligence, mixed with topical biographical notes from time to time, occasional chitchat, and angry reproaches abounding in the German version of the four-letter word (Scheisse being one of TATE's favourite expletives) when the Abwehr was not reciprocating his efficiency in kind, was tardy in meeting his demands for money, or was giving him inane tasks.

Businesslike: 'Personal observation: new balloons between Newport and Cardiff, and at Peterborough to protect Whitehead Torpedo Factory making Diesels for submarines'.

Petulant: 'You never let me know what you think of my work. An occasional pat on the back would be welcome. After all I am only human.'

Indignant: (when he was once asked to radio to the Abwehr the quality and price of loaf of bread and how it tasted) 'Don't you have anything more serious to ask? It tastes allright.'

Furious: 'What is delaying the man with the promised·money? I am beginning to think you are full of shit.'[5]

The content of his messages was first approved by the Steering Group and his superior authorities, but he was himself involved in the drafting of the text. It was very important to have a consistent style in his reporting. TAR Robertson said in a newspaper article long after the war that Harry was not always easy to handle as a double agent. Several times he refused to send a message and he always read everything before he agreed to their often unique, pungent style.

During the war, Wulf Schmidt, now named Harry Williamson, lived in Round Bush in the Watford area, north-west of London. It is possible that he was involved in the interpretation of photographs taken by aerial reconnaissance aircraft over Germany and occupied countries.[6] He later worked, from the summer of 1943, for the firm 'Greville's Photography' on Queens Road in Watford, and was also a freelance photographer for the newspaper *West Herts Post*.[7] According to colleagues, he was a skilled and accurate photographer. He was even offered the job of travelling to the Western Front in 1944 as a photo journalist, which of course was hardly realistic.[8]

TATE was never formally arrested, but there was a standing order under the Treachery Act 18b, in case it should be needed. He did have papers which showed that he was a British citizen.[9] In May 1945, the Double-Cross committee had a meeting regarding the future of TATE.[10] If they gave him full British citizenship, they might have better control of him; his experiences during the secret war were, of course, utterly sensitive. But on the other hand, they could, if he remained a Danish citizen and was registered in the name of Wulf Schmidt, threaten him with deportation if he revealed any delicate and secret information. The committee understood that he was really eager to visit Denmark, but it was probably best if he stayed on in Britain for a few years as there was a substantial risk that courts in Denmark would investigate his work for the Nazis before the war.[11] After all, he had been a member of the NSDAP-N party, and had taken part in Nazi demonstrations in his home town. Also, in 1940 he had not declined when he knew that his employer for the job he was offered in Hamburg was the Abwehr, and he had even been on missions for them in Denmark. These facts could hardly be denied, and could be considered as a distinctly negative factor after the war in Denmark, in spite of his later efforts for the Allies.[12] Wulf, however, had stated during his interrogation by the British, that he was not particularly pro-German. Because of his travels abroad, he felt almost like a man without a homeland, but it had been impossible to get a job and the Germans generously promised employment in the colonies after the war.[13] The date he finally received his British citizenship in the name of Harry Williamson is not clear, but in July 1945 it was discovered that he was registered to vote in the forthcoming election (which Churchill lost). Since Harry was still under a cloud of secrecy, it was necessary to discourage this.[14]

Harry had met Irene 'René' Esther Mytton, born in 1921, from Letchmore Heath near Watford, and married her in 1946 at Watford

Registry Office. She had lost her mother, like Harry, when she was a child. After the marriage, they lived at 55 Leggatt Wood Avenue in North Watford, where Harry remained for the rest of his life.[15] They soon had a daughter, who was named Helena. Dr Dearden at Camp 020 had considered him to be homosexual, so the marriage may have been a surprise for MI5. The daughter, Helena, argued that it was almost an arranged marriage. Harry had been ordered to marry, and had met his future wife at a local dance event. They were engaged at the end of the war but it turned out to be an unhappy marriage. She was originally engaged to another man, and had plans of opening a hairdresser's which were never realised. His wife was also obliged to keep silent about Harry's activities during the war, under the Official Secrets Act which prevented citizens from exposing sensitive secrets. She thus came to live a restricted life, not even being able to make friends unless they were approved by those at MI5 who still controlled Harry, and she almost immediately broke off contact with her family. Harry was a perfectionist, demanding a household in perfect order, and he was not always satisfied.[16]

He had now started working full time as a photographer for the newspaper the *Watford Observer*, where he eventually became chief staff photographer,[17] and also as a freelancer for the much larger *Daily Mirror*.[18] John Wheatly remembers that Harry's pride and joy was his Speed Graphic 5x4 plate camera. He met Harry when he was taking photos of a play performed by Boy Scouts. John was interested in photography, and used to spend Saturday mornings with Harry in his darkroom, where he watched 'The Master' at work, and was taught the art of copying. Harry later photographed John's wedding when he was married in 1954.[19]

His job meant photo assignments for the papers, and Harry was often away from home for longer periods. The relationship became more and more miserable, and suddenly one day his wife took their daughter Helena and left the house and Harry for ever. But the habit of taking care of the household was still there, and before she left the house she made up the beds and took out clean clothes for Harry. The divorce was finalised in 1952 and they never saw each other again, his ex-wife dying at the age of fifty-two in 1974. Harry later wrote in his autobiographical letter to his cousin Gisella Alloni that the marriage had been a mistake.[20]

His daughter never had any close contact with her father while growing up, and experienced a reserved relationship with him, marked by total obedience and often critical judgements from him. She remembers visiting TAR Robertson at Roundbush House in Radlett, where she was asked to be quiet and behave well. It was not until she was a teenager that she resumed contact with her father and she asked Harry why he had never made contact with her. But Harry said that if she was worth something, he knew that she would come to him one day. His daughter continued to have an unhappy relationship with him. The first time they met, at a café in Windsor, he said that 'he would tell about himself; he was one of the most famous spies during the war and he was still engaged in this. If she told anyone anything at all, she would get in trouble.' Only after this did they start to talk about family and other everyday subjects.[21] Now that she had met him again, she soon became the same obedient girl as when she was small. When she visited him she had to wait on him, and he often wrote lists of errands she should perform. Every day at 6.00 p.m. he would solve the crossword in the newspaper, and interference was forbidden. He often ate at a Chinese restaurant at the end of Leggatt Wood Avenue, or used their take-away service. He did not have a close relationship with his neighbours, but was friendly, and could, for example, lend them a ladder if needed.[22] Harry did not drink, and said he had not appreciated the time he was given whisky in Camp 020 by Dr Dearden in 1940 – he insisted that they had tried to get him drunk. However, he was a heavy smoker with nicotine-stained yellow fingers on his left hand, as he was left-handed. Harry liked to live alone, apart from contact with his male acquaintances. Family life had never meant anything to him and he felt no need for it. He was a rather egocentric person and a perfectionist, who would not tolerate negligence or weaknesses in others.

Harry never really liked England. His daughter said that he had never even learned to pronounce the 'W' at the beginning of his last name correctly, and in his first years after the war sometimes spelled nouns with capitals, as in German or Danish. He was extremely vigilant and afraid that people from his past life, or others in his present life, would contact him. In the house in Watford, there were several safety devices, and he had a special phone number which he could call anytime, day or night, if he should feel threatened. There were cameras and microphones in every room including the bedrooms and toilets. He had equipment in a cabinet, which his daughter was forbidden to open, but she did it anyhow when he was not at home. The cupboard was full of surveillance cameras, radio equipment and listening devices. He was very reluctant to let strangers into his house.[23] In his biographical letter to Gisella, he concluded with: 'I have already revealed too much, and although I am safe in England, you never know ...'[24] Harry did have some friends, including members of the police force, visit his home in Watford. Sometimes some of them even lived in the house[25] and one of them was, according to his daughter, asked to keep an eye on Harry.

A colleague said that Harry was an interesting man, but very quiet about his background. One time, he had accompanied him on a holiday to Denmark, where they met some of Harry's relatives, who were financially well off and significant members of the community. He was very surprised when everyone called him something else other than Harry. During the trip, Harry had problems with abdominal pain. He knew that Harry had had his appendix removed under local anaesthetic when he was in Argentina. According to his daughter, who saw the scar after his death, he also had surgery for a peptic ulcer.

Harry hesitated for a long time before he returned to Hamburg after the war; it took a full ten years. There he met his brother Kai, a Luftwaffe veteran, and his sister Hildegard in Bremen. Kai lived in East Germany while Gertrud, his other sister, had moved with her husband to Bogotá in Colombia after the war. According to Harry's daughter, the move to Bogotá was almost an escape from Germany, but why this was necessary is still not clear. She would spend most of her life there inside the house, tormented with fear that something from her past life would catch up with her.[26] At last Harry received his two Iron Crosses from his brother Kai, and the suitcase kept in Hamburg since his departure to England in 1940. It had been delivered to his sister in September 1944, after sensitive documents had been removed.[27] It is doubtful if his 2,600 old Reichsmarks were worth anything as the Reichsmark had been replaced by the Deutsche Mark in 1948. She did not stay long,[28] and he did not reveal the truth about what he really had been doing during the war. Harry came to make several trips to Germany, sometimes with his daughter as company, but he was always worried during every visit, despite his British passport. The fear that the past would take its revenge remained. Some of the trips were for family gatherings, as when his stepmother, Tante Mieze, celebrated her sixtieth or seventieth birthdays. Helena was then also invited, but was not able to go.

After retiring as a photographer from the *Watford Observer*, he worked as an interpreter and export manager for WEMCO, an electronics company in Watford on Whippendale Road, which produced electric switchgear. Harry also took photographs of their products. In addition to his salary, he also received the British state pension, and could have applied for a German pension as well, but it is uncertain whether he did. He lived, however, a spartan existence, but one thing he was extremely careful with was his personal appearance, and he was always well dressed with a smart haircut. The house had the austere original furniture and carpets which remained from the day he moved in.[29] According to one of his friends from WEMCO, Harry was a reclusive person, choosing to stay indoors after work, and any visits to the grocery shop were made late at night. He was most comfortable being indoors at home, rolling his cigarettes and drinking tea, with every window heavily draped. On rare occasions he wosuld ride on the back of his friend's motorcycle to visit places such as the London Zoo, but always after dark, and always wearing his crash helmet, scarf and goggles. They often talked into the early hours, and Harry taught him how to listen to music and pick out each instrument. Harry took great pleasure in photography, and once showed a photo of a military rally, where he had inserted a picture of a high-ranking officer which he had cut with a razor blade from a different photo. He re-photographed the doctored picture, and it was impossible to detect the deception.[30]

His great passion was canaries – he was one of the leading breeders of canaries in the country – and he was also a judge in exhibitions around the country[31] and, according to his friend at WEMCO, even published a book on canary breeding,[32] which we, however, have not managed to find. Harry built an aviary connected to one of the windows of the house, but he finally stopped breeding canaries when he had an outbreak of psittacosis, a very contagious disease in birds, and had to have all his birds destroyed. Billiards[33] and football[34] were other interests, and he could remember various past football results. It has been said that he worked as an official for the local football club but his daughter Helena has no recollection of any interest in football and Harry did not like to be in large crowds. But he, at least, went to matches with a relative in the early 1950s.[35] Music was a great interest and he had a record collection of classical music and a rather old Philips gramophone which looked like a small suitcase. He later acquired a stereo system. His favourite composer was Brahms but he did not like opera, romantic or Russian music. In his childhood, he was, like all members of the family, supposed to learn to play an instrument. His father decided on the violin, which Wulf hated. He did not achieve any success with this instrument but, when older, he played a concertina, a small accordion.[36] He was a keen writer of letters to his family, and he had most contact with his cousin Gisella Alloni. He also wrote frequent letters to his sister Gertrud, until she died in Bogotá in Colombia in May 1986. Three months before that his brother Kai had died in East Berlin, shortly before the wall was taken down.

ON THE TRACK OF AGENT 3725

In the early 1960s, Günter Peis, a German journalist, managed to track down the mysterious Agent 3725, whose fate no one seemed to know very much about. Peis managed to find more evidence, from the radio operator Richard Wein (probably Brandt), and the owner of the Hotel

Phoenix, Mr Harbeck, which led him to Denmark. There he found Wulf
Schmidt's uncle George Bruhn. Thus he gradually came to the conclusion
that Harry Williamson in Watford was the man he was looking for. Peis
was given the assignment by his newspaper to write about Agent 3725,
and he finally managed to get Williamson to agree to a meeting at his
house in Watford. The first impression of the house when he entered was
that a bachelor was living there with little comfort in his surroundings,
and Harry gave the impression of a recently divorced man. He was
extremely reluctant to say anything, or acknowledge who he really was.
But when Peis mentioned the pilot Gartenfeld to Harry, he asked what
Captain Gartenfeld did nowadays. Peis had not said anything about a
captain. Eventually, Harry Williamson began to talk, but only about tiny
fragments of his life. He showed certificates, signed by Hitler, relating
to his Iron Cross. He also had a black leather notebook in which he
said everything was written down, but written in a secret code. Several
times Williamson reminded Peis about how little he really knew, and
that Harry certainly would not reveal much. He had met with both the
King and Churchill, and his house had been bought with money from
the Third Reich, which Canaris had sent him as an agent. Sometime
during the war he had four policemen living with him in the house.
Harry Williamson felt that he simply did not have the right to reveal
any secrets. He was forbidden to talk about his past, because he would
risk disclosing the identities of his friends, who were still attached to
official British security services, and thus endanger them. He was forced
into silence by the Official Secrets Act. He said: 'Forget that you ever
met me and what I have told you! Tell your boss at the newspaper that
you never managed to trace me.'[37] Before they parted, Williamson said
that he no longer had anything to lose in life, and that with a telephone
call he had the ability to stop further prying about his past at any time,
via London or Bonn. Cryptically he added that 'there was still much at
stake, particularly in the case of the Russians'.[38] If someone threatened
to reveal Harry Williamson, he just had to pick up the phone to MI5
in Gower Street.[39] The German newspaper later tried to bribe him with
a six-digit sum to make him talk, and even move to Germany. But the

answer from Harry Williamson was: 'Keep your money and leave me in peace.'[40]

His granddaughter saw the book, which he kept on the table next to his bed and kept an eye on, even during the last days of his life,[41] and his daughter Helena was also well aware of this mysterious notebook, which she was able to read soon after his death.[42] It was filled with extremely detailed notes about everything that happened after he landed in England, and in the back there were code names of all contacts and agents, with details of where they lived. He kept the book in a safe place and watched it closely. When he died, Helena received orders from above to take it from his hospital room to the house on Leggatt Wood Avenue. What happened to it after that is unclear. A friend had taught him how to use a computer, and for several years he wrote biographical notes, which he saved on floppy disks, as the large diskettes were then called. Harry possibly hoped to publish his story one day, something that was probably inconceivable because of the sensitive information it contained. These diskettes disappeared after his death. MI5 took his Iron Crosses, but he possibly eventually got them back. He was very proud of these awards, which he might have kept in a cabinet, with medals he had won for his canaries. One Iron Cross is possibly on display at the Imperial War Museum, but the other has disappeared. He won many awards for his canaries, and his granddaughters were sometimes given these prizes as presents (the pretty rosettes, for example). Once when he was away for a while, an elderly neighbour offered to feed them in his absence. Unfortunately, she passed away during this time, and his canaries sadly died. He kept, in an old shoebox, his old identity documents, photos and passports, and a half set of gold-plated dinner cutlery from his parents (his brother Kai had the other half of the set); these also disappeared. His daughter Helena was not included in his will.[43]

Towards the end of the 1960s, a British journalist, Patrick Brangwyn, also began investigating the mysterious story of Harry Williamson's background and started looking in newspaper archives. As Williamson had been an official of the local football club it should have been easy to find sources. But in the two articles he found on Harry Williamson (from November 1947 and September 1948), two photos were carefully cut out with only two square holes left. Later, Brangwyn's apartment was burgled and, though nothing was stolen, his collection of background material for his work as a journalist had been examined, and muddled up. He took the hint, and stopped his investigation into the life of Harry Williamson.[44]

Later on, according to Peis, another journalist, Len Adams, was also on the trail of Williamson. He found him in 1971 in the Scottish Highlands and started a conversation with him, but Williamson declined to say anything. He admitted that he had a sensational story to tell but definitely could not reveal it as it would affect too many people in high positions; what he had done had saved millions of lives.[45] Mr Peis's book *The Mirror of Deception*, which describes the life of TATE, was published in 1976 though his name was never revealed in full. There are many mistakes and errors in the book; it is indicated, for example, that Schmidt and Caroli jumped by parachute together, and landed near Salisbury. However, the author had in all likelihood no access to MI5's files which, through the Freedom of Information Act, were opened to the public only in the 1990s.

Harry's name was first revealed in the *Sunday Express* by Barry Penrose in the 1990s. This was because Harry Williamson was an active protester against the Poll Tax introduced by Margaret Thatcher. There was violent opposition which partly contributed to her fall. Harry was one of 'The Poll Tax Four', which led the opposition against this tax. Harry was upset as this tax was not income or wealth based, but in many ways penalised those who tried to save and support themselves. He was cited in a newspaper saying that the 'Poll Tax punishes those who have 'been thrifty".[46] His concern for his well-protected secret identity was thus in vain. According to his daughter, there were several articles during that time, with titles containing phrases like 'Nazi Spy' and 'Hitler's Pearl', but that these articles had been removed from the newspaper archives on orders from above, and that journalists were stopped from writing more about it.[47]

His old case officer, TAR Robertson, announced that there was no longer any demand from the authorities that he must keep silent, according to the Official Secrets Act. The first thing Harry Williamson then did was to ask MI5 to give him back his Iron Crosses, which was refused, at least for the time being. This led an angry Harry Williamson to reveal his story.[48]

The well-known author and expert on intelligence Nigel West wrote a chapter about him in his 1991 book *Seven Spies who Changed the World*, which was based on Harry's own story. Harry Williamson now knew that he was suffering from cancer, and perhaps he feared that the end of his life was near, which could have been the reason why he decided to tell the truth. Nigel West met Harry several times in the course of preparing the book, and his impression of Harry Williamson was that he was a man with a somewhat dry humour, easy to get along with and very careful. He gave the impression of being relieved and delighted to finally unburden himself, and with an open heart to reveal his past. He was full of anecdotes, and seemed pleased to be able to talk at last about his experiences during the war, even negative ones, like the stay at Camp 020, where he had felt humiliated. Harry Williamson's biggest concern about the book was that his relatives would now know all his secrets,[49] and Harry was annoyed with some errors in the book due to the risk of censorship.[50] Events would prove that Harry was correct in his fear of the reactions of his relatives.

The revelations came as a complete surprise to his relatives, many of whom believed that Wulf had been a German agent during the war. Harry's second granddaughter, born in 1980 (the first was born in 1977), came to have a good relationship with her grandfather and really loved him very much. She tried later, after his death, to find out more about the family. There is a family book, *Familien Aufzeichnungen*,[51] a sort of family tree, where the whole family is carefully recorded with all the details from 1662 onwards, which his granddaughter now owns. Harry was involved in researching the American branch of the family which was sometimes frustrating work, because he did not find all the information he needed – they were rather uninterested in this. It was his sister Hildegard who had taken on the responsibility of keeping this book up to date after 1910, and before she died in January 1977 she gave it to Helena, who in turn gave it to her daughter, who had taken a particular interest. Soon Harry's granddaughter would discover that the attitude of many in the family had changed. Harry, or Wulf Schmidt, as he was known among his relatives, was not a popular topic in parts of the family. In fact several relatives, who had previously been friendly and who had close relationships with her grandfather, refused to meet or speak with her again when she mentioned his name.[52] The granddaughter was making her enquiries after Nigel West's book had been published (she has a copy of it, filled with marginal notes by Harry), and that is probably the reason why many in the family had turned against Wulf after his revelations. It was rather strange that his relatives, so long after the war, still saw Wulf's deception as a betrayal. One would think that their sympathy should have changed over time, given all the awful revelations which had shown what really went on during the war in Germany.

There also seems to be little knowledge of Harry's life after the war in German circles. The 1958 book *They Spied on England*, written by Charles Wighton and Günter Peis, was based on the diary of General Lahousen. He had been the head of Abwehr section II, which mainly dealt with sabotage. This is how Schmidt, i.e., TATE was described:

> ... Schmidt was one of the most reliable and trusted German spies in Britain. He was used only on special missions, and listened at agreed times to receive orders. He transmitted only when necessary and as seldom as possible ... all through the earliest parts of the Blitz Schmidt, at great danger for his own life, was in the heart of the bombed areas ... and made reports by his radio ... in a response to special inquiries from the German High Command, Schmidt reported concentrations of Canadian troops around the Southampton area just before the Dieppe raid in 1942 ... in the spring and early summer of 1944, he ... made long reports on the preparations for D-Day on 6 June 1944. Day by day he moved about the restricted coastal area of southern England ... In the months after the landing ... Schmidt sent long and accurate messages about the American divisions

he discovered concentrated in south-western England ... he also sent important information about the V-1 and V-2 rockets ... Schmidt sent his last signal at the beginning of April 1945 as Field Marshal Montgomery's 21st Army Gruop closed in on the Hamburg radio centre.[53]

Nikolaus Ritter wrote in his 1972 autobiography, *Dr. Rantzau*:

Hansen (i.e., TATE) was advised by his English girlfriend to give himself up to the British authorities, when his position in England had become increasingly difficult and we could not help him any more. He was incarcerated for [a] relatively short time, and the British Intelligence Service maintained a long relationship with us, using his name, so in the belief that we took his message as the absolute truth. She waited for him when he was released and he married her. Today, he is well and lives with his wife and children in England.[54]

Mainz is the twinned town of Watford and Harry Williamson was sent there in 1959 as an envoy for Watford as an English guest of honour. As a gift he handed over two records of Beethoven's Ninth Symphony to the Mayor. No one had the slightest idea who Harry Williamson really was.[55] According to his daughter, he received several similar official missions, although he was actually apprehensive about the attention and the photos.

In an article in *After the Battle* in 1991 (No. 74), concerning Latchmere House and Camp 020, there are several photographs of Williamson along with Nigel West, and in Willingham where he visited the field where he had landed fifty-one years before. Also TAR Robertson and the radio operator Russell Lee joined the reunion, which then ended with a nostalgic dinner.[56]

Two years before his death (in 1990) he was taken ill with cancer of the larynx and six months later also with lung cancer. Smoking is a major risk factor for both forms of cancer, and Harry was a heavy smoker. In the summer of 1992, he had a major brain haemorrhage, but Harry managed with help, and minor alterations to the interior, to stay in the house after that. But then he had a second stroke and was admitted to Watford General Hospital. According to his daughter Helena, she was asked by MI5 (who were still keeping a watchful eye over Harry) to move into the house until further notice. But Harry resolutely forbade this and, even when he was told that MI5 was involved, he resisted. According to Helena, Harry had contact with Alan Gilling of MI5 during the last part of his life. Harry was a difficult and demanding patient, perhaps affected by his severe illness, and he was moved to a single room during his last days. He became increasingly ill and his daughter was urgently called again. She rushed to the hospital by car, often exceeding the speed limits. Harry had had another major stroke and Helena sat there during the night until he died at 8.04 a.m. on the morning of Monday 19 October 1992, almost eighty-one years old. Obituaries were written in several major newspapers.[57, 58] In his will he had indicated his desire to be cremated and to have the ashes scattered, and there should be no headstone or memorial.[59]

Wulf Schmidt, Agent 3725, TATE, Harry Williamson, had reached the end of a very unusual and exciting life, full of drama, which had left deep scars. With his work for the Allies, he saved many lives and helped to remove a perverted evil regime.

Appendix I

Interrogation of Gösta Caroli, 7 September 1940

Gösta Caroli was interrogated at Camp 020 on 7 September 1940 (the day after he had landed), when he revealed that Wulf Schmidt, *Leonhard*, was coming as the next agent. After a promise that his friend Wulf's life would be spared, he started to talk. The interrogator was mainly Lieutenant Colonel 'Tin-eye' Stephens (KV 2/61):

Q: First of all I think we should have a description of your friend – what is his full name?
A: Wulf Schmidt.
Q: When is he due to arrive? He will use that name?
A: He will give that name. He is due to arrive any day.
Q: Do you know where he is due to land?
A: North of London.
Q: How far?
A: I don't know exactly.
Q: All you know is that he'll be landed north of London?
A: Yes. And he is coming by London to Northampton in that direction.
Q: Between London and Northampton?
A: Yes.

Q: And he will come by air and be dropped by parachute and he will have the same apparatus as yourself?

A: Yes, not quite the same.

Q: What is the difference?

A: One box and in that box is only a sender but then he has a small outfit on his breast where it doesn't break to pieces when he is landing, he can put that into the other one and receive also.

Q: So that he has got a receiver as well?

A: Yes, but the receiver is different.

Q: So he has two pieces of apparatus, the receiver and the sender?

A: Yes.

Q: And do you know what the apparatus he carries look like? Is it a black box or black leather case?

A: No, a brown leather case.

Q: And he has only two pieces of apparatus?

A: Yes, but the second is only like in air cushions – the small one – that you can blow up.

Q: The small one is packed in air cushions?

A: Yes.

Q: That is the sender, is it?

A: No, that is the receiver.

Q: And the sender?

A: The sender is in the large brown container.

Q: Has your friend been in England before?

A: No.

Q: Does he speak English?

A: He has been in the colonies.

Q: Which colony was he in?

A: The Cameroons.

Q: In the Cameroons. Do you know the time which he came?

A: Yes, he came in January or February from the Cameroons.

Q: And you have known him since January?

A: No, only since July. We made this course together.

Q: In case we do not find him when he comes down, where would he go?

A: I don't know. He don't himself, he's got to stay in the country out there.

Q: He would not move very far?

A: No, he is supposed to be between London and Northampton.

Q: Well, you were going to contact him, weren't you?

A: Yes.

Q: How?

A: In Northampton on the 20th.

Q: You were going to reach him in Northampton on the 20th. Where?

A: Yes, outside the Black Boy.

Q: What time?

A: Every hour from noon.

Q: Now describe him to us.

A: He is small, about 165, light hair, sharp nose and face – er, narrow face – clean shaven, and one of the teeth is coming out a bit farther than the other one.

Q: How many more were you going to meet at the Black Boy?

A: Nobody else.

Q: Just you two?

A: Yes – we made it up privately.

Q: And if you don't turn up?

A: He will know something is wrong.

Q: You think he will be there, do you?

A: Yes, if he can.

Q: Supposing he is late, do you go on day by day?

A: No, the 20th, and then 10 days later.

Q: 10 days later, the 30th, that's a private arrangement?

A: Yes.

Q: And then?

A: Every month the same, if we don't meet.

Q: Look, that's on the 20th and on the 30th.

A: The next 10th. We only made up three times – if we don't meet after three times we ...

Q: That's the 20th, the 30th and the 10th?

A: Yes.

Q: Every hour until when?

A: Until 6 o'clock in the evening.

Q: Were you to dress in any particular way or show any particular signs?

A: No, nothing at all.

Q: Do you know the frequency of his set?

A: No, I don't.

Q: What is he going to pose as, you say he doesn't know England at all, is he just going to wander about?

A: Yes, and if he is getting caught he has a Danish passport.

Q: Under what name?

A: The same name, he was born in Aabenraa in the German part of Denmark.

Q: But he is a German subject?

A: Yes.

Q: Have you any idea when he is coming?

A: No, it was said when the weather is good – he was at first meant to come before me.

Q: So he may be coming any day now?

A: Yes.

Q: How many people were landing at the same time as you were?

A: I was alone.

Q: You were alone – what about this friend of yours? I thought he took the course at the same time?

A: No – he was first of all supposed to come before me – there was room for only one to land from the plane.

Q: That isn't the question the gentleman wanted to know – he wanted to know who learnt with you.

A: Yes there was that friend of mine.

Q: Just the two of you?

A: Yes.

Q: Did you have any practice with parachute before?

A: No.

Q: It was unpleasant wasn't it?

A: Yes (laughter).

Q: About this friend of yours, if you think they were rather foolish in sending you here, that the risks were very considerable, they're much greater in this case aren't they – you know your way about a bit and he doesn't know his way at all?

A: No.

Q: What is he supposed to be – is he supposed to be a refugee or something?

A: Yes a refugee from Denmark.

Q: What about his identity card? He'd have to have an identity card as well as a passport.

A: Well he's got one the same as I in Hamburg.

Q: And the identity card is exactly the same as his passport – same name, made out as though he had been here since the beginning of the war.

A: Yes, no not since the war – he has come from Denmark in a fishing boat in wartime.

Q: You had an identity card didn't you? A civilian identity card? That was to make it look as though you'd been here since the war?

A: Yes.

Q: He hasn't been here at all, has he? – was he to have the same thing?

A: He still has a passport and when the war is over he will claim his thing from Denmark after.

Q: Well what about that has he got one?

A: No.

Q: The point is –

A: I understand exactly – it was the same for me. I didn't have any Alien's book. I did want an identity card to help me.

Q: Didn't they understand that. Do you gather they didn't understand that or they hadn't got the things to give you?

A: They didn't have the things to give me.

Q: So you had to take a chance on that – lost your book etc. And the same applies to him?

A: Yes.

Q: And these addresses in Birmingham that you asked about, you weren't to go to them?

A: No.

Q: Did you understand the road signs had all been removed and he wouldn't find his way about in the country?

A: Yes, but by good maps, it is possible.

Q: Even the best of maps, you didn't have a map did you?

A: Yes.

Q: But you did know there were no road signs, didn't you?

A: Yes I knew that – but I thought if it only was that question I could always find out – if you go into a pub you can always hear where you are and from there make your way.

Q: But he wouldn't be in such a good position, would he?

A: No.

Q: Does he speak better English than you?

A: Yes, but Colonial.

Q: So that he would excite less questions than you would?

A: Yes.

Q: Was he in South Africa as well in the Cameroons?

A: Only in Cameroons. I am absolutely not certain if he is coming or not because he tries to back out and he is nervous but I think he will come.

Q: How old is your friend?

A: About 20, I don't know, about 30 I think. 29 or 31 I am not quite certain.

Q: Any idea how he will be dressed?

A: Yes, I have seen his clothes, brown, nearly khaki sports jacket and grey trousers.

Q: Grey flannel trousers?

A: Yes.

Q: And the sports jackets, is it tweed or –

A: No, it looks like khaki.

Q: But what kind of cloth?

A: Smooth.

Q: Do you know the colour of his boots?

A: Yes, they're brown.

Q: Does he wear boots or shoes?

A: Shoes.

Q: Has he a hat?

A: Yes.

Q: What colour is that hat?

A: Bluish.

Q: Is it a felt hat?

A: Yes, a felt hat.

Q: Does he wear a collar and tie?

A: Yes.

Q: Do you remember, a white collar?

A: No it was slightly blue.

Q: What colour tie?

A: I don't remember.

Q: Did he wear spectacles?

A: No. He has got spectacles when he is reading.

Q: Would he bring those with him?

A: I suppose so.

Q: And he's clean shaven isn't he?

A: Yes.

Q: And the only prominent feature is the one tooth protruding out?

A: Yes. He's lost the gold stopping.

Q: Was he going to use the same cipher?

A: No, er, the same kind but it was a different key.

Q: Would the method of sending be the same? Would he use the same procedure?

A: Yes.

Q: The only difference would be the key?

A: His key is 'L'.

Q: It is actually the same as this but you set it differently?

A: No, it is not, because it is not written the same as here.

Q: So he has a different machine?

A: Yes.

A final interrogation on 9 September:

Q: There are one or two more things I would like to ask you. This friend of yours, do you remember the date you saw him last?

A: Yes, it was in Brussels on the 5th. He was out on the Airfield when I left.

Q: Who is called Wilhelm?

A: I don't know at all. I never heard about him before here.

Q: You are quite sure *Leonhard* was in Brussels on the 5th?

A: Well, if there are not two *Leonhards*.

Q: Your friend, the number of his cipher?

A: No. 2.

Q: His letter was 'L'?

A: Yes.

Q: What was the frequency of his set?

A: I don't know. It was a fixed frequency. I never noticed it.

In a summary of the interrogations from 9 September, one can also read that they trained together in Hamburg for six weeks, and that the expected dangers made them forge strong personal bonds – the planned meeting at the Black Boy was a private enterprise arrangement. Caroli thought that if Wulf had arrived in England first he would have revealed the same things as he himself had done. But there was no pre-arranged deal that they were going to try to negotiate with the British authorities. The two never discussed the possibility of failure, only success.

Wulf brought a spade for hiding his parachute, and probably also the radio equipment. Caroli never saw the map Wulf had been given, and did not know in which sector he was going to work. After landing, he would travel by bus or train, in any possible way. He had to use his own initiative concerning washing, shaving, and changes of clothes. Wulf was going to investigate the same areas of interest that Caroli had been given orders to investigate. Caroli now had the opinion that everything had been badly organised. He did not know what frequencies Wulf was going to use on his radio, but gave further descriptions of Wulf Schmidt – he was swift-footed, with brown eyes, a black spot on one tooth, the hair was parted on the right side, he spoke good German and Danish, he was very scrupulous with his clothes, always dressed in fashion, smoked Gold Flake cigarettes, took a drink sometimes, and did not look particularly German – he could be just anybody.

Appendix II

The Cipher

The German agents who communicated with Germany via radio during 1940 used a simple substitution cipher and all agents were equipped with a cipher disk. The principle was the same for everyone, but the order of the letters in the inner rotatable disc varied.

Enciphering began with the agent putting a letter on the internal disc directly opposite the current date. For TATE the letter was 'L' (as in *Leonhard*, his German code name). In the photograph of TATE's cipher disc we see that 'L' is opposite the 9 as if it were the 9th today. There are only numbers up to 26 – from the 27th onwards, 10 was subtracted, i.e., on the 29th they put the code-letter against 19. After that, they could begin to encipher with letters of the inner disc being replaced with the corresponding letters of the outer solid disc. The message was sent in groups of five letters in Morse. An 'X' was included between sentences. The sentence 'I will go to London need more money', or IWILL GOTOL ONDON NEEDM OREMO NEY, would in enciphered form be: XRXBB CKGKB KINKI IHHLF KVHFK IHO. Also numbers were enciphered, but with XX surrounding the cipher, 95 would for example be XLIX.

All messages began with a call sign of three letters. For TATE that was the 1st, 3rd and 5th letter of the second outermost ring, clockwise starting with the day's date. On the 9th this would thus be BDF. The

217

Germans responded with letters 2, 4 and 6, i.e., CEG. This was TATE's call sign the next day, on the 10th.

The messages began with the date, time, number of the telegram (three-digit, the first was 001) and how many characters the message would contain. International abbreviations, such as the Q code, were used, for example, QRM = disturbance, AR = end of message, 73 = best greetings (National Archives KV 2/61).

Appendix III

TATE's Reports Between October 1940 and July 1944

From his first message in the middle of October 1940 until July 1944 TATE sent at least 1,091 intelligence reports to his German employers, based on the reports that are kept at the National Archives in Washington today. This material is not complete as transmissions sent from August 1944 to May 1945 are missing. In spite of this, the material gives a comprehensive view of TATE's reports, the frequency of them, and what they contained. During autumn 1940 there is an increase in the number of reports, and TATE was most active during 1941, 1942 and the first months of 1943. Most reports were sent in August 1941, but the number does not give the whole picture. Of the fifty-seven reports sent in August 1941 forty-eight were weather reports, and only eight contained messages about British airfields and one about a building project outside Cambridge. TATE did not receive many questions from the Abwehr, but his own transmissions were frequent.

It is more revealing to study what TATE reported about during his years as a double agent. If we omit the reports sent during the last three months of 1940, the reports about airfields and other Air Force matters are numerous during 1941. TATE, in 1941, sent at least eighty-five reports about Air Force subjects, but only nineteen about the Army and seventeen about various industries. The following year, 1942, the frequent reports about the food situation are obvious, but also reports about Navy issues. TATE then sent forty-two reports concerning food and agriculture, because of an increased interest from the Germans. However, during that year he also sent reports on military issues: thirty-three about the Navy, twenty-eight about the Air Force, and sixteen about the Army. The number of reports decreased during 1943, but he sent thirty reports concerning the Army, eighteen about Air Force, and eighteen about Navy subjects. In the same year he transmitted sixteen reports about the results of the bombing of British cities by the Luftwaffe. It is more difficult to draw conclusions about 1944 as the material available only covers the time up to July, mostly disinformation about the forthcoming Allied invasion of Normandy. However, we know that TATE was actively involved with questions about the V1 and V2, and the fictitious minefield south of Ireland from autumn 1944 to spring 1945, and it is very likely that the number of reports increased during that period.

Notes

INTRODUCTION

1. Pedersen, E., *FamilieJournalen*, 8 March 1993, no. 10, p. 10.
2. Pedersen, E., *FamilieJournalen*, 8 March 1993, no. 10, p. 10.
3. *Siden Saxo*, vol. 11, no. 4, 1994, pp. 28–35.
4. Helen-Jayne B., *Familien Aufzeichnungen*, personal communication 19 July 2010.
5. Pedersen, E., *FamilieJournalen*, 8 March 1993, no. 10, p. 10.
6. National Archives, KV 2/61.
7. National Archives, KV 2/61.
8. National Archives, KV 2/61.
9. National Archives, KV 2/61.
10. Statspolitiet Aabenraa, police report, 10 November 1938.
11. National Archives, KV 2/61.
12. Peis, G., *The Mirror of Deception*, Weidenfeld & Nicholson 1977, p. 19.
13. Pedersen, E., *FamilieJournalen*, 1993, no. 11, p. 10.
14. National Archives, KV 2/61.
15. National Archives, KV 2/61.
16. National Archives, KV 2/60.
17. National Archives, KV 2/61.
18. Crowdy, T., *Deceiving Hitler: Double-Cross and Deception in World War II*, Osprey Publishing 2008, pp. 36–46.
19. Masterman, J. C., *The Double-Cross System in the War of 1939 to 1945*, Yale University Press 1972.

20. Pujol, J. & West, N., *GARBO. The Personal Story of the Most Successful Double Agent*, Weidenfeld & Nicholson 1985.

21. Seaman, M., *GARBO – The Spy who Saved D-Day*, Public Record Office 2000.

22. Miller, R., *Codename Tricycle*, Pimlico 2005.

23. MacIntyre, B., *Agent ZigZag – a True Story of Nazi Espionage, Love, and Betrayal*, Harmony Books 2007.

24. Booth, N., *Zigzag – The Incredible Wartime Exploits of Double Agent Eddie Chapman*, Portrait 2007.

25. Peis, G., *The Mirror of Deception*, Weidenfeld & Nicholson 1977.

26. Farago, L., *The Game of the Foxes: British and German Intelligence Operations and Personalities Which Changed the Course of the Second World War*, David McKay Company, Inc. 1971.

27. Kahn, D., *Hitler's Spies – The Extraordinary Story of German Military Intelligence*, Arrow Books 1978.

28. West, N., *MI5: British Security Operations, 1909–45*, The Bodley Head 1981.

29. West, N., *Seven Spies Who Changed the World*, Secker & Warburg 1991.

1 ENGLAND NEXT

1. National Archives, KV 2/61.

2. National Archives, KV 2/61.

3. National Archives, KV 2/31.

4. National Archives, KV 2/61.

5. National Archives, KV 2/61.

6. National Archives, KV 2/61.

7. West, N., *Seven Spies Who Changed the World*, Secker & Warburg 1991, p. 36.

8. National Archives, KV 2/61.

9. National Archives, KV 2/61.

10. West, N., 'A Nazi spy who was for turning', *Mail on Sunday* 1991.

11. West, N., *Seven Spies*, p. 35.

12. The Black Boy Inn was a traditional inn dating from the 1700s.

From the late 1800s it was a hotel in Nottingham, prominent on the skyline with a massive tower. It was demolished in the late 1960s to be replaced by an ugly commercial building.

13. National Archives, KV 2/61.

14. West, N., *Seven Spies*, p. 34.

15. National Archives, KV 2/61.

16. Oakington was built in 1939 and went into service in July 1940. In September 1940, 218 Squadron with Stirling bombers was stationed there; in November also Spitfires from the 3rd Photo Reconnaissance Unit. The airfield was a grass field which had posed problems for the heavy Stirling aircraft.

17. *After the Battle*, no. 74, p. 53.

18. National Archives, KV 2/61.

19. West, N., *MI5, British Security Service Operations 1909–45*, Triad Books; New edition 1983, p. 239.

20. West, N., *MI5*, p. 183.

21. Hoare, O., *Camp 020*, p. 368.

22. *After the Battle*, no. 25, p. 13.

23. Andrew, C., *The Defence of the Realm*, Allen Lane 2009, p. 250.

24. Hoare, O., *Camp 020*, p. 6.

25. *After the Battle*, no. 74, p. 50.

26. Hoare, O., *Camp 020*, p. 7.

27. Hoare, O., *Camp 020*, pp. 33–104.

28. Hoare, O., *Camp 020*, p. 33.

29. Dearden, who lived between 1883–1962, was a successful author, especially in criminology. But he also wrote a theatre play, *Interference*, which made 412 performanes at St James' Theatre in London. This gave Dearden an income of £40,000. However, he became bankrupt and was involved in a controversy with 'Tin-eye' Stephens, who held the opinion that this was a trick to avoid taxes.

30. Deacon, R. & West, N., *Spy! Six Stories of Modern Espionage*, Crown Publications 1980, p. 154.

31. *After the Battle*, no. 74, p. 52.

32. Hoare, O., *Camp 020*, p. 114.

33. National Archives, KV 2/60.
34. Hoare, O., *Camp 020*, p. 109.
35. Hoare, O., *Camp 020*, p. 140.
36. Hoare, O., *Camp 020*, p. 14.
37. Hennessey, *Spooks*, p. 237.
38. Booth, N., *Zigzag – The Incredible Wartime Exploits of Double Agent Eddie Chapman*, Portrait 2007, p. 137.
39. West, N., *MI5*, p. 186.
40. Hoare, O., *Camp 020*, p. 138.
41. Pedersen, E., *FamilieJournalen*, 1993, no. 12, p. 30.
42. Farago, L., *The Game of the Foxes: British and German Intelligence Operations and Personalities Which Changed the Course of the Second World War*, David McKay Company, Inc. 1971.
43. Kahn, D., *Hitler's spies – The Extraordinary Story of German Military Intelligence*, Arrow Books 1978.
44. Peis, G., *The Mirror of Deception*, Weidenfeld & Nicholson 1977.
45. West, N., ed., *The Guy Liddell Diaries, Vol. I: 1939–1942*, Routledge 2005, p. 98.
46. National Archives, KV 2/61.
47. National Archives, KV 2/61.
48. Hoare, O., *Camp 020*, p. 140.

2 RECRUITED DOUBLE AGENT

1. National Archives, KV 2/61.
2. Pedersen, E., *FamilieJournalen*, 1993, no. 11, p. 10.
3. National Archives, KV 2/61.
4. Pedersen, E.: *FamilieJournalen*, 1993, no. 11, p. 10.
5. Hoare, O., *Camp 020*, p. 140.
6. National Archives, KV 2/61.
7. Pedersen, E., *FamilieJournalen*, 1993, no. 12, pp. 30-31.
8. *Times online*, 15 May 2007.
9. *Mail on Sunday*, 1 May 2005.
10. *The Times*, 16 May 1994.
11. Crowdy, *Deceiving Hitler*, p. 43.

12. Deacon & West, *Spy*, p. 156.

13. Harry Tate was a Scotsman and lived between 1872–1940, a well-known comedian and Music Hall performer, who appeared in six films. He had a bushy moustache that he used to enhance the expression of his feelings. The artist Harry Tate often did things in his act badly and in the wrong order, but everything turned out well in the end.

14. Fort, A., *The Prof. The Life of Frederick Lindeman*, Pimlico 2004, pp. 58–59.

15. Forces Reunited. The British Armed Forces Community.

16. National Archives, KV 2/61.

17. National Archives, KV 2/61.

18. MacIntyre, B., *ZIGZAG*, p. 125.

19. National Archives, KV 2/62.

20. National Archives, KV 2/61.

21. National Archives, KV 2/61.

22. Olsson & Jonason, *Gösta Caroli – Dubbelagent SUMMER.* Unpublished manuscript.

23. National Archives, KV 2/61.

24. Bower, T., *The Perfect English Spy*, Heinemann 1995, p. 41.

25. Masterman, J. C., *The Double-Cross System in the War of 1939–45*, Yale 1972, pp. 66–67.

26. Booth, *Agent ZIGZAG*, p. 51.

27. Masterman, J. C., *Double-Cross*, p. 62.

28. Masterman, J. C., *Double-Cross*, p. 58.

29. Crowdy, *Deceiving Hitler*, p. 77.

30. Masterman, J. C., *Double-Cross*, pp. 17–33.

31. Miller, R., *Codename Tricycle. The True Story of the Second World War's Most Extraordinary Double Agent (Dusko Popov)*, Secker & Warburg 2004, p. 44.

32. *The Guardian*, 18 March 2004.

33. Knightley, P., *The Second Oldest Profession*, W. W. Norton 1986, p. 152.

34. Masterman, J. C., *Double-Cross*, p. 15.

3 GREAT BRITAIN DURING THE FIRST YEARS OF THE WAR

1. Calder, A., *The People's War: Britain 1939–45*, Jonathan Cape 1969, p. 44.

2. Calder, A., *The People's War*, p. 72.

3. Gardner, J., *Wartime Britain 1939–1945*, Headline 2004, p. 61.

4. West, N., *MI5*, p. 139.

5. Ziegler, P., *London at War*, Alfred. A Knopf 1995, p. 95.

6. *The Sun*, 5 September 2005.

7. Smithies, E., *Aces, Erks & Backroom Boys*, Cassell 2002, p. 182.

8. Moffat, J., *I Sank the Tirpitz*, Corgi 2010, p. 124.

9. Gardiner, *Wartime Britain*, p. 590.

10. Calder, A., *The People's War*, p. 155.

11. Gardiner, *Wartime Britain*, p. 179.

12. Ziegler, *London at War*, p. 47.

13. Calder, A., *The People's War*, p. 468.

14. Gardiner, *Wartime Britain*, p. 161.

15. Gardiner, *Wartime Britain*, p. 166.

16. Brown, M. & Harris, C., *The War Time House*, Sutton 2001, pp. 74–75.

17. Longmate, N., *How We Lived Then*, Arrow 1971, pp. 266–267.

18. Brown, M. & Harris, C., *The Wartime House*, pp. 40–42.

19. Brown, M. & Harris, C., *The Wartime House*, pp. 68–69.

20. Calder, A., *The People's War*, p. 581.

21. McKay, S., *The Secret Life of Bletchley Park*, Aurum 2010, Chapter 11.

22. Ramsey, W., ed., *The Blitz Then and Now. Vol. 2, After the Battle* 1988, pp. 306–325.

23. Evans, M., *Invasion: Operation Sealion, 1940*, Longman 2004, p. 80.

24. OKW Directives for the invasion of U.K. – Operation *Seelöwe* – Summer and Autumn 1940.

25. Coggins, E.V. & Coggins, E., *Wings that Stay On*, Turner 2000, p. 56.

26. Evans, M., *Invasion: Operation Sealion, 1940*, p. 91.

27. Gardiner, *Wartime Britain*, p. 224.

28. A conservative politician born in 1897 and Home Secretary for several periods: 1935–38, 1940–45 and 1951–55. He was Prime Minister 1955–57, during the Suez crisis. During this time he was taken ill, partly because of his use of Benzedrine (an amphetamine substance), and finally had to resign.

29. *The Independent*, 23 July 2010.

30. Gardiner, *Wartime Britain*, p. 227.

31. *The Independent*, 23 July 2010.

32. Gardiner, *Wartime Britain*, p. 241.

33. *Times Online*, 5 January 2009.

34. Hayward, J., *Myths & Legends of the Second World War*, Sutton 2003, p. 122.

35. McKinstry, L., *Lancaster. The Second World War's Greatest Bomber*, John Murray 2009, p. 322.

36. Ziegler, *London at War*, p. 96.

37. Other sources mention 1,054 interned.

38. Ironside was born in 1880. He was wounded twice in the Boer War. He commanded a brigade on the Western Front in the First World War. After this war he was an enthusiast for the need of a mechanised army. It was generally thought that he would be given the post of commander of the British Expeditionary Force (BEF) in France in 1940, but this was given to Lord Gort with whom cooperation was difficult. After a short period as Commander-in-Chief Home Forces, i.e. the invasion defence, he was replaced due to his age. He was promoted to Field Marshal, but did not take part in any operations or have any official post after that. In 1941 he became a baron.

39. Calder, *The People's War*, p. 154.

40. Hayward, J., *Myths & Legends of the Second World War*, History Press Tempus Publishing 2009, p. 11.

41. Calder, *The People's War*, p. 155.

42. Gillies, M., *Waiting for Hitler: Voices from Britain on the Brink of Invasion*, Hodder & Stoughton 2006, p. 45.

43. The radio programme *Germany Calling* was broadcast from Hamburg throughout the entire war. It had several British programme

presenters, but Joyce was the most well known. He was sentenced to death for treason, and hanged in 1946.

44. Calder, *The People's War*, p. 156.

45. Tyler Kent was a cipher clerk at the American embassy, where Joseph Kennedy (the father of the famous Kennedy brothers) was ambassador, and known to have been hardly an anglophile. Tyler Kent stole thousands of copies of documents from the embassy, which he shared with pro-German organisations, such as Archibald Ramsay's *The Right Club*, where also a certain Anna Wolkoff was an important member. Among the documents were secret communications between Churchill and President Roosevelt concerning American aid to Britain, which was a very delicate and sensitive issue in politics in the USA. Tyler Kent and Anna Wolkoff were sentenced to several years in prison.

46. West, N., *The Guy Liddell Diaries, Vol. 1*, p. 196.

47. Ziegler, *London at War*, p. 98.

48. Gardiner, *Wartime Britain*, p. 239.

49. Longmate, *How We Lived Then*, p. 97.

50. Hayward, *Myths & Legends*, p. 26.

51. Hayward, *Myths & Legends*, p. 23.

52. Calder, A., *The People's War*, p. 585.

53. Hayward, *Myths & Legends of the Second World War*, p. 119.

54. Hayward, *Myths & Legends of the Second World War*, p. 113.

55. Glover, *Invasion Scare 1940*, p. 189.

56. Glover, *Invasion Scare 1940*, p. 164.

4 TATE STARTS HIS WORK

1. The information in at least thirty-eight reports is based on the numbering of the reports from TATE to the Abwehr in Hamburg, which are kept at NARA in Washington today.

2. Pedersen, E., *FamilieJournalen*, 1993, no. 12, p. 31.

3. National Archives, KV 2/61.

4. The Abwehr had several agents in Ireland, the most well-known being Herman Götz, Günther Schütz and Adolf Mahr.

5. National Archives, KV 2/61.

6. National Archives, KV 2/61.

7. Howard, M. & Hinsley, H., *British Intelligence in the Second World War, vol. 5*. Stationery Office 1990, p. 10.

8. Howard, *British Intelligence in the Second World War, vol. 5*, p. 14.

9. NARA, T-77, R-1541, p. 70, Report from TATE, 14 February 1941.

10. Brize Norton (about twelve miles east of Oxford) is today the RAF's largest air base with, in particular, much of the transport aircraft for British army movements, but it is a fully equipped base with fighter jets. During the war 99 Squadron was stationed there, with Wellington and Halifax bombers, the latter being sometimes used for dropping containers for the resistance movements in Europe.

11. Kahn, *Hitler's Spies*, p. 334.

12. Kahn, *Hitler's Spies*, pp. 334–335.

13. West, *Seven Spies*, p. 40.

14. National Archives, KV 2/61.

15. *After the Battle*, no. 74, p. 53.

16. National Archives, KV 2/61.

17. National Archives, KV 2/61.

18. Hinsley, H. & Simkins, C., *British Intelligence in the Second World War, vol. 4*. Stationery Office 1990, Appendix 8, pp. 331–334.

19. Howard, *British Intelligence in the Second World War, vol. 5*, pp. 10–11.

20. National Archives, KV 2/61.

21. National Archives, KV 2/61.

22. National Archives, KV 2/61.

23. National Archives, KV 2/61.

24. Bushey Museum, personal communication.

25. Nigel West, personal communication.

26. Farago, L., *The Game of the Foxes*, pp. 287–288.

27. National Archives, KV 2/61.

28. National Archives, KV 2/61

5 FINANCIAL PROBLEMS

1. National Archives, KV 2/61.
2. National Archives, KV 2/60.
3. National Archives, KV 2/61.
4. The Regent Palace Hotel was built in 1914 and was then the largest hotel in Europe with 1,028 rooms. The location was excellent, just off Piccadilly Circus, and it was seen initially as luxurious, but became with time a popular tourist hotel. It ceased trading at the end of 2006.
5. National Archives, KV 2/61.
6. National Archives, KV 2/61.
7. National Archives, KV 2/61.
8. National Archives, KV 2/61.
9. Masterman, *Double-Cross*, p. 25.
10. The large hotel the Strand Palace is still standing on the Strand.
11. National Archives, KV 2/61.
12. National Archives, KV 2/61.
13. Miller, *Codename Tricycle*, pp. 15–18.
14. Miller, *Codename Tricycle*, p. 65.
15. Kahn, *Hitler's Spies*, p. 278.
16. Miller, *Codename Tricycle*, p. 224.
17. Miller, *Codename Tricycle*, p. 79.
18. Miller, *Codename Tricycle*, pp. 88–89.
19. National Archives, KV 2/61.
20. National Archives, KV 2/61.

6 KAREL RICHTER

1. National Archives, KV 2/61.
2. National Archives, KV 2/31.
3. National Archives, KV 2/31.
4. National Archives, KV 2/31.
5. One of the RAF Bomber Command's bases. Units with various bombers, such as Wellingtons, Mosquitoes and Lancasters, were stationed there at different times.
6. West, N., *The Guy Liddell Diaries*, Vol. 1, p. 129.

7. Hoare, O., *Camp 020*, p. 155.

8. Hoare, O., *Camp 020*, pp. 115–116.

9. West, N., *MI5*, p. 326.

10. West, N., *The Guy Liddell Diaries, Vol. 1*, p. 128.

11. Hoare, O., *Camp 020*, p. 116.

12. National Archives, KV 2/31.

13. Sharp, M. & Bowyer, M., *Mosquito*, Faber & Faber 1967, p. 55.

14. *After the Battle*, no. 11, p. 28.

15. Hoare, O., *Camp 020*, p. 164.

16. *After the Battle*, no. 11, p. 28.

17. Hoare, O., *Camp 020*, p. 164.

18. National Archives, KV 2/31.

19. Hoare, O., *Camp 020*, p. 165.

20. National Archives, KV 2/31.

21. National Archives, KV 2/61.

22. National Archives, KV 2/30.

23. National Archives, KV 2/61.

24. National Archives, KV 2/31.

25. Hoare, O., *Camp 020*, p. 166.

26. National Archives, KV 2/61.

27. National Archives, KV 2/61.

28. *After the Battle*, no. 11, p. 24.

29. Evans, C., *The Father of Forensics*, Icon 2007, pp. 297–298.

30. West, N., *MI5*, p. 328.

31. *Times Online*, 21 October 2009.

32. National Archives, KV 2/31.

33. Pierrepoint, A., *Executioner: Pierrepoint*, Harrap 1974.

34. National Archives, KV 2/61.

7 1942

1. NARA, T-77, R-1541, Report from TATE 10 January 1942.

2. Helen-Jayne B., personal communication.

3. National Archives, KV 2/61.

4. One of the bases for seaplanes and the fleet, which was located on

the west side of Loch Ryan, near Stranraer on the south-west coast of Scotland.

5. Tower-like defence plants made of concrete, known as Maunsell Forts, which were placed in the sea in the Thames Estuary and in the Mersey near Liverpool. They were either intended for the Navy, or as platforms for anti-aircraft defences.

6. National Archives, KV 2/61.

7. National Archives, KV 2/61.

8. Farago, L., *The Game of the Foxes*, p. 293.

9. National Archives, KV 2/61.

10. Farago, L., *The Game of the Foxes*, p. 299.

11. National Archives, KV 2/61.

12. National Archives, KV 2/1067.

13. A large secret store of ammunition in a tunnel near Bristol.

14. National Archives, KV 2/61.

15. The Junior Carlton Club was founded in 1864 and had its premises on Pall Mall. It sought to emulate the venerable Carlton Club, which was opposite. The club had been linked to the Conservative Party. The building in Pall Mall was destroyed by a direct hit during the Blitz. In 1977 the club was closed, and was incorporated into the Carlton.

16. National Archives, KV 2/61.

17. Masterman, *Double-Cross*, p. 76.

18. National Archives, KV 2/61.

19. Montagu, E., *Beyond Top Secret U*, Corgi 1979, p. 119.

20. Holt, T., *The Deceivers*, Weidenfeld & Nicholson 2004, p. 560.

21. Howard, *British Intelligence in the Second World War, vol.* 5, p. 223.

22. Montagu, *Beyond Top Secret U*, pp. 118-119.

23. Howard, *British Intelligence in the Second World War, vol.* 5, p. 226.

24. Gannon, M., *Black May*. Aurum 1998, p. 64.

25. Montagu, *Beyond Top Secret U*, pp. 126-127.

26. Satchell, A., *Running the Gauntlet*, Chatham 2001.

27. Blair, C., *Hitlers Ubåtskrig vol.* 5 (Hitler's U-boat War), Hjalmarson

& Högberg 1996, p. 173.

28. HMS *Illustrious* was launched in 1939 and participated in November 1940 at Taranto, where much of the Italian fleet was obliterated. In January 1941 it was badly damaged by a German dive bomber. In 1942 it had twenty-one Martlets, six Fulmars and eighteen Swordfish. Later on it participated in the war against Japan. It was scrapped in 1954.

29. HMS *Indefatigable* was launched in December 1942 and took part in the war against Japan. In July and August 1944 she took part in the attack on *Tirpitz* in Norway. It was scrapped in 1956.

30. Montagu, *Beyond Top Secret U*, p. 117, and in Howard, *Intelligence in the Second World War, vol. 5*, p. 225.

31. Hinsley, *British Intelligence in the Second World War, vol. 4*, p. 123.

32. Masterman, *Double-Cross*, p. 109.

33. Montagu, *Beyond Top Secret U*, pp. 132-133.

34. Montagu, *Beyond Top Secret U*, p. 135.

35. Gannon, M., *Black May*, p. 105.

36. *Mail Online*, 3 March 2009.

8 1943

1. NARA, T-77, R-1541, Report 745 and 761 from TATE.

2. Greville's was a reputable family photo business for many years. During the war Theodore Greville was owner, but the firm was later taken over by his three sons, who became well-known photographers in Watford and have left an extensive collection of photographs. The house on 46 Queens Road has been demolished.

3. West, N., *The Guy Liddell Diaries, Vol. II:1942–1945*, Routledge 2009, pp. 82, 86.

4. National Archives, KV 2/61.

5. Miller, *Codename Tricycle*, p. 156.

6. West, N., *Seven Spies*, p. 60.

7. Masterman, *Double-Cross*, p. 150.

8. Hinsley, *British Intelligence in the Second World War, vol. 4*, p. 221.

9. National Archives, KV 2/1333.

10. Masterman, *Double-Cross*, p. 150–151.

11. Hesketh, R. & West, N., *Fortitude, the D-Day Deception Campaign*, Overlook 2002, p. 55.

12. Farago, L., *The Game of the Foxes*, p. 294.

13. National Archives, KV 2/61.

14. National Archives, KV 3/205.

15. Of the 1,104 reports from TATE archived at NARA in Washington, 604 are weather reports.

16. Greenland. Warcovers.dk 29 May 2010.

17. Llewellyn Evans, M., *Great World War II Battles in the Arctic*, Greenwood 1999, p. 61.

18. Selinger, F., 'Meteorological Operations' *in the North Atlantic 1940–45*, 15 July 2000.

9 1944 & 1945

1. Farago, *The Game of the Foxes*, pp. 646–647.

2. Farago, *The Game of the Foxes*, p. 652.

3. 'Sichere Quelle' was code for the intercepted radio transmissions of the Allies.

4. Farago, *The Game of the Foxes*, p. 652.

5. Hesketh, *Fortitude*, p. 59.

6. National Archives, KV 2/61.

7. National Archives, KV 2/61.

8. McKee, A., *The Mosquito Log*, Souvenir 1988, pp. 144–145.

9. National Archives, KV 2/61.

10. Masterman, *Double-Cross*, p. 161.

11. Howard, *British Intelligence in the Second World War, vol. 5*, p. 45.

12. Hinsley, *British Intelligence in the Second World War, vol. 4*, p. 240.

13. British air reconnaissance was already engaged in missions over Sweden. The western part was covered, including the major city of Malmoe, close to Copenhagen, and the second largest city in Sweden, Gothenburg, was photographed in four missions in 1941–43. This was mostly carried out by Mosquitoes flying much higher than the Swedish

fighter aircraft. *Expressen* 24 August 2008.

14. Crowdy, *Deceiving Hitler*, pp. 232–233.

15. Hesketh, *Fortitude*, pp. 166–167.

16. Hesketh, *Fortitude*, p. 105.

17. National Archives, KV 2/61.

18. General Lloyd Fredendall, who took part in Operation TORCH, had been appointed by Eisenhower, who soon regretted his decision. Fredendall was not a success in that campaign and after this he was posted to the USA. Some comments about him were: '... one of the most inept senior officers to hold a high command during World War II', 'a son of a bitch', or 'a moral and physical coward'.

19. Hesketh, *Fortitude*, p. 105.

20. Hesketh, *Fortitude*, pp. 95–96.

21. National Archives, KV 2/61.

22. Hesketh, *Fortitude*, pp. 95–96.

23. Hesketh, *Fortitude*, p. 121.

24. Kahn, *Hitler's Spies*, p. 336.

25. Seaman, M., *GARBO – The Spy who Saved D-Day*, Public Record Office 2000, p. 205.

26. Hesketh, *Fortitude*, p. 148.

27. Hesketh, *Fortitude*, p. 225.

28. Hesketh, *Fortitude*, p. 226.

29. Hesketh, *Fortitude*, p. 226.

30. Hesketh, *Fortitude*, p. 265.

31. Hesketh, *Fortitude*, p. 287.

32. Hesketh, *Fortitude*, p. 297.

33. Hesketh, *Fortitude*, p. 311.

34. Hesketh, *Fortitude*, pp. 472–478.

35. Kahn, *Hitler's Spies*, p. 336.

36. Hesketh, National Archives, KV 2/62.

37. Hesketh, *Fortitude*, pp. 328–329.

38. Hesketh, *Fortitude*, p. 336.

39. National Archives, KV 2/61.

40. Masterman, *Double-Cross*, p. 185.

10 New Threats From the Sky

1. Launius, R., *Frontiers of Space Exploration*, Greenwood 2004, p. 108.

2. Ward, B., *Dr. Space: the Life of Wernher von Braun*, Naval Institute Press 2005, p. 16.

3. Brown, L., *Technical and Military Imperatives – A Radar History of World War II*, Taylor & Francis 1999, p. 104.

4. Boog, H., Krebs, G. & Vogel, D., *Germany and the Second World War: Volume VII: The Strategic Air War in Europe and the War in the West and East Asia 1943–1944/5*, Oxford University Press 2006, p. 494.

5. Reuter, C., *The A4 (V2) and the German, Russian and American Rocket Program*, S. R. Research and Publishing 1998, pp. 44–45.

6. Reuter, C., *The A4 (V2) and the German, Russian and American Rocket Program*, pp. 46–47.

7. Jones, R. V., *Most Secret War – British Scientific Intelligence 1939–1945*, Coronet 1979, p. 525.

8. Jones, *Most Secret War*, p. 527.

9. MacIntyre, B., *Agent ZigZag – En sann historia om kontraspionage, kärlek och svek*, Ekerlids Förlag 2008, p. 280.

10. Jones, *Most Secret War*, p. 531.

11. Jones, *Most Secret War*, p. 534.

12. Jones, *Most Secret War*, p. 532.

13. Jones, *Most Secret War*, p. 535.

14. Jones, *Most Secret War*, p. 534.

15. Harris, *GARBO*, pp. 243–244.

16. Harris, *GARBO*, pp. 248–249.

17. Harris, *GARBO*, p. 249.

18. Harris, *GARBO*, p. 250.

19. Harris, *GARBO*, p. 251.

20. Harris, *GARBO*, pp. 260–261.

21. Andrew, *The Defence of the Realm*, p. 312.

22. West, *The Guy Liddell Diaries, Vol. II*, 7 July 1944.

23. MacIntyre, *Agent ZigZag*, p. 298.

24. MacIntyre, *Agent ZigZag*, p. 298.
25. Andrew, *The Defence of the Realm*, p. 313.
26. Brentford & Chiswick Local History Society, *The Chiswick V2 Memorial*, 8 September 2004.
27. Andrew, *The Defence of the Realm*, p. 314.
28. Andrew, *The Defence of the Realm*, p. 315.
29. National Archives, KV 2/61.
30. National Archives, KV 2/61.

11 THE MINEFIELD THAT NEVER EXISTED
1. National Archives, KV 2/61.
2. National Archives, KV 2/61.
3. Olsson & Jonason, *Gösta Caroli – Dubbelagent SUMMER*, Unpublished, p. 42.
4. Howard, *British Intelligence in the Second World War*, vol. 5, p. 223.
5. Howard, *British Intelligence in the Second World War*, vol. 5, p. 223.
6. National Archives, KV 2/61.
7. National Archives, KV 2/61.
8. National Archives, KV 2/61.
9. National Archives, KV 2/61.
10. National Archives, KV 2/61.
11. National Archives, KV 2/61.
12. National Archives, KV 2/61.
13. National Archives, KV 2/61.
14. National Archives, KV 2/61.
15. Stanfords is a well-known bookshop established in 1901, specialising in travel books and maps.
16. National Archives, KV 2/61.
17. 'Milk cows' were ten specially built large type XIV U-boats. They carried an extra 600 tonnes of diesel fuel, with which they could supply the type VII and IX U-boats, and in this way prolong their operating range in the Caribbean and round the south of Africa. The extra diesel oil was enough to replenish about ten U-boats. There was also lubricating oil, torpedoes, fresh water, and 30 tonnes of supplies, such

as fresh food, available to distribute, and there was a doctor on board. This operation, which involved great risks, took place in the middle of the Atlantic, outside the operating range of the Allied aircraft. At most these U-boats only completed five or six missions before they were sunk by the Allies. John White, *U boat tankers 1941–45*, Airlife 1998.

18. Blair, C., *Hitlers ubåtskrig, vol. 5*, p. 358.

19. Howard, *British Intelligence in the Second World War*, p. 228.

20. Howard, *British Intelligence in the Second World War*, p. 228.

21. Naval Historical Center, T-4066, PG 30347, 16–30 November 1944: Kriegstagebücher (KTB) Des Führers/Befehlshaber der Unterseeboote, 17 November 1944.

22. Naval Historical Center, T-4066, PG 30347, 16–30 November 1944: Kriegstagebücher (KTB) Des Führers/Befehlshaber der Unterseeboote, 18 November 1944.

23. Naval Historical Center, T-4066, PG 30347, 16–30 November 1944: Kriegstagebücher (KTB) Des Führers/Befehlshaber der Unterseeboote, 24 November 1944.

24. Naval Historical Center, T-4066, PG 30361, 16–31 December 1944: Kriegstagebücher (KTB) Des Führers/Befehlshaber der Unterseeboote, 29 December 1944.

25. Naval Historical Center, T-4066, PG 30361, 16–31 December 1944: Kriegstagebücher (KTB) Des Führers/Befehlshaber der Unterseeboote, 31 December 1944.

26. National Archives, DEFE 3/739: ZTPGU 34919.

27. Howard, *British Intelligence in the Second World War*, p. 228.

28. McKay, S., *The Secret Life of Bletchley Park*, Aurum 2010, p. 276.

29. National Archives, DEFE 3/740: ZTPGU 35227.

30. Naval Historical Center, T-4066, PG 30362, 1–15 January 1945: Kriegstagebücher (KTB) Des Führers/Befehlshaber der Unterseeboote, 14 January 1945.

31. Naval Historical Center, T-4066, PG 30362, 1–15 January 1945: Kriegstagebücher (KTB) Des Führers/Befehlshaber der Unterseeboote, 14 January 1945.

32. Naval Historical Center, T-4066, PG 30362, 1–15 January 1945:

Kriegstagebücher (KTB) Des Führers/Befehlshaber der Unterseeboote, 15 January 1945.

33. National Archives, DEFE 3/741: ZTPGU 36330.

34. The German Navy had a navigation and positioning system where the Atlantic and the Mediterranean Sea were divided into squares (*grossquadraten*) marked with two letters, the sides of each box being about 486 nautical miles. A U-boat that went from Germany to Newfoundland passed through boxes BF, BE, BD, BC and BB. Each square was divided into nine smaller squares, and each of these smaller boxes in turn was divided into nine parts, giving 81 boxes numbered from 11 to 99. Each such smaller box was divided again in the same way, giving 81 small boxes with sides of six nautical miles. A position in this area of 6x6 nautical miles had a name, such as BD 6312 or AF 1236. An interesting fact is that the British did not know about this in detail until 9 May 1941, when they managed to board *U-110* (Kptlt Lempe), and in addition to the Enigma rotors also obtained this chart. This was of course of huge advantage, helping to understand and read the German Enigma coded messages at Bletchley Park. (Gannon, M., *Black May*, Aurum 1998, p. 50.)

35. National Archives, DEFE 3/742: ZTPGU 37374.

36. Blair, *Hitlers Ubåtskrig vol. 5*, p. 358.

37. Blair, *Hitlers Ubåtskrig vol. 5*, p. 461.

38. Blair, *Hitlers Ubåtskrig vol. 5*, pp. 455–459.

12 AFTER THE WAR

1. West, *MI5*, p. 241.

2. Masterman, *Double-Cross*, p. 161.

3. Masterman, *Double-Cross*, p. 53.

4. National Archives, KV 2/31.

5. Farago, *The Game of the Foxes*, pp. 292–293.

6. Peis, *The Mirror of Deception*, p. 19.

7. L. Hayward, Watford Museum, personal communication.

8. Masterman, *Double-Cross*, p. 53.

9. West, *The Guy Liddell Diaries, Vol. II: 1942–1945*, p. 110.

10. West, *The Guy Liddell Diaries, Vol. II*, p. 295.
11. West, *The Guy Liddell Diaries, Vol. II*, p. 295.
12. Lauridsen, J. T., *Agent A.3725 og TATE*. Information.dk 25 July 2007.
13. National Archives, KV 2/61.
14. Masterman, *Double-Cross*, p. 53.
15. Pedersen, *FamilieJournalen*, 1993, no. 12, p. 31.
16. Helena B., personal communication.
17. J. Wheatly, personal communication.
18. *After the Battle*, no. 74, p. 53.
19. J. Wheatly, personal communication.
20. Pedersen, *FamilieJournalen*, 1993, p. 98.
21. Helena B., personal communication.
22. Helen-Jayne B., personal communication.
23. Helena B., personal communication.
24. Pedersen, *FamilieJournalen* 1993, no. 10, p. 10.
25. Peis, *The Mirror of Deception*, p. 18.
26. Helena B., personal communication.
27. Masterman, *Double-Cross*, p. 185.
28. West, *Seven Spies*, p. 65.
29. Helena B., personal communication.
30. A friend of Harry Williamson, personal communication.
31. West, *Seven Spies*, p. 33.
32. A friend of Harry Williamson, personal communication
33. Helena B., personal communication.
34. Pedersen, *FamilieJournalen*, no. 13, p. 99.
35. Helen-Jayne B., personal communication.
36. Helena B., personal communication.
37. Peis, *The Mirror of Deception*, p. 32.
38. Peis, *The Mirror of Deception*, pp. 10–15.
39. West, N., 'A Nazi spy who was for turning', *Mail on Sunday*, 1991.
40. Peis, *The Mirror of Deception*, p. 34.
41. Helen-Jayne B., personal communication.
42. Helena B., personal communication.

43. Helena B., personal communication.

44. Peis, *The Mirror of Deception*, p. 180.

45. Peis, *The Mirror of Deception*, pp. 250–252.

46. Helen-Jayne B., personal communication.

47. Helena B., personal communication.

48. *After the Battle*, no. 74, p. 53.

49. Nigel West, personal communication.

50. Helena B., personal communication.

51. The complete name is: *Aufzeichnungen über die Familie von Johann August Schmidt Pastor zu Steinbergkirche – Gesammelt von William Schmidt Rechtsanwalt u. Kgl. Notar in Apenrade*, written by Wulf's father and published in 1910.

52. Helen-Jayne B., personal communication.

53. Wighton, C. & Peis, G., *They Spied on England*, Odhams 1958, pp. 99–100.

54. Ritter, N., *Deckname Dr. Rantzau. Die Aufzeichnungen des Nikolaus Ritter, Offizier im Geheimen Nachrichtendienst*, 1972, p. 315.

55. Peis, *The Mirror of Deception*, pp. 17-18.

56. Nigel West, personal communication.

57. *The Times*, 24 October 1992, Obituary. Harry Williamson.

58. *The New York Times*, 23 October 1992, Bruce Lambert: 'Harry Williamson, 80, a Top Spy For the British, Prized by Hitler'.

59. Pedersen, *FamilieJournalen*, 1993, no. 14, p. 99.

Bibliography

BOOKS

Andrew, C., *The Defence of the Realm – The Authorized History of MI5*, Penguin 2009.

Blair, C., *Hitlers Ubåtskrig vol. 5* (Hitler's U-boat War), Hjalmarson & Högberg 1996.

Boog, H., Krebs, G., Vogel, D., *Germany and the Second World War: Volume VII: The Strategic Air War in Europe and the War in the West and East Asia 1943–1944/5*, Oxford University Press 2006.

Booth, N., *Zigzag – The Incredible Wartime Exploits of Double Agent Eddie Chapman*, Portrait 2007.

Bower, T., *The Perfect English Spy*, Heinemann 1995.

Brammer, U., *Spionageabwehr und Geheimer Meldedienst*, Rombach 1989.

Brown, L., *Technical and Military Imperatives – A Radar History of World War II*, Taylor & Francis 1999.

Brown, M., Harris, C., *The War Time House*, Sutton 2001.

Calder, A., *The People's War*, Granada 1971.

Centner, J., *Codename Magpie; The Final Nazi Espionage Mission against the U.S. in WW II*, BookSurge 2005.

Coggins, E. V., Coggins, E., *Wings that Stay On – The Role of Fighter Aircraft in War*, Turner 2000.

Crowdy, T., *Deceiving Hitler: Double-Cross and Deception in World War II*, Osprey 2008.

Deacon, C. R., West, N., *Spy!: Six Stories of Modern Espionage*, Parkwest 1984.

Evans, C., *The Father of Forensics*, Icon 2007.

Evans, M. M., *Invasion! – Operation Sealion – 1940*, Longman 2004.

Farago, L., *The Game of the Foxes: British and German Intelligence Operations and Personalities Which Changed the Course of the Second World War*, David McKay Company, Inc. 1971.

Fort, A., *The Prof. The Life of Frederick Lindeman*, Pimlico 2004.

Gannon, M., *Black May*, Aurum 1998.

Gardiner, J., *Wartime – Britain 1939–1945*, Headline Review 2005.

Gillies, M., *Waiting for Hitler – Voices from Britain on the Brink of Invasion*, Hodder & Stoughton 2006.

Glover, M., *Invasion Scare 1940*, Leo Cooper 1990.

Hayward, J., *Myths & Legends of the Second World War*, Sutton 2003.

Hennessey, T., Thomas, C., *Spooks – The Unofficial History of MI5*, Amberley 2009.

Hesketh, R., *Fortitude: The D-Day Deception Campaign*, Overlook 2002.

Hinsley, H., Simkins, C., *British Intelligence in the Second World War*, *vol. 4*, Stationery Office 1990.

Hoare, O., *Camp 020: MI5 and the Nazi Spies - The Official History of MI5's Wartime Interrogation Centre*, Public Record Office 2000.

Holt, T., *The Deceivers*, Weidenfeld & Nicholson 2004.

Howard, M., *British Intelligence in the Second World War, vol. 5: Strategic Deception*, HMSO 1990.

Jones, R. V., *Most Secret War – British Scientific Intelligence 1939–1945*, Coronet 1979.

Jörgensen, C., *Hitler's Espionage Machine: The True Story Behind One of the World's Most Ruthless Spy Networks*, Lyons 2004.

Kahn, D., *Hitler's Spies – The Extraordinary Story of German Military Intelligence*, Arrow 1978.

Knightley, P., *The Second Oldest Profession*, Penguin 1988.

Kristensen, H. S., *I hemmelig tysk tjenste – Hvis lille kat er du, Max Pelving?*

Lauridsen, J. T. (ed.) *Over Stregen – Under besættelsen*, Gyldendal 2007.

Launius, R. D., *Frontiers of Space Exploration*, Greenwood 2004.

Longmate, N., *How We Lived Then*, Arrow 1971.

Llewellyn, E. M., *Great World War II Battles in the Arctic*, Greenwood 1999.

MacIntyre, B., *Agent ZigZag – A True Story of Nazi Espionage, Love, and Betrayal*, Harmony 2007.

MacIntyre, B., *Agent ZigZag – En sann historia om kontraspionage, kärlek och svek* (Agent ZigZag – a True Story of Nazi Espionage, Love and Betrayal), Ekerlids Förlag 2008.

MacIntyre, B., *Operation Mincemeat*, Bloomsbury 2010.

Masterman, Sir J. C., *The Double-Cross System in the War of 1939 to 1945*, Yale University Press 1972.

McKay, S., *The Secret Life of Bletchley Park*, Aurum 2010.

McKee, A., *The Mosquito Log*, Souvenir 1988.

McKinstry, L., *Lancaster: The Second World War's Greatest Bomber*, John Murray 2009.

Miller, R., *Codename Tricycle: The True Story of the Second World War's Most Extraordinary Double Agent*, Pimlico 2005.

Moffat, J., *I Sank the Tirpitz*, Corgi 2010.

Montagu, E., *Beyond Top Secret U*, Davies 1977.

Olsson, S., Jonason, T., *Gösta Caroli – Double agent SUMMER*, Unpublished manuscript.

Peis, G., *The Mirror of Deception*, Weidenfeld & Nicholson 1977.

Pierrepoint, A., *Executioner: Pierrepoint*, Harrap 1974.

Pujol, J., West, N., *GARBO. The Personal Story of the Most Successful Double Agent*, Weidenfeld & Nicholson 1985.

Ramsay, W., (ed.) *The Blitz Then and Now: Volume 2*, Battle of Britain Prints International 1988.

Reuter, C., *The A4 (V2) and the German, Russian and American Rocket Program*, S. R. Research and Publishing 1998.

Ritter, N., *Deckname Dr. Rantzau. Die Aufzeichnungen des Nikolaus Ritter, Offizier im Geheimen Nachrichtendienst*, Hamburg: Hoffmann und Campe Verlag 1972.

Satchell, A., *Running the Gauntlet*, Chatham 2001.

Seaman, M., *GARBO – The Spy who Saved D-Day*, Public Record Office 2000.

Sharp, M., Bowyer, M., *Mosquito*, Faber & Faber 1967.

Smithies, E., *Aces, Erks & Backroom Boys*, Cassell 2002.

Ward, B., *Dr. Space: the Life of Wernher von Braun*, Naval Institute Press 2005.

West, N., *MI5*, The Bodley Head 1981.

West, N., *Seven Spies Who Changed the World*, Secker & Warburg 1991.

West, N., (ed.) (2005): *The Guy Liddell Diaries, Vol. I: 1939–1942*, Routledge 2005.

West, N., (ed.) *The Guy Liddell Diaries, Vol. II: 1943–1945*, Routledge 2009.

White, J., *U boat Tankers 1941–45*, Airlife 1998.

Wighton, C., Peis, G., *They Spied on England*, Odhams 1958.

Wilke, K., *Die deutsche banane – Wirtschaft und Kulturgesichte der Banane im Deutschen Reich 1900–1939*, Phil.Diss. Hannover 2004.

Ziegler, P., *London at War*, Mandarin 1995.

Øvig Knutsen, P., *Efter Drabet*, Gyldendal pocket 2001.

ARTICLES

Aabenraa Ugeavis, 20 January 2010 (Jan Sternkopf): *Aabenraaér var med til at aendre krigens gang.*

After the Battle, no. 11.

After the Battle, no. 25.

After the Battle, no. 74.

Brentford & Chiswick Local History Society (2004): 'The Chiswick V2 Memorial, 8 September 2004'.

FamilieJournalen, no. 10, 1993 (Erik Pedersen): *Ukendt dansk mesterspion forkortede Den 2. Verdenskrig – Han reddede tusinder af menneskeliv* (Unknown Danish master spy shortened the second World War – He saved thousands of lives).

FamilieJournalen, no. 11, 1993 (Erik Pedersen): *Spionen, der kom ned fra himlen* (The spy who came down from heaven).

FamilieJournalen, no. 12, 1993 (Erik Pedersen): *Hitler belønnede mig med jernkorset* (Hitler rewarded me with an iron cross).

FamilieJournalen, no. 13, 1993 (Erik Pedersen): *Min far fik ikke nogen gravsten* (My father had no gravestone).

Hamburger Abendblatt, 11 August 2007 (Günther Stiller): *Wohin führen Vera Schalburgs Spuren?*

Information.dk, 25 July 2007 (John T. Lauridsen): *Agent A.3725 og TATE.*

Knobelspiesse, A. V. (1996): 'Masterman Revisited'. CIA Historical Review Program, 2 July 1996.

Mail Online, 3 March 2009 (John Garth): 'Revealed: Allied invasion of North Africa was only saved by arrest of spy'.

Mail on Sunday, 1991 (Nigel West): 'A Nazi spy who was for turning'.

Mail on Sunday, 1 May 2005 (Alastair Robertson): 'How MI5's man in 'passion pants' saved D-Day'.

Siden Saxo, vol. 11, no. 4, 1994, pp. 28–35 (Hans Chr. Bjerg): *TATE – 3725.*

Siden Saxo, vol 27, no. 2, 2010, pp. 30-37 (Simon Olsson & Tommy Jonason): *Wulf Schmidt og den tyske militære efterretningsvirksomhed i Danmark 1940* (Wulf Schmidt and the German military intelligence in Denmark 1940).

The Guardian, 18 March 2004: 'Ghosts of wartime spies haunt Welsh hotels'.

The Independent, 23 July 2010 (Rob Hastings): 'Don't panic! The story of the real Dad's army'.

The New York Times, 23 October 1992 (Bruce Lambert): 'Harry Williamson, 80, a Top Spy For the British, Prized by Hitler'.

The Sun, 5 September 2005 (Tom Newton Dunn): 'Nazi chocolate bombs plot'.

The Times, 24 October 1992, 'Obituary. Harry Williamson'.

The Times 16 May 1994: 'Obituary. T. A. Robertson'.

Times Online, 5 January 2009 (Michael Evans): 'Secret army of 'scallywags' to sabotage German occupation'.

Times Online, 21 October 2009: 'Rudolf Hess's prescription for insomnia in the Tower sold for £750'.

INTERVIEWS
Roy Baker, Leece Museum.
Helen-Jayne B.
Helena B.
Alan Franklin, Manx National Heritage Library and Archive Service.
Steffen Harpsøe, *Siden Saxo*.
Lindsey Hayward, Watford Museum.
Henrik Lundtofte, HSB.
Jim Munsey, The Alberta Railway Museum.
René Rasmussen, Historisk Samfund for Sønderjylland.
Hans Schultz Hansen, Landsarkivet for Sønderjylland.
Henrik Skov Kristensen, Frøslevlejrens Museum.
Mike Smith.
John Wheatly.
Nigel West.

ARCHIVES
Bushey Museum and Art Gallery, Bushey.
Joint Services Command and Staff College Library, Watchfield.
Landsarkivet for Sønderjylland, Aabenraa.
National Archives, Kew.
National Archives and Records Administration, Washington.
Naval Historical Center, Washington.
Northamptonshire Police Archive, Northampton.
Riksarkivet, Stockholm.
Statens Arkiver, Copenhagen: Arkivalieronline.
Watford Museum.

OTHER DOCUMENTS
Landsarkivet for Sønderjylland, Aabenraa: 'Statspolitiet i Aabenraa, police report, 10 November 1938'.

Joint Services Command and Staff College Library, Watchfield: 'OKW Directives for the invasion of U.K. – Operation Seelöwe – Summer and Autumn 1940'.

National Archives, Kew: File KV 2/14 (Vera Eriksen), KV 2/30 (Karel Richter), KV 2/31 (Karel Richter), KV 2/60 (Gösta Caroli), KV 2/61 (Wulf Schmidt), KV 2/62 (Wulf Schmidt), KV 2/1067 (John Moe), KV 2/1333 (Julius Jakob Böckel), KV 2/85-88 (Nikolaus Ritter) and KV 3/205 (IM Nest Bremen).

National Archives, Kew: DEFE 3/739, DEFE 3/740, DEFE 3/741 and DEFE 3/742.

National Archives and Records Administration, Washington: Records of the Headquarters of the German Armed Forces High Command, Part 1, T-77, R-1540 & R-1541.

Naval Historical Center, Washington: T-4066: *Kriegstagebücher (KTB) Des Führers/Befehlshaber der Unterseeboote.*

Riksarkivet, Stockholm: Archive of the Security Police: File HA1240/45.

Selinger, F., 'Meteorological operations in the North Atlantic 1940–1945', A lecture to be held at the Conference 'War in the Arctic 1939–1945' arranged by the Pomor Stare University, ArKahngelsk, Russia (15 July 2000).

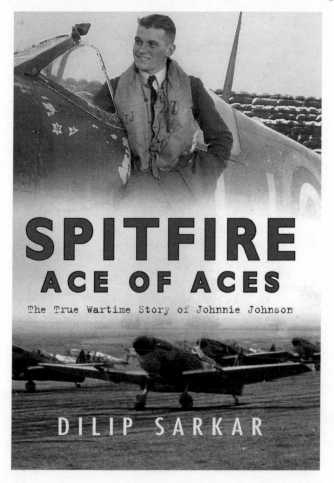

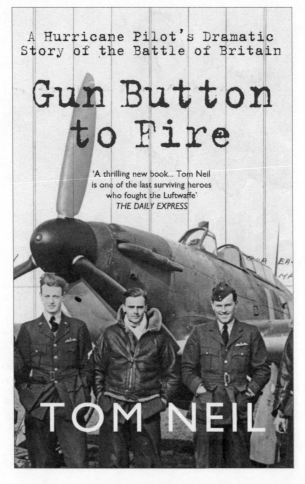

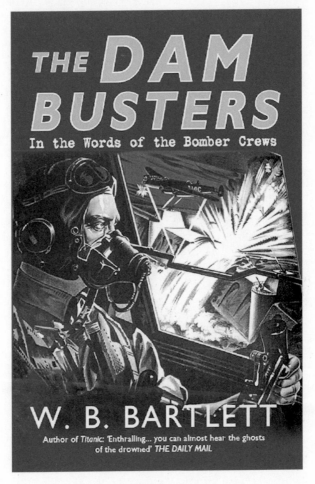

Also available from Amberley Publishing

How to fly the legendary fighter plane in combat using the manuals and instructions supplied by the RAF during the Second World War

'A Must' *INTERCOM: THE AIRCREW ASSOCIATION*

An amazing array of leaflets, books and manuals were issued by the War Office during the Second World War to aid pilots in flying the Supermarine Spitfire, here for the first time they are collated into a single book with the original 1940s setting. An introduction is supplied by expert aviation historian Dilip Sarkar. Other sections include aircraft recognition, how to act as an RAF officer, bailing out etc.

£9.99 Paperback
40 illustrations
264 pages
978-1-84868-436-2

Available from all good bookshops or to order direct
Please call **01453-847-800**
www.amberleybooks.com

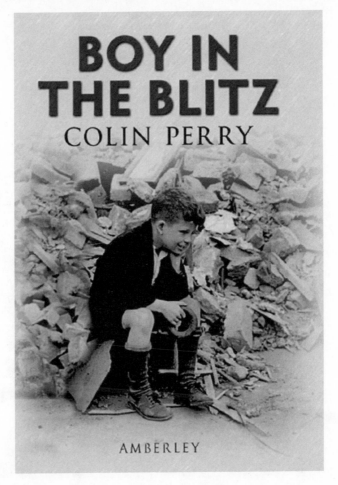

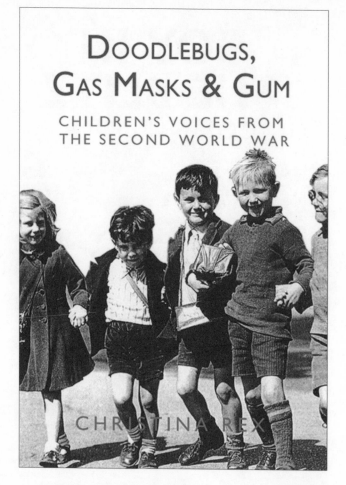

Index